Psychoanalysis Outside the Clinic

Also by Stephen Frosh:

For and Against Psychoanalysis
Hate and the Jewish Science: Anti-Semitism, Nazism and Psychoanalysis
Critical Narrative Analysis in Psychology: A Guide to Practice (revised edition; with P. Emerson)
Key Concepts in Psychoanalysis
After Words: The Personal in Gender, Culture and Psychotherapy
Young Masculinities: Understanding Boys in Contemporary Society (with A. Phoenix and R. Pattman)*
The Politics of Psychoanalysis: An Introduction to Freudian and Post-Freudian Theory (second edition)*
Sexual Difference: Masculinity and Psychoanalysis
With Glaser, D. Child Sexual Abuse (second edition)*
Identity Crisis: Modernity, Psychoanalysis and the Self
Psychoanalysis and Psychology: Minding the Gap
The Politics of Mental Health (with R. Banton, P. Clifford, J. Lousada and J. Rosenthall)

** Published by Palgrave Macmillan*

Psychoanalysis Outside the Clinic

Interventions in Psychosocial Studies

STEPHEN FROSH

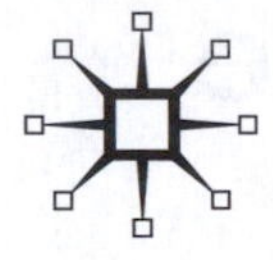

First published 2010 by
PALGRAVE MACMILLAN

Palgrave Macmillan in the UK is an imprint of Macmillan Publishers Limited, registered in England, company number 785998, of Houndmills, Basingstoke, Hampshire RG21 6XS.

Palgrave Macmillan in the US is a division of St Martin's Press LLC, 175 Fifth Avenue, New York, NY 10010.

Palgrave Macmillan is the global academic imprint of the above companies and has companies and representatives throughout the world.

ISBN 978–0–230–21031–8 hardback
ISBN 978–0–230–21032–5 paperback

This book is printed on paper suitable for recycling and made from fully managed and sustained forest sources. Logging, pulping and manufacturing processes are expected to conform to the environmental regulations of the country of origin.

A catalogue record for this book is available from the British Library.

A catalog record for this book is available from the Library of Congress.

10 9 8 7 6 5 4 3 2 1
19 18 17 16 15 14 13 12 11 10

Printed in China

Contents

Acknowledgements

I would like to thank my colleagues in the Department of Psychosocial Studies at Birkbeck College, University of London, for their support over the past few years. I am particularly grateful to Lisa Baraitser for her generosity in allowing me to develop for this book a number of articles originally written jointly with her.

Some sections of this book have previously been published in different forms, as follows.

Part of the section of Chapter 3 entitled 'The Destructive Element: Kleinianism and its Literary Resonances' appeared in S. Frosh (2003), 'Psychoanalysis in Britain: The Rituals of Destruction', in D. Bradshaw (ed.), *A Concise Companion to Modernism*, Oxford: Blackwell.

Chapter 4 is based on S. Frosh (2010), 'Psychoanalytic Perspectives on Identity: From Ego to Ethics', in M. Wetherell and C. Mohanty (eds), *The Sage Handbook of Identities*, London: Sage, and on S. Frosh and L. Baraitser (2009), 'Goodbye to Identity?', in A. Elliott and P. du Gay (eds), *Identity in Question*, London: Sage, both reproduced by permission of SAGE Publications, London, Los Angeles, New Delhi and Singapore.

Parts of Chapter 5 are based on S. Frosh (2008), 'Elementals and Affects or On Making Contact with Others', *Subjectivity, 24*, 314–24, reproduced with permission of Palgrave Macmillan; S. Frosh (2009), 'What Does the Other Want?', in C. Flaskas and D. Pocock (eds), *Systems And Psychoanalysis: Contemporary Integrations in Family Therapy*, London: Karnac; and on S. Frosh and L. Baraitser (2009), 'Goodbye to Identity?', in A. Elliott and P. du Gay (eds), *Identity in Question*, London: Sage, reproduced by permission of SAGE Publications, London, Los Angeles, New Delhi and Singapore.

Chapter 7 is based on S. Frosh and L. Baraitser (2008), 'Psychoanalysis and Psychosocial Studies', *Psychoanalysis, Culture and Society, 13*, 346–65, reproduced with permission of Palgrave Macmillan.

I would like to thank Kelly Noel-Smith for the reference to Freud's account of Empedocles in Chapter 1. I am grateful to the members of the Freud Reading Group at Birkbeck College in 2007–9 for insights into Freud's literary and artistic writings, reflected in the discussion in Chapter 2.

Acknowledgements

Chapter 1

The Applications and Implications of Psychoanalysis

Psychoanalysis in and outside the clinic

Psychoanalysis arose at the end of the nineteenth century as a practice rooted in the 'clinic'. This clinic had a specific location in Freud's consulting room in his home in Vienna, but it rapidly became a metaphorical space referring to the setting for an encounter between a patient, defined as someone in a certain amount of psychological distress, and an analyst, who, through listening and interpreting, could alleviate that distress. Borrowing the terminology of medicine, both because this gave it prestige and also because most of the early analysts were doctors, the consulting room became the model for psychoanalysis thought of as a *treatment*. The procedures developed therein – for example, the use of a couch for the patient to lie on, the regulation of the duration of sessions to 50 minutes, the 'abstinence' of the analyst from undue emotional involvement with the patient – drew on the practices of medicine and came to govern the activities of psychoanalysts as professional therapists. As time went on, increasingly sophisticated theories about mental life arose from the work carried out along these lines, and these in turn influenced further developments in clinical work. In a very concrete sense, therefore, the therapeutic clinic became the source of psychoanalysis' vitality, and its theories and practices were developed to apply in the clinic.

This clinical focus is still characteristic of psychoanalysis, as is the locus of its theories as applied to the speech of individual 'patients' (technically, 'analysands'). In an important sense, this makes psychoanalytic knowledge 'artificial', in that it arises from, and refers back to, a very particular situation specially created to be different from the normal environment of everyday life. In few other places does a person have the opportunity to engage in a largely uninterrupted flow of talk with an attentive listener whose role it is to try to understand what is being said and to help the speaker make sense of it. Everywhere else, transactions of this kind are pedagogic (one person speaks in order to teach the other something), or instructional in a 'performative' sense (for example, giving orders or making or responding to requests), or conversational. In the psychoanalytic setting, however, what transpires is at least an exaggeration of, and possibly radically different from, any other situation in which someone might speak. The analyst does not aim to teach or to make the patient do something; and when the analyst does speak, it is usually with considerable caution about revealing too much about her or his own life. *Reciprocity* of a certain kind exists, as the analyst tries to engage with integrity in the conversation with the patient; but *mutuality* in the sense of equivalence of contact does not. The 'clinic' therefore is a physical space (a bounded zone relatively free from interruption), but it is also a description of a kind of relationship, in which one person makes her or himself available to interpretation by another, and both obey a set of procedural rules recognisable as psychoanalytic practice. This means that the expertise of psychoanalysts is primarily in how to deal with patients in a peculiar situation, and there is no obvious reason why that expertise should generalise to any of the other, very different, circumstances in which people might interact with each other.

Of course, this is nowhere near the whole story of psychoanalysis. The clinic has often been extended significantly to refer, for example, to group situations, to hospital wards, schools, therapeutic communities and learning environments. In each of these cases, some core aspects of the psychoanalytic setting are retained, but others are varied. Sometimes, what is retained is little more than a theoretical orientation that accepts a notion of the 'unconscious' as crucial for understanding motivation and behaviour; at other times, for instance in psychoanalytic group therapies or play-oriented therapy with children, the processes involved may closely mimic the traditional practices of dyadic psychoanalysis. The clinic, in this sense, is *portable*; its key element is the speech of the analysand or analysands, interpreted according to the principles of psychoanalysis by an analyst who is present in that live encounter but occupies a different position – that of the one who is available to think about what is going on, without speaking (too much) of her- or himself. The metaphorical status of the clinic is thus more important than its physical location because it operates as an organising structure for the relationship between any persons who engage with one another in this peculiar, but powerful, way.

If the clinic can be thought of like this, then what becomes central to psychoanalysis is not only a set of specific theoretical constructs (crucially, the existence of a dynamic unconscious, but also including notions such as free association, transference and interpretation), but also a live encounter between people, albeit of a special kind. This 'liveness' seems absolutely crucial to the practice of psychoanalysis. This is because the capacity of the analyst to understand the patient, and of the patient to benefit from that understanding, depends on the two of them being locked into a visible relationship which can be tracked and reflected upon. What analysts focus on are often tiny moments of emotional exchange, small slips or revelations, slight changes; similarly, patients are ever-alert to the timing and nuance of comments and interpretations. Psychoanalysis is a kind of microscopic examination of patterns of speech enacted in a relationship of often long duration (sometimes years of meeting several times a week), and hence of considerable depth. In its clinical form it depends on the actual presence of the people concerned, who can explore their interactions with one another as a way of understanding the 'dynamics' that are at work. This is why, for example, psychoanalytic interpretation is much more than just an intellectual affair in which the analyst explains to the patient what the reality is of her or his unconscious wishes or conflicts. As I have discussed in some detail elsewhere (Frosh, 2006), interpretation depends on the *context of the relationship* between analyst and patient. At the core of this – and what makes the relationship distinctively *psychoanalytic* – is the *transference*, understood as the unconscious way in which the patient relates to or 'uses' the analyst, and usually coupled with the reciprocal *countertransference*, referring to the analyst's response to this. In its strongest version, for example in the work of contemporary Kleinian psychoanalysts, the interpretation arises from the analyst's ability to reflect on her or his countertransference feelings, which are generated by the patient's transference; and the patient's response to the interpretation is in turn governed by the state of the transference. Even without unpacking all the niceties of this complex interchange, it is immediately obvious that interpretation depends on the co-presence of analyst and patient in relationship with one another and cannot take place reliably at a distance. Conventionally, it is even *defined* in terms of such an interpersonal relationship. For example in Sandler, Dare and Holder's (1973) influential account of psychoanalytic concepts, interpretation is referred to as 'all comments and other verbal interventions which have the aim of immediately making the patient aware of some aspect of his psychological functioning of which he was not previously conscious' (p.110). This quotation shows how what is being envisaged is a situation in which the 'verbal intervention' of the analyst draws out a response from the patient that is 'immediate', implying the presence of the two protagonists together. Without analyst and patient both being there, locked into their transferential relationship, interpretation in the psychoanalytic sense cannot take place.

The clinic out of which psychoanalysis has developed, the crucible for its concepts and its practices, is thus a metaphorical space surrounding a live encounter. This liveness is necessary for it and integral to the processes that go on within it. Anything else, therefore, is not psychoanalysis, however much appeal there is to the language or theoretical constructs of psychoanalysis. So when a literary author's work is interpreted in terms of childhood trauma, it is not psychoanalysis; or when a political commentator draws on ideas about unconscious national impulses, it is not psychoanalysis; or when a social psychologist or philosopher uses ideas about intimacy and stability of selfhood to understand identity conflicts, it is not psychoanalysis. None of these intellectual activities (including the writing of books about psychoanalysis), however carefully they employ psychoanalytic ideas, are in fact psychoanalysis, because they lack the specific kind of encounter that constitutes the psychoanalytic clinic. This seems clear, if not necessarily to everyone's taste. However, it leaves open another set of questions. If the practice of psychoanalysis depends on the clinic, what happens when it is *in fact* taken outside, and psychoanalytic ideas are used to make sense of non-clinical phenomena? Even if one agrees that this is not the same thing as being involved in, or conducting, a psychoanalysis, one might still claim that it offers a distinctive and productive approach to interpreting human actions, social phenomena and cultural products 'outside' the clinic. If the theoretical constructs generated inside the clinic by psychoanalysis have any robustness, why should they not be at least suggestive aids to comprehension of complex events that in their unexpectedness or emotional intensity seem to show the traces of the unconscious? Why vacate the field and have nothing to say just because the context is not exactly the same as the core psychoanalytic setting? Or is it actually the case that moving outside the clinic strips psychoanalytic concepts of their meaning, so that when they are applied in this way they actually produce a kind of nonsense? There is in this a challenge to those who would apply psychoanalysis in social and cultural spaces outside the clinical sphere, for example to literary texts, films, or biographies, without access to psychoanalysis' characteristically detailed processes of intersubjective contact. If psychoanalysis is a specially staged live event, as claimed, then it loses its potency and legitimacy in being applied outside its conditions of emergence, the clinical encounter itself. On the other hand, perhaps psychoanalysis' capacity to theorise moments of irrationality and eruptions of fantasy is just too great to be ignored when such moments are visible outside the clinic; and if this is the case, then the challenge becomes not that of *justifying* psychoanalysis, but rather of deploying it creatively and yet with integrity. Perhaps the way in which psychoanalysis embodies an encounter provides a model for understanding and promoting all occasions on which 'something happens', so long as one recognises the possible consequences of the leap being made from the clinic to its outside.

As it happens, psychoanalysis has had a contentious but productive history of engagement with the intellectual world outside the clinic, specifically with the humanities and social sciences, since its inception; and it is still a widely used yet also controversial element in the critical armoury of those working in these disciplines. Early forays into literary and artistic theory by Freud and his circle (e.g. Freud, 1907, 1910a) had a significant impact on biographically-oriented work and also in opening out a domain of interpretive activity that was new in its orientation and its possibilities. In some areas, such as art history, literary criticism and film studies, the effect of psychoanalysis has been profound, provoking rich seams of research that touch on fundamental questions of structure, motivation, representation and response (e.g. Stokes, 1955; Ehrenzweig, 1967; Mulvey, 1989; Stonebridge, 1998; Žižek, 1991, 2006a). In philosophy, politics, history and law, psychoanalysis has at times provided a set of tools for conceptual work (e.g. Hirst, 1979; Wolfenstein, 1981), and offered a vocabulary and set of perceptions that have troubled or channelled major areas of social debate such as 'sexual difference' in gender studies or feminist philosophy (Brennan, 1989; Irigaray, 1985), 'otherness' in the context of racism (Kovel, 1995; Frosh, 2006) and various notions of personal and political emancipation as applied in social and political theory (Marcuse, 1955; Habermas, 1968; Whitebook, 1996). Despite fluctuations in the extent to which psychoanalysis is regarded as having cultural currency, it continues to be a significant intellectual resource in the humanities and social sciences, with especially influential recent deployments in some major works on art and politics, sexuality, violence and war (e.g. Žižek, 2006b; Rose, 1996, 2003; Butler, 2008). In part this attests to the cyclical pattern of repudiation and resurrection that psychoanalysis seems to undergo within academic settings. But it also shows very cogently that whatever the force of the argument that psychoanalysis really belongs only to the clinic (albeit in the broad sense described here), it has actually migrated elsewhere and become one of the most significant tools available to those who wish to understand the social world. This being so, the issue of whether psychoanalysis 'belongs' outside the clinic or not is of less significance than questions about the *effect* of this migration: what happens when psychoanalysis is used in this way, what are its benefits for the domains in which it is applied, what are the dangers, what insights are gained and what distortions are introduced? And if this is not to be a one-way street, in which the only thing considered is the *use* of psychoanalysis, one should also ask, what difference does it make *to* psychoanalysis itself when it is used in this way? Does it learn anything, does it change, are its own gaps in understanding revealed, is it added to in constructive ways? All this is to say that psychoanalysis may have something to offer, and it may benefit from this engagement with the outside world; but there is a great deal to unpick here, and many dangers to skirt.

Psychoanalysis as social critique

There is an important characteristic of psychoanalysis that should be noted at the outset of this examination of questions of translation and impact as psychoanalysis moves outside the clinic. This concerns the tension that it repeatedly enacts between what might be thought of as its *critical* capacity and a tendency to back away from what this criticism reveals, and instead fall into what one can only term a 'conformist' way of dealing with its own discoveries. What is meant here is that one part of the psychoanalytic tradition is to 'unsettle' situations by revealing the unconscious elements that feed into them; this unsettling capacity becomes *socially* critical when it seeks to expose power situations that rely on the denial of opposition and the pretence that it is necessary to maintain existing patterns of domination. 'Critical theory' in the tradition of the Frankfurt School, which from the middle of the twentieth century was a significant influence on politically radical social theorists, knew this well and explicitly drew on psychoanalysis to inform its insights (e.g. Adorno, 1967; Marcuse, 1955). Similarly, many contemporary writers of the left have been very inclined to see psychoanalysis as a route for a continued critique of power (see Frosh, 1999). There is an obvious reason for this, based on the idea that psychoanalysis has the capacity to disrupt the complacent acceptance of the status quo by revealing both the disturbance that lies behind it, and the way *nothing* is stable because there is always a pressure towards change, whether this be as a consequence of an excess of love or of destructiveness. This idea of the disturbing nature of psychoanalysis can be traced back to Freud, whose startling originality lay in identifying an underside to knowledge –how the unconscious subverts and disrupts whatever one thinks of as certain or clear. What Freud discovers is the unsettledness of psychic life, in which the tendency to rest at ease with oneself is undermined by the appalling capacity of unconscious elements to introduce something fantastic and full of desire. Whenever we believe we know something – even psychoanalysis – we are tripped up uncomfortably by our *wish* to know it. This wish always has unconscious components; it is spoken from a place within us about which we have little understanding, and over which we have even less control. Even this terminology, which makes the unconscious a 'place' and implies a modicum of stability, is of course wrong: what Freud emphasises is the *fluidity* of psychic life, in which the apparent concreteness of objects and thoughts is undermined by the appalling capacity of unconscious life to seep into it, to make of what should be 'real' something which is 'in reality' fantasy, with a life of its own. This kind of fantasy flows oddly along the riverbeds of the nocturnal and the dreamlike, the infantile and the wishful. *Nothing* is solid; there is nowhere to run to, no real 'container' for anxiety, no firm holding that can totally relieve worry. Everything fades as one comes close to it. The dreamscape is the dominant motif of Freudian life: we may bump into things all the time, they may hurt; we may feel the knives and caresses of other humans; we may seek certainty and believe we have found it, for instance in religion or in the material solidity of home, or in the wiring of the brain; we may feel that love, or death, are ultimate foundational boundaries for being, and make it meaningful. In each case, however, not only does fantasy inhabit these things, translating them into wishful entities with blurred boundaries, making them indecipherable at least to some degree, and incommunicable to an even greater extent; but unconscious impulses always impishly trip us up as we approach them.

This is the joy and challenge of psychoanalysis: it populates the world with fantasies, and in so doing it dissolves all certainties. As Freud himself noted, it is an attack on the narcissism of the individual because it displaces each one of us from the centre of our own agency. Famously aligning psychoanalysis with the scientific advances of Copernicus and Darwin, which damaged the 'self-love' of humans by showing that they are not the centre of the universe, Freud argues that society's resistance to psychoanalysis is in part produced by the way it decentres the individual still further. Not only are we not the centre of the universe, we are not even in control of ourselves.

> But human megalomania will have suffered its third and most wounding blow from the psychological research of the present time, which seeks to prove to the ego that it is not even master in its own house, but must content itself with scanty information of what is going on unconsciously in its mind. We psychoanalysts were not the first and not the only ones to utter this call to introspection; but it seems to be our fate to give it its most forcible expression and to support it with empirical material which affects every individual. Hence arises the general revolt against our science, the disregard of all considerations of academic civility and the releasing of the opposition from every restraint of impartial logic. (Freud, 1917a, p.285)

We are spoken by, and enacted through, something else or *other* that is more 'real' than the reality we think we know, something which gives rise to resistance yet is scientifically irrefutable. This something is not to do with identity, or a 'true self' that one then spends one's life seeking out; it is rather the precise opposite of this, insisting that there is no such 'self' – an insistence that is now a routine legacy of poststructuralism and postmodernism. The language of the self still has a hold, of course, in ordinary speech and in the technical lexicon of many psychotherapeutic and social psychological enterprises, including much that passes for psychoanalytic psychotherapy, but this does not make the self *real* in any meaningful sense. What psychoanalysis insists on, with its fundamental displacement of the locus of subjectivity away from anything that can fulfil the functions of selfhood, is that there is always something else speaking *in the place of the subject*. This means that there may be a fantasy of selfhood, but it is undermined, dispersed, even mocked by the relentless pressure that comes from unconscious life. It is as if the human subject is plugged into something else that gives it its energy 'from outside', yet presents the fiction that this comes from within. The shock occurs when the source of this power makes itself directly felt.

The problem – one which resonates through this book – is that the 'shock' of the unconscious is often too much to bear. One of the difficulties psychoanalysis has always had is in sustaining the clarity of its vision about the way unconscious life disturbs the scenery. Freud refers to the resistance to psychoanalysis that comes from its critics ('the general revolt against our science'), but even in his lifetime there were *insiders* whose deviations from psychoanalytic orthodoxy were interpreted as resistance to its major discoveries – notably Jung and Adler, both of whom tried to significantly reduce the emphasis on sexuality. In Freud's view, this move was mainly in order to make their own theories more easily acceptable to outsiders. However, it could also be seen as a symptom of a more general resistance amongst analysts themselves towards accepting the implications of their own discoveries. Throughout the history of psychoanalysis, this resistance has been expressed in a mode of conformity that seeks theoretical and social respectability and professional status, as against the more subversive and 'radical' position which questions the possibility of incorporating psychoanalytic knowledge into conventional academic and professional structures. Both these tendencies begin with Freud's own work, for instance in the encounter with hysteria, in which what is revealed is a split between Freud as 'man of science' and as disrupter of the rationalist assumptions of science itself. In an observation that has always seemed particularly astute, Toril Moi (1989) notes:

> Psychoanalysis is born in the encounter between the hysterical woman and the positivist man of science. It is in this reversal of the traditional roles of subject and object, of speaker and listener, that Freud more or less unwittingly opens the way for a new understanding of human knowledge. But the psychoanalytical situation is shot through with paradoxes and difficulty. For if Freud's (and Breuer's) act of listening represents an effort to include the irrational discourse of femininity in the realm of science, it also embodies their hope of extending their own rational understanding of psychic phenomena. Grasping the logic of the unconscious they want to make it accessible to reason. (pp.186–7)

In the context of femininity, always a fraught area for psychoanalytic work, Moi's reading suggests that psychoanalysis was founded in a gap between what could be known and what one might wish to know. The former requires an acknowledgement of lack: there are limits to what can be known; perhaps even nothing can be known reliably, given that the unconscious disrupts everything. The latter, however, represents a repression of this understanding, built up into the claim that an expert (the 'man of science') might get to know everything, a position later named by Lacan (1991) as 'the discourse of the Master'. This tension between knowing and disrupting knowledge is a key one for current debates about how psychoanalysis might be deployed outside the consulting room. Does it contribute to knowledge understood as a cumulative project in which things are waiting to be discovered, or can it be used to query such claims to knowledge, and if so, in the name of what does it do that? Perhaps the dilemma here is that although the project of bringing psychoanalysis into the 'academy' (to put it at its most theoretical) is an important one both for complementing and for challenging other approaches within the disciplines it encounters there, psychoanalysis tends to lose its socially critical power once it is appropriated as a mode of institutional knowledge (Frosh, 2006). This is, of course, a familiar dynamic in other 'critical' areas such as feminism and Marxism: when they enter into common use they can be appropriated or colonised in the interests of the thing they might have been set up to criticise. Adorno (1967) pointed out, and Althusser (1971) elaborated in a rather different theoretical language, that this is exactly how the 'administered society' operates: it co-opts its critics. As Freud himself knew (e.g. Freud, 1925), *accepting* a disturbing thesis can be a way of denying its truth: it can become defanged, a norm, just like any other knowledge.

The suggestion here is that if the co-option of an apparently critical discourse into a normalising one is a widespread phenomenon (for instance, it is visible in the continuing vitality of capitalism as it manoeuvres its dissidents into being sources of profit), there may be something specific, or at least exemplary, in the way in which this happens with psychoanalysis. Despite a great deal of historical optimism that it might have something important to offer as a critical approach to sociality, psychoanalysis has at least equally often been portrayed as a bureaucratising and conformist practice, in which adaptational and wishfully integrationist thinking is primary, trouble and trauma are individualised, and social relations are either ignored or made visible in a way that leaves them undisturbed (e.g. Jacoby, 1975). This accusation has usually been focused on ego psychology, the dominant form of psychoanalysis in America after the Second World War, but this is now an old and perhaps partial appraisal. Indeed, whilst ego psychology concentrated on that side of psychoanalysis that stresses the necessity for control of unconscious impulses and adaptation to society and hence seems clearly at odds with the radical critique of society articulated by the 'Freudo-Marxists' (e.g. Marcuse, 1955; Frosh, 1999), it can also be understood as an honest response to the destructive explosion of *irrationality* embodied in fascism and Nazism. That is, despite its many and obvious limitations, one should not be too single-minded about pillorying ego psychology's attempt to reinstate rationality as a moral force, given the historical context out of which it emerged. However, something more general is at stake here: not just ego psychology as a mode of conformist psychoanalysis, but the tendency for the most demanding, most difficult ideas of psychoanalysis to give way to a kind of conformist moralism, a common sense which one might argue it is precisely the task of psychoanalysis to disrupt. Moi (1989, p.197) comments in relation to sexual difference and the tendency of psychoanalysis to 'colonise' in the sense of imposing a grid of rationality on the unconscious, that 'When the colonising impulse gains the upper hand, psychoanalysis runs the risk of obliterating the language of the irrational and the unconscious, repressing the threatening presence of the feminine in the process.' Writ large, this refers to an overwhelming trend in much psychoanalytic work to *normalise*, to create another edifice that mimics all the edifices of the disciplines and professionals around it, with grades of seniority and legitimate and illegitimate credentials, with graduation ceremonies and evaluation criteria, and with true and false knowledge.

Laplanche (1999) calls this psychoanalysis' tendency towards 'going-astray' from its own most radical insights. Using Freud's idea about being akin to Copernicus in decentring the human subject, Laplanche comments:

> If Freud is his own Copernicus, he is also his own Ptolemy. The revolution in astronomy lasted nearly two millennia, with some intuitions of the truth almost from the start, but also with an initial going-astray. In psychoanalysis everything, essentially, is produced by a single man – *simultaneously: the discovery*, affirmed at a very early stage, and which is conjointly (and for me indissociably) that of the unconscious and that of seduction – *and the going-astray*, the wrong path taken each time there was a return to the theory of self-centring, or even self-begetting. (p.60)

Laplanche's reference to the 'wrong path' refers to loss of the radical awareness of the causal nature of otherness that psychoanalysis makes possible. However, it has another resonance: one in which 'self-centeredness' is a *political* act that backs away from engagement with the other and in doing so loses its principles. The starkest instance of this in the history of psychoanalysis is its failure in Germany to appreciate the implications of Nazism and to take a stand against it; as a consequence, psychoanalysis lost its moral valence, and can be thought of as taking a 'wrong path' that was very much a 'going astray' (Frosh, 2005). In language that serendipitously parallels Laplanche's vocabulary, the Mayor of Hamburg, Klaus von Dohnyani (1986), introducing the 1985 International Psychoanalytic Association Congress there, made some powerful accusatory comments about German psychoanalysis. These comments suggest a potential link between the kind of theoretical abandonment described here, and the loss of moral direction that can have significant political consequences:

> It therefore is my opinion that your colleagues who have described the weaknesses of psychoanalysts and their associations in the years leading up to and during National Socialism have helped to free us from historical entanglements by showing us how it really was – with respect to psychoanalysts, too, even Sigmund Freud. For fear of losing everything, bit by bit was sacrificed, every step being rational – and yet at the same time always in the wrong direction. Here a compromise concerning persons, there a compromise of principles, but always in the pretended interest of preserving the whole – which in the end was lost. (p.4)

Not all compromises lead to collaboration with Nazism, of course, and to accuse psychoanalysis of always having lost its way like this would be a gross calumny. Nor is it the case that psychoanalysis is any worse in this regard than other professions – law and psychiatry immediately come to mind. But if one is trying to hold onto what might be called the 'critical tradition' in psychoanalysis, which pays its full dues to its capacity for resisting conformist pressures (the opposite kind of resistance from that outlined by Freud when describing social responses to psychoanalysis itself), one has to ask about the connections between theoretical 'going astray' and the wandering down blind, or at least morally questionable, political alleys. This is one of the issues taken up by Jacoby (1983) in his account of the fate of European psychoanalytic radicalism (embodied especially by Otto Fenichel) once transplanted into America, so the point here is not only about Nazism, but about all occasions on which psychoanalysis fails to withstand the bureaucratising and conformist pressures placed upon it.

For Laplanche, the key issue is the extent to which *otherness* can be engaged with as the source of psychic life, his argument being that Freud's appreciation of other-centredness is both radical and precarious, always retreating back into claims for egoic mastery. More generally, this relapse into the hope of mastery is a retreat from recognition of the *essential* alienness of human subjectivity, a retreat that is not accidental, but inherent in the material. As John Fletcher (1999) writes in his introduction to Laplanche's *Essays on Otherness*:

> To this dialectic between a decentring to which Freud officially aligns himself and a recurrent recentring, Laplanche joins the diagnostic notion of a wandering or going-astray of Freudian thought. . . . The covering over and occlusion of the discovery of the radical otherness of the unconscious and sexuality in Freud's thought, Laplanche suggests, trace out the movements of just such a covering over in the human subject itself. (p.3)

Awareness of the extent to which what is other dominates our existence is too painful, too terrifying, to be maintained; instead, both the subject and psychoanalysis itself 'wander' back from the momentary vision of this truth, to the fantasy of completeness, of narcissistic selfhood. There is something to be alert to here in reflecting on the impossibility of acceptance of the other, or at least on how painful such an acceptance can be. Laplanche comments (1999, p.67), 'One could endlessly demonstrate how the domestication of the unconscious never ceases to operate in Freudian thought, and this with regard to each of the foremost aspects of its alien-ness.' *Politically*, as well as 'scientifically', one might then say that each of its most profound inventions or discoveries is a threat to ease-of-mind, whether personally (as each individual analysand comes across something troubling in their speech to the analyst, for instance the racism that slips out, or the unwanted wish) or ethically/morally, as one comes across a claim made by psychoanalysis that disturbs the vision of human subjecthood that one would rather have. In each case, individually or institutionally, there is a tendency to 'wander', to back away from the insight that might itself have been painfully won, and take refuge instead in the safety of a knowledge that seems whole and reassuring, but instead is based on a damaging self-willed blindness towards what has already been seen.

This section has addressed a second theme of this book, which complicates the broader questions around what happens to psychoanalysis when it moves outside the clinic. The claim here is that psychoanalysis has an intrinsic link to radical social critique, because its concern is with unconscious impulses understood as destabilising and subversive of social as well as personal norms. In particular, psychoanalysis' positing of something 'alien' at the core of the human subject – an unconscious that somehow speaks 'through' the subject without being completely under the subject's control – draws attention to the central importance of *otherness* in personal and social life. Preserving this critical function of psychoanalysis is an important step in keeping psychoanalysis alive and preventing it from ossifying into a form of expert received knowledge that can be easily accommodated into technologies of social control. However, not only is psychoanalysis subject to the same pressures towards bureaucratisation as are critical movements in other disciplines, but it also has its own internal momentum towards conformism derived from the disturbing nature of its discoveries. This suggests another set of issues which need to be addressed as one moves away from the clinic: can the direct engagement of psychoanalysis with social and cultural phenomena lead to a renewal of psychoanalysis itself, as it lays itself open to critical scrutiny in a more 'public' domain?

Normalising tendencies inside the clinic

Although this book is concerned with psychoanalysis outside the clinic, it is important to note, albeit briefly, criticisms of psychoanalytic clinical work that parallel the account of its drift into moralism and conformism as an academic discipline. Psychoanalysis is not divided into a radical clinical practice that sometimes loses its sharpness when it directly addresses culture or society. Rather, the tension between critique and conformity is *endemic* to psychoanalysis in all its manifestations – which is the point of Laplanche's previously quoted claim that 'the domestication of the unconscious never ceases to operate in Freudian thought.' Psychoanalysis as a clinical discipline has often demonstrated normalising approaches to patients. This has occurred most obviously in the case of homosexuality, where psychoanalysis has only recently, and partially, emerged from a long night of explicit and often highly damaging homophobia (Frosh, 2006; Isay, 1985). It also arguably applies generally in its adherence to models of family life based on an Oedipal norm that makes the relationship with the mother 'narcissistic' and that with the father (representing the prohibiting voice of the social law) the emblem of 'reality'. Issues here include the postulation of a normative developmental trajectory in childhood, giving a kind of 'teleological' feel to psychoanalytic theory (i.e. that there is a predictable developmental sequence resulting in mental health and that departures from this sequence are pathogenic); the promotion of particular familial organisations as if they are universal and necessary, especially in the context of gender relations; and ethnocentric assumptions about 'race', ethnicity and culture that may acknowledge the allure of 'other' cultures but neglect consideration of their specific characteristics when met with in treatment, and which also underplay the impact and historical cogency of racism and colonialism. The conservatism of the psychoanalytic profession itself has also frequently been commented upon. This is evidenced in the tight regulation of acceptable versus unacceptable practice (the standardised 'fifty-minute hour' of treatment, for example); the compromises wrought by private practice; training regimes that reward conformity and militate against creative and critical thinking; and an aura of stiffness, fear of spontaneity and social conservatism that seems to pervade psychoanalytic societies. It does not take much imagination to see this as another manifestation of Laplanche's 'wandering'. Faced day-to-day with the slipperiness and determined challenge of the unconscious as it manifests in speech, with the disturbance it engenders and the erotic or aggressive embarrassments it perpetrates on, against, or in collusion with the analyst (not to speak of the *analyst's* unconscious and what it acts out in the clinical situation), perhaps it is not surprising that a covering-over and turning-away is provoked, so that there is not too much evidence left behind that something extreme happened here, something worrying and discomfiting. Living their professional, bourgeois lifestyle, perhaps it is too much to require of analysts that they should remain permanently plugged into the life-energy so delicately and waveringly uncovered by Freud. Is it really possible for their world to be restlessly populated by desire in all its peculiarities, without judgement or moralism, without platitude or denial? How does one go home to one's spouse and children, how does one remain a respected member of the community of doctors, lawyers and teachers, after a day spent so relentlessly grubbing around in the dirt? Perhaps it is only by dressing conservatively, metaphorically as well as literally, that this can be managed, that the veneer of respectability can be maintained, for oneself as well as the world. The sheer *effort* involved in remaining attuned to the surprises, insults and affections of the unconscious – again, one's own as well as one's patients – is exhausting and personally potentially damaging, as one struggles to withstand the assaults on one's identity and sense of coherence, on one's *integrity* in every sense of the word.

This is no excuse, of course, for the crass normalisations one sees in so much psychoanalytic clinical writing, let alone for its repeated failure to really address issues to do with the grounding of its clinical claims and the effectiveness of its treasured techniques (Frosh, 2006). Nevertheless, there is also something gallant about the continued willingness of these labourers of the soul to put themselves in the firing line, to take on the task of subjecting themselves to the daily assaults of unconscious missiles, day in day out, week after week, month after month, year after year (often with the same patient). Not only do they have to have a phenomenal capacity to withstand boredom (or to daydream), but they need to combine skins sufficiently thick to deal with the constant assaults on their narcissism from patients who repeatedly tell them how useless they are, with a capacity for relatively calmly imbibing tales of terror and disgust, and with a further ability to ignore or parry overtly as well as implicitly erotic advances. All this has to be managed alongside retaining some alertness to the sensitive handling of deeply unhappy people. A close read of current clinical literature and exposure to clinical presentations suggests that many analysts carry this difficult feat off remarkably well, even allowing for the likely rewriting of reality that such unaudited accounts suffer from. Interestingly, there is also a heroic tradition of reporting therapeutic *failures*, from Freud onwards, that is perhaps even more impressive than the more conventional way in which a successful piece of analytic work is presented (in anonymised, hence distorted form) as a vignette supporting analytic theory. Freud's efforts in this vein, for example in the 'Dora' case history (Freud, 1905) in which his work came to an abrupt end by the patient walking out on him, show him trying both to learn from the events and also to legitimise his actions. No failure is truly a failure, but rather the manifestation of a resistance, or the consequence of a choice of patient known to be impermeable to treatment from the start (e.g. Freud, 1920a). This is often regarded, probably correctly, as a defensive response on Freud's part. However, the wish to make sense of failure is in itself not a malicious one, whether or not Freud was open enough about his own shortcomings, a point which also applies to later analysts. What is less common in the clinical literature is reflection on the assumptions underpinning analysis. Success or failure tends to be given in terms of an undeconstructed notion of therapeutic progress (albeit characteristically with caution about use of the troubling term 'cure'), using at best rather conventional notions of mental health. These often reference Freud's idea that improvement in a patient's capacity for love and work should be the goal, or possibly that 'The business of psychoanalysis is to secure the best possible psychological conditions for the functioning of the ego; when this has been done, analysis has completed its task' (Freud, 1937, p.402). It is far less common to find reference to the *critical* potency of the analytic process as something relevant to analytic aims.

An example might be useful here. Ann Smolen (2009) reports a case of child analysis with an adopted son of two gay male parents. This case went on for some years and was eventually broken off by one of the fathers, evidently against the wishes of the boy and his analyst. The case is beautifully described, with rich examples of the clinical encounter with the young boy and one of the fathers, and is followed by three respectful and insightful commentaries by other analysts. These commentaries are predominantly technical. One includes a parallel case of a daughter of a lesbian couple (Herzog, 2009) and there is also interest in the 'new family form' involved, giving rise to some cautiously balanced comments about the importance of maintaining 'a strict analytical attitude', defined as 'what I mean is that it is necessary to try to observe and tend to reflect' (Ungar, 2009, p.28). There is much to be learnt from the case presentation and commentaries, and much to admire in the sensitivity of the work and the simple care and patience demonstrated by the analyst. Indeed, as regards the professional ethics of psychoanalysis the case is exemplary: despite all pressures to the contrary, the analyst does her best to stick with the patient whilst he tries to work things out and through for himself. There seems no question of a contracted period of time in which the therapy has to be concluded, but rather a recognition that what might often be needed is a pacing of work that reflects the reality of an intimate encounter, that is, that it has to unfold, that it has its ups and downs, that it can be difficult, and that much of its meaning resides simply in its durability. What is *not* visible, however – and, in a way, why should it be in an account that aims to promote professional practice, rather than question the assumptions of the profession itself? – is a mode of reflexivity that moves beyond the unquestionable capacity of the analyst to think about herself in relation to the boy, to further consider what *becomes of* psychoanalysis in such circumstances. What does this case do to the normative assumptions on which psychoanalysis is premised – not just in the sense of demanding liberal tolerance of 'new family forms', which still are seen as requiring special 'explanation' to the children who grow up within them (Ungar, 2009, pp.28–9)? What expectations are disrupted, what new thing is learnt, what assumptions about adulthood and childhood and the relations between them, as well as the relations between adults and children, are put into question; what, in a word, is there by way of *surprise*? My point here, as should be clear, is not that the work described is bad, neglectful, deceitful or retrograde; it is, rather, that it is *bureaucratic* in the sense evoked by Lacan's (1991) 'discourse of the university': it makes knowledge into technology, rather than exploring the way in which it can be explosive. How might psychoanalysis, as the discipline of the disruptive unconscious, maintain its capacity to shock? Only by itself being open to newness, to discovering something that it did not previously know existed. This is hard, in clinical work as elsewhere, though there is something to be said for the possibility that the clinical environment is more rather than less promising for this to happen: at least the patient is always present, to refuse to comply with the analyst's pre-existent schema. But when this is written about, in the case studies that comprise much of the analytic world's internal communication system, it is rare to find instances that say, 'my theory failed, I learnt something new.'

Constructions of psychoanalysis as a colonising science

The question of how to renew psychoanalysis so that it continues to be a shocking discipline, to itself as well as to others, is perhaps especially paradoxical in relation to applications of psychoanalysis outside the clinic. These applications reflect the ambition of psychoanalysis to be a 'general' theory, seeking out the materialisation of the unconscious in all areas of human activity. They also reproduce a specifically modern imaginary of the scientist as moralist, as the person (in fact, the man) who might be called upon to pronounce on the great issues of life and death. For Freud, the temptation to enact this role was too strong to be resisted. Psychoanalysis, he thought, was more profound than philosophy in that it dealt with the same issues, but in a way that was scientific – which also contrasted it with that other contender for the governing of human passions, religion, dismissed as an 'illusion' (Freud, 1927). Philosophy, Freud claimed to his friend Fliess, had been his first love: 'As a young man my only longing was for philosophical knowledge, and now that I am changing over from medicine to psychology I am in the process of fulfilling this wish' (Freud, 1896/1961, p.241); but once psychoanalysis emerged, he no longer respected the armchair creations of the philosophers. The key difference in his mind was the material, empirical foundation of psychoanalysis compared with the speculative nature of philosophy. For example, discussing the relationship between the ideas of the Greek philosopher Empedocles and his own theory of the life and death drives, Freud (1937, p.245) comments, 'But the theory of Empedocles which especially deserves our interest is one which approximates so closely to the psychoanalytic theory of the instincts that we should be tempted to maintain that the two are identical, if it were not for the difference that the Greek philosopher's theory is a cosmic phantasy while ours is content to claim biological validity.'

In this light, it is a well-known irony that a major criticism of psychoanalysis is over its *lack* of empirical grounding and its wobbly relationship to biological reality. Contrariwise (a good term for psychoanalysis in general), it is the great imaginative sweep of the discipline as well as its focus on questions of meaning rather than cause, that endears it to so many followers who are less than impressed with scientific reductionism. As often noted (e.g. Frosh 2006), this was not Freud's preferred path; for him, the scientific 'Weltanschauung' was the one that psychoanalysis should follow. But what can be termed the 'colonising' tendency in psychoanalysis has its origins in Freud's own proselytising activities, his claims for the universal validity of psychoanalysis, or at least its relevance to all fields in which people tread. How can one write on literature and art, on religion and war, on social structures, dreams and daydreams, on jokes and sex, without exciting those who wish to make psychoanalysis a universal critical schema; and at times without drawing in the lost souls who want to make it a way of life? The clinical setting provides some of the frisson of psychoanalysis, with its opportunity for intense immersion in the lives of others – but as already noted, this is opposed by the responsibility entailed in this kind of contact, not to mention its repetitive and mundane quality, its sheer boredom and difficulty. 'What do they want from me?' might be the call of the experienced, honest analyst or therapist, facing her or his schedule of patients for yet another day. This mundanity grounds the speculative thrill of psychoanalytic theory, so that it is less likely to float away. 'Applied' psychoanalysis, using that term to signify the use of psychoanalytic theory outside clinical settings, has no such obvious grounding; there is nothing intrinsic to it to hold it in place. Hence its excitement and its risks: for those attracted to speculation, it is an open invitation to indulge. Freud himself claimed aversion to wildness in imagining psychoanalytic truths, yet also showed a tendency to engage in it, as he admitted in one of his most ambitious and important texts, *Beyond the Pleasure Principle* (Freud, 1920b, p.295): 'What follows is speculation, often far-fetched speculation, which the reader will consider or dismiss according to his individual predilection. It is further an attempt to follow out an idea consistently, out of curiosity to see where it will lead.' This is not to say that *anything* goes: constraints are imposed by the theory of psychoanalysis, by the traditions of the specific disciplines into which the psychoanalytic thinker might wander, and by the restrictions of common sense; but as will be seen, these constraints are not always effective in tethering psychoanalytic ideas to something resembling plausibility. And the contrary argument, of course, goes as follows: why should they be so tethered? If psychoanalysis is not simply an expression of whatever is already known and commonsensical, is not in league with normativeness and regulation, is not therefore, a bourgeois discipline, the work of which is simply to confirm the everyday in its greyness; then why should it not multiply fantasies, provoke breaks in the ready-made and received, the *obvious*? That is, why bother to deploy psychoanalysis if all it does is reproduce what everyone already accepts as true? Again, there is some danger in following this logic in the clinical situation, where one might do harm with one's mad speculations; but perhaps outside it, such madness can be indulged.

It is not difficult to see problems with this argument, notably that ideas have consequences even without the immediate danger of the misuse of power in the clinical situation. People go to war for ideas; ideas maintain conflicts between and within nations, in families and groups; people liberate themselves and enchain themselves in the service of what they think and believe. The notion that ideas are harmless, or else that they are merely froth, bouncing about on the surface of economic and political waves, is no longer seriously maintained by anyone. In the specific case of psychoanalysis, the impact of ideas is especially pronounced, and is observable in the saturation of contemporary culture with psychoanalytic notions (Parker, 1997). This is not only a statement about the *marketing* of psychoanalytic ideas, for example in advertising or in novels. It is, additionally, a comment on the extent to which the reflexive self-understanding of contemporary western societies draws on psychoanalysis as a prominent 'discourse'. It might even be claimed that if psychoanalysis was only *partly* 'true' when Freud invented it, it is much truer now, at least in the cultures in which it has had high levels of intellectual penetration. The unconscious exists, even more than in Freud's day: it is a routine way in which people understand themselves and others, a discourse they draw on to make sense of their experiences, a tool to be used when struggling to manage their own behaviour and that of other people. Elementary notions in everyday life, such as that a person might be lying to her or himself, posit the existence of an area of unconscious mental functioning that draws implicitly on Freudian premises; displacement, projection, denial and repression are all widely used explanatory ideas, with or without their technical vocabulary. The broad psychologisation of culture is rife, and the contribution of psychoanalysis to that trend is highly pronounced. Hence, the interpretive claims that are made – especially if they are repeated endlessly – make a difference; at times, they might even be a matter of life and death.

This all puts some responsibility on those who apply psychoanalysis to find ways to constrain their activities that might parallel the procedures governing the clinical freedom of psychoanalysts to imagine all sorts of impossible things. How can these constraints be developed? One problem with the notion of 'applying' psychoanalysis is that it suggests that one well-formed discipline is going to be used to elucidate the obscurities of another – for example, that psychoanalysis has insights into art history that the historians themselves may not have – and that as a general theory it can be stretched across widely disparate areas of intellectual activity. Not only does this neglect the specifics of *psychoanalysis'* conditions of emergence and the question of the limits of its applicability; more to the point it neglects the specifics of the disciplines to which it is being applied. For example, can psychoanalysis speak of literature without using literary tropes? Is it fair to import it into music or art without deep knowledge of the conventions and technical apparatuses of those two immensely rich terrains? Is social research the same as clinical activity when it comes to questions of interpretation and reflexivity? What do sociologists and political theorists know of group relations and conflicts that psychoanalysts know not? Did psychoanalysis 'cause' cinema, which grew up at exactly the same time, or was the direction of effect the other way around, or mutual?

This last example is a particularly apposite one, as it reminds us of the extent to which psychoanalysis is itself a modernist construction, with porous boundaries in relation to other such constructions. Like psychoanalysis, cinema burst on the scene from nowhere; like cinema, psychoanalysis has always dealt with illusions, fantasies and dreams. Gabbard (2001) describes this mutuality well:

> In 1895 there were two auspicious births. The Lumière brothers invented a rudimentary film projector, signifying the birth of the cinema, and *Studies in Hysteria* appeared, inaugurating the new science of psychoanalysis. Throughout the twentieth century the two new disciplines have been inextricably linked. As early as 1900 a writer would describe his psychotic episode in terms of 'the magic lantern' effects of the nickelodeons... In 1931 the American film industry was already being called a 'dream factory' ... reflecting the close resemblance between film imagery and the work of dreams. (p.1)

Given this context, the idea that psychoanalysis could hold the truth of cinema seems far-fetched; Gabbard (pp.4–5) notes that, 'Obviously, when one applies a psychoanalytic lens to the text of a film, one cannot hope for a definitive reading. A more modest goal is to emphasise how clinical psychoanalytic theory can illuminate what appears to be happening on the screen and the manner in which the audience experiences it.' The term 'illuminate' here reveals the complexities of the situation. 'Illumination' (even 'Lumière') is precisely the activity of cinema, and one might argue that the vocabulary and technology of film is exactly what is needed to help us understand psychoanalysis itself. That is, maybe it is only amongst a population that is used to the play of images on a screen, out of which a narrative is made, that the distinction between conscious perception and unconscious significance makes sense; or perhaps it requires familiarity with the kinds of visual glimpses and auditory hints to be found in the cinema before one can be completely comfortable with the way psychoanalysis finds meaning in small gestures and slips. The major shift of psychoanalytic film criticism towards Lacanian psychoanalysis in the 1970s (e.g. Mulvey, 1975; Metz, 1977) revealed the potency of the latter's focus on the imaginary and on representation; but perhaps it is also the case that Lacanian psychoanalysis *needs* cinema to ground it, to enable its concepts to make sense. The same might be true of psychoanalysis more generally –

its dreamscape is cinematic, and perhaps without film we could neither imagine it so thoroughly nor find it so convincing.

The argument unveiled by this example is that psychoanalysis itself is a cultural construction, a modernist project, and hence that whenever it seeks to establish its expertise, its mastery in other areas, it is exposed to a querying process in which its own conditions and assumptions are placed under scrutiny. Indeed, Rustin (1999, p.106) understands psychoanalysis as the 'last modernism', defining modernism as 'a movement which sought to understand, and develop new languages and cultural forms to represent the intractable obstacles which remained to human freedom and the powers of reason' (p.108) – a notably broad definition that incorporates most of the principled activities of the disciplines contemporary with psychoanalysis. Zaretsky (2004) similarly places its development in what he terms the 'second industrial revolution', Fordism and subsequent twentieth-century movements. If this is the case, psychoanalysis has no special position that it can exploit in order to grant it expert status in relation to other entities. It is, simply, one of a class of intellectual activities – perhaps a powerful one because of the protean nature of its concepts and the potential rigour of its methodology – itself produced by, and in the context of, other historical forces. As has many times been commented upon, psychoanalytic imagery and assumptions reflect a range of notions that were around at the time of its emergence (Frosh, 1991). Specifically, the claim that there is some interpretive depth reality which is truer than surface appearances is central to modernist views of creativity and resistance just as it is crucial to traditional psychoanalysis. It can also be detected in Freudian-based analyses of the socio-political situation, which classically emphasise the perpetual contradiction between personal desires and social necessity, with the attendant restrictions on full human happiness (Freud, 1930). *Underlying* psychological stability are unmet desires; social stability is built on the renunciation of instinctual impulses. This model of the surface threatened by 'unconscious' impulses that have been historically suppressed supplies the connection between the advent of psychoanalysis between 1895 and the 1920s and the many contemporaneous modernist images (in art, literature, music and politics) of revolution, of how what lies underneath can break through and overturn the established order. Freudian psychoanalysis spoke fully to this, and offered a route through, a way of thinking about how such elemental forces might be expressed without wiping out everything in their way. A consequence of this, however, is to *relativise* psychoanalysis: as a product of its time and locality, it too is ripe for examination and cannot be used as a sure ground on which to stand and from which others can be put in their place.

Areas of psychoanalytic influence in the arts and social sciences

That said, the impact of psychoanalysis on the arts, humanities and social sciences has been enormous. Sometimes this has transpired as a relatively straightforward and accepted mode of colonisation, but more often as a resisted practice (against which the natives take up arms), with problems and benefits both for the putative colonised group and the psychoanalytic imperialists themselves. Much of the early work was in essence crude psychobiography – for example, Freud's (1910a) own famous mis-analysis of Leonardo da Vinci, in which the artist's creativity is seen as a manifestation of his repressed homosexuality, itself linked to the speculative history of his relationship with his mother. Given the fascination of psychoanalysts with 'creativity', Freud's admiration for cultural heroes, and a rather general tendency for psychoanalysts to see themselves as kindred spirits to creative artists; and given the receptivity of artists, especially in the first half of the twentieth century, to those who might be able to speak seriously about dreams and nightmares; it is perhaps not surprising that a kind of mutual admiration should grow up between the two groups, though perhaps rather less obvious that the artistic community would appreciate the reductive interpretive propensities of the psychoanalysts. In retrospect, it is perhaps predictable that this reductionism, focusing analysis on 'personality' or 'character', should be the psychoanalytic tendency. Partly this is because psychoanalysis was an element in a psychological revolution that, far from displacing the human subject as the centre of all things (as Freud thought), rather developed or invented the *individual* as the locus of scientific and (particularly) literary concern. The emergence of the novel as the most popular literary form, for example, significantly predates psychoanalysis, but it is also part of the same movement towards individualisation that was a consequence of the industrial revolution, the 'long' period of modernity, and the gradual differentiation between private and public that was a characteristic of capitalist society (Berman, 1983). That the individual psyche should be seen as the source of artistic meaning is therefore predictable from the character and conditions of emergence of psychoanalysis itself. It was a reflection of, and a way of expressing, the pressure towards individualisation and the construction of an autonomous human subject, however self-contradictory this task should eventually turn out to be. Moreover, the push in psychoanalytic literary and art criticism to find roots for creativity in the artist's developmental history is not just a reflection of the specifics of psychoanalytic theory, but of its structure: the discipline was founded on the premise that meaning is made retrospectively, that looking backwards to childhood is necessary if one is to understand what has come 'next'. Indeed, this concept of backwardness or '*Nachträglichkeit*', translated in French as 'après-coup' and in English as 'deferred action' has become a key notion in contemporary cultural appropriations of psychoanalysis, perhaps because of its 'rediscovery' by Lacan (1953). As Eickhoff (2006) points out, these two translations actually emphasise two somewhat different senses (retroactivity and after-effect) implicit in the term coined by Freud. The former references the way meaning is conferred on an event from the standpoint of a later event that brings it to consciousness; while the latter describes the impact of early experiences on that which comes later. Despite the contradictory implications of these two ideas – the first of which emphasises the constant rewriting of the past from the situation of the present, whilst the latter has a more traditional and linear 'developmental' focus – the primacy given to a view of *history* in formulating explanations for human action is symptomatic of a specifically modernist consciousness. Yet this historical outlook also has some critical possibilities embedded within it. In its most widespread and 'classical' form, the developmental thrust of psychoanalysis promotes a backward-looking approach, in which the past is mined as the source of a linear sequence that is taken to be explanatory of the here and now. Yet clearly this is not the only way to develop notions of causality: *circular* explanations, in the sense of recurrent, repetitive time, are also rife in Freud. They are, for example, key to the notion of the death drive as summarising a universal tendency to repetition, and the unconscious has *timelessness* as one of its chief characteristics. So the reductive, linear approach is not only problematic from the point of view of art, which sees it as neglecting the specifics (formal properties and so on) of art traditions themselves; it is also very partial from the point of view of *psychoanalysis*. Whilst biography matters enormously, it only takes its meaning retrospectively, hence cannot be used unproblematically as a formula for interpreting the present (with a patient) or the produced work (in art).

What has made a profound difference to the reception of psychoanalysis in art and literary criticism, and to a lesser extent in the social sciences, has been the poststructuralist interest in the way in which knowledge is constructed *in the relation between* the material itself and the reader or viewer. This has, for example, rendered obsolete the solely biographical approach (however inviting it may be because individualism still exists) and has promoted examinations which explore the manifold ways in which meanings might be attributed to art works – that is, what they *produce*, rather than what they *reveal*. Psychoanalysis has come up with its own parallel approach, especially amongst those who have drawn on Lacanian theory, which is concerned with 'chains of signifiers' and representational practices that refuse (or intentionally fail) to pin down meaning but instead focus on opening it up. This has to do again with retroaction: Lacan holds that sense is always made post hoc, being produced by the interpreter re-reading the subject's discourse in order to even it out, to find anchor points for it and consequently to make it safe and orderly, however complexly and aesthetically this may be done. Sense-making is therefore carried out from the standpoint of something that has already happened and can be molded into shape in the light of where one now finds oneself, a process of 'après-coup' if one is to use the distinctions within *Nachträglichkeit* mentioned above. As it unfolds, however, the chain of signifiers has no particular meaning, it just moves on, throwing out shards from which retroactive sense is then made. The role of psychoanalysis is to stay connected to the signifying process itself; it aims not to make narrative sense in which the unconscious is drawn on as an 'explanation', but rather to *disrupt* sense, to examine the building blocks out of which sense is being produced as a kind of epiphenomenon. This means that there is no specific 'truth' of the work of art to be uncovered; instead, interpretive – or, better, *reading* – strategies continuously revolve the art work to reflect different moments of connection and resonance, of light, off its surface. If one is concerned with this kind of productivity, with what amounts to the *effects* of an art work, then interpretation will shift moment by moment, and its purpose will be to fix meaning for only so long as for it to have an impact, and then to move on, disrupting the meaning that has just been found. Such an approach reduces the risk of psychoanalysis presenting itself as a master discourse that can uncover the truth, and sustains at least some element of its subversiveness. It seeks continually to undermine the temptation to take refuge in the belief that one has mastered the complexities of the art work, that one knows what it is about; in this way, it retains a link with the unpredictable seditiousness of the unconscious. But this is at a price: just like critics said about the excesses of postmodernism, psychoanalysis may become more playful and fluid, but less satisfying, less capable of taking a stand.

The examples of law and sexual difference

Many of the issues that arise in relation to the arts also emerge in social science disciplines such as social psychology, philosophy, politics, history and law. These particularly involve the use of psychoanalytic interpretations and concepts to make sense of social phenomena; that is, psychoanalysis is deployed as a way to augment the explanatory power of the disciplines concerned. For example, there is a long history of discussion in law of how psychoanalytic accounts of the superego and the Oedipus complex can contribute to understanding legal authority and its transgression, and of the power of the law to 'inhabit' its subjects so that they regulate themselves, feeling guilty when they transgress law's injunctions, even at the same moment as experiencing enjoyment. This tradition really starts with Freud's (1913a) *Totem and Taboo* and his (1921) *Mass (or Group) Psychology and the Analysis of the Ego*, both of which deal with the way in which groups and societies enhance their control over their subjects through psychic regulation, particularly in the form of internalised constraints derived from external authority. The development of the concept of the superego, which is articulated fully in *The Ego and the Id* (1923), made it possible for Freud to theorise the route taken to this internal policing system, which he presents, in *Civilization and its Discontents*, through a simile of colonisation. 'Civilization ... obtains mastery over the individual's dangerous desire for aggression by disarming it and by setting up an agency within him to watch over it, like a garrison in a conquered city' (Freud, 1930, p.316).

Prior to this, there had already been legal discussion of the place of the superego in preserving social order, for example in a long paper by the jurist Hans Kelsen that appeared in the *International Journal of Psycho-Analysis* in 1924, which constituted an important and erudite partial refutation of Freud's own views on mass psychology. The significant point here is that psychoanalysis provides an explanatory account of how the seemingly arbitrary rules developed by a society to manage its activities can be *experienced* by its members as binding; and conversely, how there can be pleasure in transgressing these rules even when that transgression produces anxiety and guilt. This explanation is given primarily in developmental terms (Frosh, 1999): the Oedipal encounter with the father generates aggression and the fear of aggression, materialising as castration anxiety; this is dealt with by being incorporated into the psyche and appears 'institutionalised' in the superego. This internalised aggression is experienced as guilt, the most obvious price of civilisation; guilt which does not depend on actions, but which is plugged into wishes and unconscious life. 'Whether one has killed one's father or has abstained from doing so is not really the decisive thing. One is bound to feel guilty in either case, for the sense of guilt is an expression of the conflict due to ambivalence, of the eternal struggle between Eros and the instinct of destruction or death' (Freud, 1930, p.325).

Guilt arises as the external threat of punishment and is 'taken in' and given structural permanence in the superego, where it is free to judge wishes with the same sadistic vigilance with which it would previously have judged actions. Nothing can be hidden: the psyche is set against itself, hedging in the thoughts and behaviours of the individual with proscription and punishment. Thus guilt has two origins, first a fear of authority, second a fear of authority internalised, the superego. Of these two, it is the latter that is more destructive to the happiness of the individual. 'The first insists upon a renunciation of instinctual satisfactions; the second, as well as doing this, presses for punishment, since the continuance of the forbidden wishes cannot be concealed from the super-ego' (Freud, 1930, p.319).

Ironically, the super-ego is an escalating phenomenon: created by instinctual renunciation (of Oedipal desire), it demands more and more renunciation as its aggression is turned against unconscious wishes; the stronger the repressions, the stronger the sense of guilt. Society needs this to happen, according to Freud. Obeying an erotic compulsion to form people together to protect them against nature and each other, it demands harnessing of externalised aggression and its replacement with this internal agency of control.

One can perhaps see why this is an attractive set of ideas for legal theorists interested in the hold that law has over people even in the absence of strong constraints, and conversely in the reasons why transgression occurs even when it seems not to be in the interests of the transgressor. In the superego and in the Oedipal scenario, there is a mechanism proposed that can explain these phenomena, and can in particular provide a language for expressing the intensity of feeling that accompanies legal events – ranging from playground complaints of unfairness to complex judicial questions of culpability and punishment. 'Inside' the mind there is an agency that judges; this agency has a life of its own, and is fuelled both by inner, wishful impulses and by external constraints, by the rigours and irrationalities of the social order. This theory has the added advantage of linking social and personal, and hence different kinds of law – from actual physical enforcement through to the subtle and formative manoeuvrings of ideology (Hirst, 1979). Law becomes infested with emotion, bought into by the human subject as she or he wrestles with conscience and the unconscious, with ideals and reprimands all experienced as deeply personal and hence carrying more weight than if they were 'merely' external. And as psychoanalysis never tires of showing, each prohibition exists *because* there is an impulse towards transgression (the incest taboo is universal because incestuous desires are universal) but also as an *invitation* to transgression – for example, a social taboo on miscegenation actually promotes it as exotic and exciting. Thus it becomes easier to understand why crime pays, emotionally if not always in reality, as people only do wrong because there is wrong to do. The law has its perverse underside, both in the way it operates (Kafka being the great chronicler of this), but also in the temptation, even encouragement, it offers people to break it: in formulating prohibitions, it names their desire.

These are genuinely profound insights and liberate law from a rationalism that can only address subjects in mechanistic terms and will always remain confused by the failure of people to behave according to simple cost-benefit analyses. Law invites transgression, not only structurally (a law defines what lies outside it) but emotionally too. Moving away from the specifics of the Freudian theory of the superego, psychoanalysis here offers a considerable amount of further leverage on legal issues through its interest in what the Lacanians term 'imaginary' and 'symbolic' orders. The former relates to the illusion provided by the law, that human behaviour can be perfectly regulated and hence is perfectible. It is imaginary, in the sense of idealising and illusory, to think of anything in this way; and in the case of human behaviour, it is downright dangerous. The idea that law can provide answers to everything leads to repressive states, using that term to reference both social orders and states of mind; it is also 'regressive' in the sense of aspiring to something imagined to be early and utopian, a state of narcissistic oneness in which there is no contradiction, in which nothing disturbs the surface of bliss. The symbolic, on the other hand, follows on from the discussion of the superego: it asserts the primacy of the signifying chain in which the individual subject is placed. Whilst it is more familiar to understand this as a linguistic issue – Lacanian psychoanalysis being concerned with the practice of language – the rich description that Lacanian theory offers of how the symbolic works reinforces the notion of an external law that is crucial to psychosocial being. That is, law regulates, and within it the subject finds its location.

This account stresses the benefits to legal studies of using some elements of psychoanalytic theory, but there are also ways in which law has challenged psychoanalysis, particularly in terms of the structural relationship between social contracts and subjectivity. For instance, psychoanalysis' propensity to postulate universal psychic mechanisms that become formulated as legal injunctions (the incest taboo as a universal outcome of incestuous desire being the primary case) is punctured by evidence that radically distinct legal systems exist, and that they can and do shift as a consequence of social change. In addition, classical psychoanalytic identification of the Oedipal triad as the forum for the encounter with 'reality' is challenged by legal theory that sees law as itself arbitrary and contractual – not 'real' at all – though this criticism can be offset by the Lacanian rendering of the symbolic as a non-naturalisable 'order' that always, in important ways, fails.

The challenge to psychoanalysis can also be seen in some other areas of social scientific application of psychoanalytic thinking, where the role of psychoanalysis has been questioned even when its concepts are being deployed. The clearest examples here are where psychoanalysis has mapped across to areas of political as well as intellectual struggle, in particular being used as a resource to 'explain' or at least help theorise the motivations of political actors. Sometimes this has led to psychoanalysis being attacked as a bourgeois, oppressive discipline; at other times psychoanalysis has been turned back upon itself, so that its own investment in the troubles it is analysing becomes a topic for consideration and concern. The most important instance of this kind is that of gender and sexual difference, to which psychoanalysis has attended from the start, when received notions of heteronormativity were challenged by the formulation of sexuality as inherently bisexual, but supported by other psychoanalytic concepts such as penis envy. For Freud, as is well known, sexual difference was the 'bedrock' of psychoanalysis, beyond which it could not go, and this took the specific form of the refutation of femininity and the pursuit of masculinity. This was contested from very early on, in the work of psychoanalytic writers of the 1920s and 1930s, and the general sexual normativeness of psychoanalysis has continued to be the object of critique, both from feminists and from gay and lesbian writers (see Frosh, 1999, 2006). However, especially since the publication in 1974 of Juliet Mitchell's book, *Psychoanalysis and Feminism*, psychoanalysis has also been drawn upon by many theorists in a search for theoretical leverage on gender and sexuality. This does not mean that Mitchell's promotion of psychoanalysis as a sexually progressive discipline has gone unchallenged. Indeed, psychoanalysis' conservatism in this area is well documented: in theory and in clinical work it has rarely supplied convincing recruits to the radicalisation of gender politics or to the ranks of sexual revolution. More importantly, however, there is now a sense of banality about many of the psychoanalytic claims concerning gender and sexual difference. Freud's phallocentrism and misogyny, as well as his confusion over feminine development and sexuality, is so clearly documented as to require no detailed repetition. Virginia Goldner (2003), in a paper exploring the relationships between contemporary psychoanalytic thinking on gender and on sexuality, points out how gender is now commonly discussed in an ironic tone, to accentuate the way in which its taken-for-granted status has been thoroughly undermined. With the exception, she claims, of 'a band of Euro-Lacanians and a few surviving True Believers, Freud's theoretical contrivances on behalf of the penile phallus are now taken as prima facie evidence of his ambivalent homophobia, casual misogyny, and traditional family values' (pp.113-14). The issue of 'penis envy' no longer has much resonance outside stand-up comic routines, and even the object relational idea that girls, because of their close ties with their mothers, struggle with issues of autonomy and separation whilst boys trip up over intimacy, can now be seen both as a truism and as a tautology, describing a socially induced state of affairs without grasping hold of the complexities of the psychological mechanisms at its root. To say that girls reproduce feminine stereotypes because of their identification with their mothers, and boys become 'masculine' because of their repudiation of their mothers, is not a specifically psychoanalytic formulation: it could just as easily have been derived from social learning theory. What has replaced all this has been, as Goldner (ibid.) lists it, the work of 'Contemporary feminists, gay and lesbian scholars, queer theorists, and generations of psychoanalysts looking for better ideas about sex and gender,' which has produced what she describes as 'theories that refuse to sit still, retaining the density of the analytic perspective while digging up the ideological infrastructure of normativity, objectivism and biologism'.

Despite this healthy critique of psychoanalytic platitudes, contemporary gender theory is almost unimaginable without psychoanalytic input. Serious writers such as Judith Butler and Lynne Segal, both deeply embroiled in the political and philosophical understanding of gender, routinely deploy notions of unconscious life, albeit showing care to avoid reductiveness and individualism in so doing. Indeed, in Butler's case, the centrality of psychoanalysis to her recent thinking has been very marked, even though her highly influential early book *Gender Trouble* (1990) showed few hints that this would happen. Importantly, the key concepts she uses are not those put forward by Freud and later analysts as explaining sexual difference; it is rather the psychoanalytic formulation of more general mental mechanisms, particularly the identificatory ones described in Freud's (1917b) *Mourning and Melancholia*, that give shape to her continuing interrogation of identity and identity politics. This tendency is also visible in Jessica Benjamin's detailed psychoanalytic explorations of gender (e.g. Benjamin, 1995), which again focus on identification, and rather parallel the situation in the humanities, where the most constructive engagement with psychoanalysis has not been through its specific claims about literature or art, but rather through the tools it makes available for conceptualising psychological and psychosocial phenomena. Psychoanalysis thus enters the fray and holds its own not so much because of widespread adoption of its specific theories of sexual difference, but rather because it offers a framework for thinking through ways in which subjecthood resonates to the beat of social divides, and in particular for dissolving the simple separation between social and individual that bedevils other social psychological approaches. It is the sophistication of the psychoanalytic lexicon and its capacity for extension and disruption that attracts gender theorists, not its specific proposals about psychic development. This is even true of the Lacanian element: whilst there are aspects of Lacan's account of 'sexuation' that have had an impact on psychoanalytically inspired work in the area, it is more the general Lacanian approach that has mattered, particularly because of the centrality given to analysis of the 'phallus' in its imaginary and symbolic manifestations. It is almost as if psychoanalysis loses its liveliness in these areas when it resolves itself into a specific theoretical account, and retains it when it pumps out ideas about the symbolic mechanisms at the heart of psychosocial life.

As will be clear from this, gender theory has had a striking impact on psychoanalysis itself, querying its allegiance to a dull and normative model of heterosexuality, disputing the homophobia that seems to be close to the heart of its musings on homosexuality, and demanding that it renew itself in the context of contemporary understanding of sexuality, sexual orientation and gender politics. This has been received positively in some psychoanalytic circles, even though in the dogged work of the clinic there is perhaps less evidence of novel thinking. However, the influx of feminists into psychoanalysis (Julia Kristeva, Juliet Mitchell, Nancy Chodorow and Jessica Benjamin are all psychoanalysts, as are Muriel Dimen, Virginia Goldner and other influential figures in the gender field) has meant that there is a way of speaking to psychoanalysis from within, whatever the difficulties of holding onto one's radicalism without being co-opted, and this has resulted in some genuinely transgressive thinking. This is now extending into arenas such as mothering (Baraitser, 2009), historically the bastion of the most regressive psychoanalytic theorising, though also an area hard fought over by feminist writers. Perhaps here more than anywhere there is evidence of a reciprocal relationship between psychoanalysis and those who mine it for its insights outside the clinic; and this is despite the fact that it also contains some of the most conservative elements of the psychoanalytic approach, which see normative models of family life as sacred and treat diversions from the received heterosexual path and bourgeois family arrangements as pathological and pathogenic.

Types of psychoanalysis

This last point raises another large issue. Psychoanalysis has so far been described here mostly as if it is a homogeneous entity, albeit one riddled with tensions over what I have termed 'critical' and 'conformist' tendencies. However, as I have described in detail elsewhere (especially in

Frosh, 1999), this apparent homogeneity is far from the truth. Psychoanalysis is a very diverse field, constituted by numerous 'schools' which have certain basic ideas and practices in common (the main one being commitment to the centrality of the unconscious as an explanatory notion) and which overlap importantly with one another, but which also have significant differences. In some cases, these differences are so substantial that there is little common ground and instead a great deal of mutual antagonism; in others, the differences are so slight as to be almost invisible to an outsider, even if they are deeply felt by adherents of the different groupings. Broadly speaking, however, it is possible to discern three main approaches that have had important effects in the applied world 'outside the clinic'. The first of these is classical Freudian psychoanalysis, obviously visible in Freud's own work and in that of the early psychoanalysts, but also informing the writings of a wide range of critics in the arts and humanities, social theorists and applied social researchers. For example, the critical theorists mentioned earlier, alongside other traditional 'Freudo-Marxists', worked with Freudian notions of repression and sublimation to articulate their understanding of the machinations of society in managing the desires of its subjects. Similarly, a number of important literary and cultural critics of the mid-twentieth century (including Lionel Trilling, whose work is referenced in Chapter 3) rooted their sympathetic understanding of psychoanalysis mainly in Freud's writings. In contemporary social theory, this position is less visible, but it is extremely important in revised forms in current work that combines psychoanalysis and attachment theory, in applications of psychoanalysis to child development, and in the controversial emerging field of 'neuropsychoanalysis' (e.g. Fonagy and Target, 2007; Mayes, Fonagy and Target, 2007). In some ways, what seems to have happened is that after quite a long period of being under pressure from object relations theories to accommodate growing evidence of the social orientation of children alongside an increasingly powerful clinical literature focused on transference from a relational perspective, Freudian psychoanalysis has reinvented itself. This has involved casting off some of the more rigid perspectives of the old 'ego psychology', accepting the centrality of object relationships, and configuring its interests to be closely aligned with the more biologically oriented developmental sciences. This is producing a revitalised empirical psychoanalysis with a great deal to say about human development and with an increasingly powerful theoretical lexicon that is also influencing clinical practice, for example in the form of research-based 'mentalisation' therapies that combine brief psychoanalytic psychotherapy with some of the principles of cognitive therapy (e.g. Allen and Fonagy, 2006). However, whilst the contemporary Freudian school is making considerable contributions to the application of psychoanalysis in developmental psychology and related areas, there is relatively little evidence of impact in the wider fields of social and political theory, or in the arts and humanities.

The second broad group of psychoanalytic positions can be gathered together in what might be termed the 'relational' school of thought. This is a very large grouping with some significant differences between sub-groups – for example, some of the American 'intersubjectivists' are highly critical of Kleinian approaches to clinical work (e.g. Benjamin, 2004). Nevertheless, there is one very important factor that unites everyone, from object relations theorists and Kleinians in Britain, through to the interpersonal and intersubjectivist analysts in the United States. This is adherence to a model postulating that *relationality* is the primary concern of psychoanalysis, and also the major motivational and explanatory concept to be used both in clinical work and in broader theorising involving psychoanalysis. Psychoanalysis from this perspective involves a focus on the quality of the contact between analyst and patient as a way of addressing unconscious features of the patient's relational practices. How such unconscious features are theorised and exactly how psychoanalysis addresses them varies considerably. For example, Kleinians focus on 'inner world' features of the patient, understood to be built up out of a complex mixture of psychological drives and relationships with internal 'objects' (crudely, representations of people or parts of people). For them, the way in which unconscious phantasies attached to objects operate within the patient is demonstrated through transference-countertransference exchanges in therapy, and the analyst's task is to utilise these exchanges to help the patient recognise and work through the conflicts produced by these phantasies (e.g. Waddell, 1998; Frosh, 1999). For other analysts of the British object relations school (e.g. Casement, 2002) and the American intersubjectivists (Benjamin, 2004, 2009), there is relatively more interest in the 'reality' of the relationship between patient and analyst, in which new modes of what Benjamin and others call 'recognition' can be articulated so that the patient gains an experience of being treated as a *subject* whose needs can be understood and possibly met (Benjamin, 1995).

In Britain, Kleinian psychoanalysis in particular has a long history of use in artistic and sociological work (e.g. Stokes, 1963; Segal, 1991; Rustin, 1991), which in the early years of the twenty-first century has been strengthened by the emergence of a field of psychosocial studies drawing on Kleinian ideas for empirical as well as social investigations (Hollway and Jefferson, 2005; Roseneil, 2006). In the work of Wilfred Bion in particular it has a strong applied dimension dealing with the development of a theory of thinking (Bion, 1962, 1963, 1967) and of groups (Bion, 1959). Bion is also an example of a psychoanalyst very appreciative of the difference between analytic practice in the clinic and the process of writing about it and hence using it outside. The influence of the broader object relations tradition, particularly stemming from the work of Donald Winnicott, can be seen in much thinking on creativity and also in social democratic theorising on political processes. For example, the writings of Anthony Giddens (1991) and Axel Honneth (Fraser and Honneth, 2003), discussed briefly in Chapter 6, use this kind of psychoanalysis to help theorise the conditions of social life in late modernity. The Winnicottian perspective, which emphasises the primacy of human relationships in the construction of secure selves, has also heavily impacted on American intersubjectivist theory, which in turn has contributed to bringing psychoanalysis into an active engagement with the philosophy of ethics, an issue that will be returned to in detail in Chapter 5.

There are, however, a couple of critical points about the relational stance 'outside the clinic' that will recur in this book. The first relates to a debate about politics, inner worlds and psychoanalytic purity and reflects a tendency amongst psychoanalysts to pursue orthodoxy in the form of debates about what is 'genuinely psychoanalytic' in their own and others' work. For instance, in the context of Benjamin's account of recognition, Juliet Mitchell (2002) queries whether the non-Kleinian relational approach loses the central psychoanalytic concern with the unconscious:

> The direction in which Benjamin takes it [i.e. the notion of recognition] however, moves it away from psychic conflict, away from sexuality and destructiveness to give us a rich phenomenology of processes of recognition of sameness and difference in which the psychic world reflects the social world. This move excludes the fact that dynamically unconscious processes are different from conscious ones, that dreams and symptoms have meanings that can be deciphered but that are not reflective. Benjamin's injunction is made within a psychosocial, not a psychoanalytical framework. (p.227)

This point about the 'psychosocial' versus the 'psychoanalytic' will be returned to in Chapter 7, but it is notable here that Mitchell is holding onto a concept of 'psychic conflict' that is seen as *autonomous* in relation to social processes, whereas, she claims, the more 'psychosocial' approach of the intersubjectivists is one which understands psychic life as 'reflecting' the social world. Importantly, this critique is offered in a response from Mitchell to attacks on her own work by some who see her as having lost the political edge that characterised her feminist interventions in earlier writings (Mitchell, 1974; Segal, 2001). This tussle over what is and is not legitimately 'psychoanalytic', as well as what is and is not 'political', is characteristic of both areas. What is interesting here is that it also reflects a debate within the broad field of relational psychoanalysis about what the connections might be between the postulated 'inner world' and its outer determinants and reflections.

A second point about relational psychoanalysis is more focused on applications of Kleinian theory. Much of this work is rich and enticing, but it also demonstrates a tendency to take psychoanalytic concepts and translate them for use in the cultural and social sphere without worrying about whether this translation is actually legitimate. For example, key clinical concepts such as projective identification, transference and countertransference are entrusted with explanatory weight in investigations of phenomena such as racism (Frosh, 2006) or war (Segal, 1995). The potential problem with this, already hinted at and discussed in more detail in Chapter 7, is both that this risks reduction of social processes to psychoanalytic categories and that it significantly alters the psychoanalytic concepts being deployed, without acknowledgment that this has happened. It is arguable, for instance, that neither projective identification nor transference mean the same thing inside as outside the clinic – indeed, as will be described later, some analysts argue that transference only exists as such in the psychoanalytic encounter. Using these terms to 'give meaning' to social analysis is thus a speculative, metaphorical process, but in some work at least it can harden into an explanatory identity.

This leads into the third group of psychoanalytic approaches in this very broad classification – the Lacanian and post-Lacanian schools. Despite there being a very strong international tradition of Lacanian clinical work, it seems fair to say that the major impact of Lacanian psychoanalysis on the arts, humanities and social sciences has derived from its theoretical machinery, often as if it has nothing much to do with the clinic at all. For example, the original impact of Lacanianism in the British and American academies stemmed mainly from its position within the general pantheon of poststructuralist theories (Coward and Ellis, 1977) as well as its being part of what in the 1980s was a very fashionable wave of 'French theory' that included the work of Foucault, Derrida and Althusser as well as a variety of French feminists, some of whom drew on Lacanian theory for their own writing (Marks and de Courtivron, 1981). This meant that applied Lacanianism did not have to make the move from the clinic in the same way as did other psychoanalytic theories; rather, it was worked out, usually by non-analysts, in the context of the 'outside', for example in film theory, literature, politics and feminism. This history has attractions and problems from the point of view of the current book. On the positive side, Lacanian psychoanalysis and its derivatives and even some of its antagonists are fully incorporated into the academy and do not rely (or not solely) on the credibility given them by their clinical activities. This means that the strengths and limitations of Lacanian thought in the applied sphere can be judged in the same way as one might judge any other social or cultural theory, with less danger of an appeal to the expertise of the psychoanalyst as the one who knows the 'secrets of the unconscious' because of her or his clinical experience. There is also a specific element of Lacanian theory to add to this, which will be worked on extensively in this book. This is its own suspicion of claims to mastery, something Lacan expressed in his account of the transference as well as in his description of the 'four discourses' (Lacan, 1991), in which the 'discourse of the Master' is specifically registered as not identical to – or even opposed to- that of the Analyst. What this provokes is an approach geared not to uncovering unconscious meaning, but to repeated questioning of claims to knowledge, rather along the lines argued at the beginning of this chapter. Partly for this reason, the Lacanian stance is appealing as a way of utilising the psychoanalytic understanding that the unconscious *is disruptive* in the social and cultural field, without pinning this down to a position in which the analyst alone knows the 'truth' of what is going on.

The drawback to this is that in being set free of the clinic, Lacanianism is also highly prone to abstraction in a way that is much less true of other psychoanalytic schools. In some respects, precisely because it does not often highlight its clinical status, it also loses the specific grounds of its authority, and instead has to share a position as one amongst many potential vocabularies for theorising social phenomena. Perhaps the discomfort this produces is one reason why some Lacanians have insisted on the clinical locus of psychoanalysis and on the *illegitimacy* of straightforward translation of its concepts to the wider sphere of knowledge (e.g. Nasio, 1992). It may also be a motivation for the tantalising way in which Lacanianism often seems to undermine its own knowledge claims by expressing them in abstrusely paradoxical, technical or enigmatic ways (including mathematical formulae that may not stand up to scrutiny). The message here seems to be both that there is a superior form of abstract knowledge available in Lacanianism, and that the lesson of psychoanalysis is that no-one can ever know anything at all.

Many of the details of these schematically presented distinctions between different psychoanalytic schools will be returned to in the course of this book. What will become clear is that despite its difficulties, the primary engagement here is with the Lacanian perspective because of the way in which it highlights the disruptive potential of psychoanalysis and hence works against the ossification of psychoanalytic thought as an expert system that somehow knows the truth of the unconscious and can explain it to the world outside the clinic. However, there is also a strong presence of relational psychoanalysis in this book, particularly in the discussions on ethics and on social identity, and also use of some theorists who do not stand within any one psychoanalytic school, notably the French analyst Jean Laplanche. None of these approaches are being presented as unproblematic, for it is part of the task here to examine how they work in order to identify what they offer to the field of social criticism, and some of what they lack.

Psychoanalysis in the social sciences: a psychosocial approach

In summary, more than a hundred years after the founding of psychoanalysis, it is apparent that the influences and controversies surrounding it continue. The locus of psychoanalytic knowledge is in the clinical situation, so what is being enacted when it moves 'outside' is a translation across and extension of psychoanalytic ideas and practices, raising issues about the distortions and possibly creative alterations that take place along the way. Of particular concern is the extent to which the limitations on 'wild' analysis (Freud, 1910b) that are produced by the clinical situation (meaningless or wrong-headed interpretations might, one hopes, be constrained by the presence of an actual analysand who can speak back to the analyst) are lost once the restrictive boundaries of that situation are removed. There is also the danger of psychological reductiveness, in which the specific disciplinary constraints of the humanities or social sciences are displaced by a tendency to reduce everything to personal psychodynamics, often with a pathological slant. Nevertheless, it is arguable that psychoanalysis holds something significant for all the other disciplines – specifically, a capacity to theorise subjectivity in a way that is provocative and unique, through reference to the unconscious. In addition, the fertility of its applications reflects back on psychoanalysis itself. Some of the most important critical work applied to psychoanalysis has come from outside the clinical situation, as if the freedom to think without being concerned with the requirements of therapy is a necessary condition for theoretical development.

This book takes up these themes through a number of engagements with applied psychoanalysis. It is by no means comprehensive: part of the argument is that psychoanalysis fails when it is used without detailed knowledge of the area under discussion, and trying to cover everything would simply replicate this failure. My own interests produce a bias towards social and political issues rather than the arts and humanities. Applications of psychoanalysis in the fields of sexuality, gender and 'race' come into this in an especially powerful way, but I have written about these extensively elsewhere (Frosh, 1994, 1999, 2005, 2006) and want to focus the present discussion on some newer areas of concern. These include particularly the emergence of a psychoanalytically-inflected literature around relational ethics, linked to questions of recognition, violence and 'otherness'. Nevertheless, the reality of sexual and racial oppression haunts the current text as a kind of undercurrent that constantly questions the way psychoanalytic ideas traverse the space of the social world.

The focus of the book is therefore on the applications of psychoanalysis in what can be loosely termed the 'social sciences', though even here I am consciously selective. For example, apart from the brief discussion in this first chapter, there is little more on law and nothing on the imaginative uses of psychoanalysis that have impacted upon recent human geography (Kingsbury, 2007) or on some controversial attempts to incorporate psychoanalytic thinking into social history (e.g. Pick, 1995). There is also no account of the use of psychoanalysis in developmental theory (see Frosh, 1989, for an early discussion of this), despite its growing importance, and nothing on the clinical uses of psychoanalysis in non-analytic settings such as psychiatry or psychodynamic counselling (Spurling, 2009). On the other hand, I do offer some coverage of the engagement of psychoanalysis and literary studies with one another, even though this lies outside the arena of the social sciences. This is because I shall argue that some classical debates over the literary uses of psychoanalysis are in important respects paradigmatic for the concerns of 'applied psychoanalysis' as a whole, and can offer a template and source of ideas for the social science discussion that in particular relieves it of the temptation to descend into a controversy over psychoanalysis' 'scientific status'. Whilst this question of 'scientificity', which I have previously discussed (Frosh, 2006), has its own interest, I suggest that the example of literary studies reveals more strongly some key pointers to enlivening the encounter between psychoanalysis and another discipline. These include how to keep both protagonists open to the other and reflexive enough to change as a consequence of contact, and how to ensure that the uses to which psychoanalytic ideas are put are sufficiently grounded in the kind of evidence that is relevant to the other discipline. Freud's own 'literary' works are therefore considered early in the book, as is the vexed and thrilling issue of 'psychoanalysis and literature', to produce a kind of model in which what is advocated is a reciprocal influence of each discipline on the other – what Felman (1982a) calls the 'implication' of each discipline in the other, rather than the 'application' of psychoanalysis to a field outside itself. This demands a certain degree of openness and reflexivity within psychoanalysis, as well as modesty in its claims; but it also suggests that there are real gains to be had when psychoanalysis is brought into the sphere of activity of other disciplines, that it may help open them up or disrupt their own received wisdoms. The rest of the book proceeds through explorations of the social psychological and ego psychoanalytic notion of 'identity', which also draws on the massive interest in identities that pervade the social sciences (including ethnic, racialised and sexual identities); to debates on 'relational ethics' and examination of what it means to 'recognise others'; and to explorations of psychoanalysis in political theory. The final substantive chapter, on psychoanalysis and psychosocial studies, takes up particularly strongly the question of what psychoanalysis can offer to this attempt to think the 'social' and 'psychological' subject as one entity, and what happens to psychoanalysis along the way.

The logic of inclusion and argument here depends on an understanding of one so far unacknowledged element of my own disciplinary perspective, that of 'psychosocial studies'. The specifics of this in relation to psychoanalysis are discussed in Chapter 7, but in general what is being explored in this emerging field is the possibility of developing an approach to human subjects that manages to theorise together what are usually taken to be separate: the 'social' and the 'personal' or 'individual'. This requires an engagement with theories of subjectivity –hence, psychoanalysis – and also with theories of the appearance of the subject in the social. That is, using a term popularised by Althusser (1971), we are dealing particularly with questions of 'interpellation', which means considering how the human subject is both formed as an entity through the social order, and yet has agency within it. This paradox, that one can be both 'subject to' the workings of society and yet also be a 'subject' in the sense of being an agent with power to act on the world, is a core issue for psychosocial studies, as it is for many in the broader field of social theory. For example, Judith Butler (1997) expresses the dynamic well in her account of how power both constructs the subject and is available to the subject for use; that is, the same processes that make the human a 'subject' of power also constitute what is often taken to be the 'essence' of human subjectivity itself. She writes (p.14), 'Power acts on the subject in at least two ways: first, as what makes the subject possible, the condition of its possibility and its formative occasion, and second, as what is taken up and reiterated in the subject's "own" acting.' Written more simply and generally, the issue here is how one can describe the human subject in a way that accounts for the richness of what is usually taken to be 'inner life' (fantasies, desires, affects and the like) yet also recognises how each of us is constituted first and foremost as a social being. Psychosocial studies is a generic term for this project, and also refers specifically to a set of theories and studies that try to bring these two aspects of the subject together.

A recurrent question in this book, then, is how to approach psychoanalysis not as possessing a 'truth', but rather as opening out some questions and perceptions that enable us to think the social and the psychological together in a manner that genuinely offsets the reductive pressures that work to hold them apart. The choice of topics in the chapters that follow can be seen as an attempt at various 'interventions' to support this goal of advancing psychosocial understanding through the use of psychoanalysis. From its historical contextualisation in Freud's work in Chapter 2 to the explicit consideration of psychoanalysis in psychosocial studies in Chapter 7, the interventions I have chosen are those which combine psychoanalysis and social or cultural theory in an attempt to break down traditional society-individual differentiations. Earlier, two questions were posed for this discussion. The first was what happens to psychoanalysis when it moves outside the clinic. The second was how, when the move is made, psychoanalysis can preserve or enhance its value as a critical approach, able to challenge and disturb the disciplines with which it comes into contact, and also able to renew itself in the process. A third, related issue, is now at stake. This revolves around the 'project' of psychosocial studies, distilled into a specific question of whether psychoanalysis 'outside the clinic' can be a force through which the divide between social and personal, 'external' and 'internal', can be overcome.

Chapter 2

Freud on Art, Culture and Society

Although this book is concerned with contemporary trends in psychoanalysis as applied in the social sciences, there is, as ever, no escaping Freud. For one to understand why and how psychoanalysis has moved out of the clinic, it is important to realise just how ambitious was the psychoanalytic project from the start, and also just how much energy was spent by the early analysts in arguing over the use of psychoanalysis as an instrument of cultural study. In particular, Freud and his followers were intensely interested in ways in which artistic and cultural phenomena could act as evidence for psychoanalytic theories. The study of mythology, for example, which was a focus for many late nineteenth-century scholars, was seen as a rich hunting ground for the psychoanalysts, particularly because of the apparent parallels between myths and dreams. Indeed, as Kerr (1993) has shown, for Freud and his early follower Jung it was so central that it became a space for disputation, expressing the growing personal and professional dissension between them. Jung developed work on myths earlier and more extensively than Freud, who initially regarded the younger man's research in this area as advancing psychoanalysis' credibility and field of application. However, once their relationship had soured, the study of myth became a site for recrimination and barely coded antagonism. Freud emphasised the sexual and paternal motifs to be uncovered in mythological structures, whilst Jung immersed himself in what Freud thought to be spiritual and maternal illusions. By the time of the publication of the Freud's main text on the subject, *Totem and Taboo* (Freud, 1913a), Jung had already left the psychoanalytic fold, but Freud's book was as much a polemic against him as it was a contribution to the anthropological literature. In this way, the study of mythology became a political tool for the advancement of different versions of psychoanalysis.

This brief example flags up some of the issues to be dealt with in this chapter. 'Applied' psychoanalysis has several aims, all of which are registered in Freud's own work. One is to seek to extend the reach of psychoanalysis by showing its utility in fields outside the clinic. This 'political' advancement of psychoanalysis is coupled with a genuine curiosity about what psychoanalysis might add to understanding social and cultural materials, and an irritation with those in other disciplines who cannot comprehend the difference that the unconscious might make to their studies. Conversely, as Freud and his followers believed they were uncovering universal features of mental life, they also looked to the wider world for evidence to support their claims. Art and literature would be especially valuable here, given the supposed parallels between artistic creativity and dreaming; but broader social and cultural phenomena such as mythology would also be important sources of such evidential support. These two main purposes of applied psychoanalysis – to extend the reach of the discipline and to provide support for its claims – continue to be central motives for psychoanalysis outside the clinic. Their political significance in establishing the credentials of psychoanalysis also remains, as it was for Freud, a primary cause of the intensity of much of the succeeding debate.

This chapter explores some of Freud's own contributions to the extension of psychoanalysis outside the clinic, focusing first on what he had to say about artistic creativity, and then moving to a more central issue for this book, his views on society and some of its major features. The examples presented here show a few things quite clearly: that Freud was deeply committed to this extension of psychoanalysis; that he was often aware of its limitations and of the problems it might create; and that he was mostly engaged in an *application* of psychoanalysis where the advantage lay with his own approach, seen as casting light on phenomena that could otherwise only be partially understood. All these issues recur in later work and so contribute to the framing of the discussions in this book, but the last of them, what might be termed the 'colonialist project' of psychoanalysis, is of particular importance.

Culture on the couch

From early on in his psychoanalytic work, Freud was on the lookout for ways in which psychoanalysis might draw on evidence from outside the consulting room in order to establish itself more firmly, as well as for opportunities to use psychoanalysis for wider cultural and scientific ends in the service of knowledge in general – as part, that is, of a broader process of scientific enlightenment. The 'social', 'cultural' and 'psychological' were not fully distinct domains for Freud. Anthropology, religion, art and politics were areas in which the unconscious could be observed at work, and consequently had things to say to psychoanalysis and, even more significantly, things to learn from it. As early as 1912, Otto Rank and Hans Sachs had founded a journal, *Imago*, which was 'concerned with the application of psycho-analysis to non-medical fields of knowledge' (Freud, 1926, p.269). This journal had considerable success until the Nazis seized the psychoanalytic publishing house, the *Internationaler Psychoanalytischer Verlag*, in 1938, after which it was reinvented in America as *American Imago*. *Imago* was entertaining from the start, and involved some of the early psychoanalysts in exciting cultural speculations of a kind that, as widely read bourgeois, they immensely enjoyed. Gay (1988) comments:

> The nonclinical writings of the inner circle generated opportunities for round robins of good will and mutual congratulations. Freud welcomed Jones' weighty contribution to *Imago* on the symbolic significance of salt; Jones told Abraham that he had perused his 'charming study' of Segantini 'with the greatest interest'; Abraham for his part read Freud's *Totem and Taboo* 'twice, with ever-increasing relish.' Admittedly, some of the pathographies of artists and poets produced in the Vienna circle were naïve and slapdash, and at times they aroused Freud's outspoken irritation. But whether well done or bungled, applied psychoanalysis was a cooperative venture almost from the start. Freud found this widespread interest agreeable, but he needed no urging from others to put culture on the couch. (p.312)

Gay argues that Freud's principles when moving from the couch to culture were 'few in number, easy to state, but hard to apply: all is lawful, all is disguised, and all is connected' (ibid.). Psychoanalysis reveals how culture operates to gratify or frustrate 'hidden wishes'; hence, psychoanalysis opens out new areas of cultural understanding, and advances human knowledge in all its fields of application. 'What mattered to him,' writes Gay (pp.312–13), 'was less what he could learn from art history, linguistics and the rest than what they could learn from him; he entered alien terrain as a conquistador rather than a supplicant.' As will be seen, this is not completely true: Freud was in considerable awe of what he termed 'creative artists', who he thought had an intuitive grasp of the unconscious that could be used to provide evidence for psychoanalytic claims. But it is the case that, for better or worse (mostly the latter), applied psychoanalysis has tended to mean an attempt at conquest rather than partnership. This is perhaps justifiable for Freud and his immediate followers, who were working in a context in which what mattered most was the establishment of psychoanalysis as a discipline with something unique to offer, and for whom psychoanalysis was a revolutionary activity that overturned all traditional authority and ways of understanding the world. But even then, the complexity of the relationship between psychoanalytic knowledge and the specialised knowledge produced by the disciplines with which it is in dialogue (or with which it interferes) is considerable. Freud seems to have had more than an inkling that, whatever his own pleasure in cultural speculation, there might be limits to what his new approach could do.

These early applications of psychoanalysis came in a number of areas, but with the possible exception of mythology they were more focused on art and literature than on what might now be termed the social sciences. Later on, not just in *Totem and Taboo* but even more in the great texts on religion and society of the 1920s and 1930s, Freud turned powerfully to consider social phenomena, but in this case the application of psychoanalysis was very much one-way. Psychoanalysis was a tool to make fuller sense of social and 'civilisational' concerns than the existing (e.g. political and anthropological) and emerging (e.g. sociological) social science disciplines could do on their own. However, in considering art and literature, Freud knew he was engaging with modes of intellectual practice that had their own considerable history and potency, and whilst the 'conquistador' was very much in evidence in his attitude towards them, he also realised that there might be something psychoanalysis could learn. For this reason, if one is to seek an open psychoanalysis that can speak with other disciplines without too much arrogance and appropriative desire, a place to start might be with the problematic but also provocative musings of Freud on creative artists and their products. Before turning to some of the social applications of psychoanalysis, therefore, this chapter looks at some examples of his work on art and literature as a way of beginning to sketch something of a methodology. What emerges is a tale that will become familiar of psychoanalysis stating too much too firmly about its own knowledge, but nevertheless participating in a dialogue that has intriguing effects.

Pillaging art

Freud's approach to art and literature was that of a pillager, taking from it whatever he could to support his work. However, this was not done out of disrespect: he was steeped in admiration for literature, which formed much of the background to his thinking. His writings are peppered with literary allusions and references, marking him out as solidly within the traditions of European thought, a romantic in his belief in the power of the creative imagination. More significantly, Freud believed that the psychological processes fuelling artistic creativity were identical to those revealed by psychoanalysis in the clinic, and hence that exploration of the former would advance and deepen general psychological knowledge. A seminal example of this reasoning can be found in his paper, *Creative Writers and Daydreaming*, which presents the 'assumption' that 'a piece of creative writing, like a day-dream, is a continuation of, and a substitute for, what was once the play of childhood' (Freud,

1908a, p.139). In this short piece, Freud undertakes both to outline the sources of the creative writer's work and also its impact on readers, arguing that the continuity with childhood play reveals that the phantasies appearing in literature (especially romantic literature) are expressions of unconscious wishes, either erotic (in young women) or both erotic and ambitious (in young men). Freud acknowledges that much creative writing seems to be at a considerable distance from this kind of reductive scheme, yet states that he 'cannot suppress the suspicion that even the most extreme deviations from that model could be linked with it through an uninterrupted series of transitional cases' (p.138). But the key argument is one which directly parallels the account given in *The Interpretation of Dreams*, which postulates that dreams arise when a 'day residue' activates a childhood experience that has become wholly or partially repressed:

> A strong experience in the present awakens in the creative writer a memory of an earlier experience (usually belonging to his childhood) from which there now proceeds a wish which finds its fulfilment in the creative work. The work itself exhibits elements of the recent provoking occasion as well as of the old memory. (p.139)

Freud takes this 'wish-fulfilment' to be a very general phenomenon, explaining both the work of the writer and the response of readers to literature. According to Freud, the aesthetics of a piece of literature are a way of 'bribing' the reader with 'fore-pleasure' so that the disturbing elements of repressed material can be tolerated. Further pleasure can then be gained by the release of the underlying tension caught up with this repression:

> In my opinion, all the aesthetic pleasure which a creative writer affords us has the character of a fore-pleasure of this kind, and our actual enjoyment of an imaginative work proceeds from a liberation of tensions in our minds. It may even be that not a little of this effect is due to the writer's enabling us thenceforward to enjoy our own day-dreams without self-reproach or shame. (p.140)

Here it is the literary product that is the object of study, but behind it is an examination of patterns of psychological functioning that are seen by Freud as having general currency. They apply to dreams, daydreams, literary production and response, explaining both how creative writing comes about and how it might have an impact on a reader. Psychoanalysis is being used here not so much to interpret the 'meaning' of a piece of literature, but rather to understand the psychological processes that go into its production. As such, this approach is in line with much work on the psychology of 'creativity' and it can be argued that it lies well within the domain of psychoanalysis' expertise: what mental processes allow a creative writer to work, and what psychological factors are called into play when a reader reads with enjoyment? Freud's answers to these questions might be tendentious and speculative, but the questions themselves are legitimately psychological and both draw on and advance the burgeoning theory of psychoanalysis as it applies itself to the broader, non-clinical arena of psychic life.

The model outlined by Freud in *Creative Writers and Day-Dreaming* is seen by him as possibly applying even to nations, their myths being 'distorted vestiges of the wishful phantasies of whole nations, the *secular dreams* of youthful humanity' (Freud, 1908a, p.140). As noted above, the exploration of myth was an important area of research for the early psychoanalysts because it seemed to offer anthropological support for psychoanalysis' claims, as well as providing a possible route to 'primitive' thoughts that might be seen as foundational for the structure of modern human minds. For Freud, the power of myths as routes to engaging with basic wishes and anxieties also explained the way audiences might respond to works of art that stirred up the same 'primitive' emotions that these myths dealt with so effectively. For example, in *The Theme of the Three Caskets* (1913b), Freud takes the scene from Shakespeare's *The Merchant of Venice* in which Portia's suitors have to choose between a gold, silver and lead casket, and what he convincingly presents as the parallel situation in *King Lear*, in which the true daughter is the third one, Cordelia, and argues that this 'dumb' third is death, now made an object of choice rather than necessity:

> Choice stands in the place of necessity, of destiny. In this way man overcomes death, which he has recognised intellectually. No greater triumph of wish-fulfilment is conceivable. A choice is made where in reality there is obedience to a compulsion; and what is chosen is not a figure of terror, but the fairest and most desirable of women. (p.245)

Literature is being treated as myth (Freud also quotes myths and fairy tales in this short piece), providing insights into basic human psychic mechanisms, in this case the substitution of what is most desired for what is most feared. This also acts as a mode of resignation and had – for the lugubrious, 57-year-old Freud, now at the end of what he had hoped would be a saving relationship with that other great exponent of myth, Jung – much personal resonance:

> We might argue that what is represented here are the three inevitable relations that a man has with a woman – the woman who bears him, the woman who is his mate and the woman who destroys him; or that they are the three

> forms taken by the figure of the mother in the course of a man's life – the mother herself, the beloved one who is chosen after her pattern, and lastly the Mother earth who receives him once more. But it is in vain that an old man yearns for the love of woman as he had it first from his mother; the third of the Fates alone, the silent Goddess of Death, will take him into her arms. (ibid., p.247)

Literary analysis is being deployed here, remarkably successfully in many ways, to identify a symptom revealing a general human psychological state. That is, it is being used in the service of psychoanalysis, to advance understanding of psychic mechanisms (wish-fulfilment and reversal, for example) and to gain access to the way that residues from the past of humanity provide motive power for observable regularities in individuals' mental defences.

Occasionally, and less frequently than would be the case with later analysts, Freud applies psychoanalysis in order to enhance the understanding of the work of art itself, with his remarkable if rather unpersuasive analysis of *The Moses of Michelangelo* being a prime example (Freud, 1914). Freud's stance here is ostensibly naïve and rationalistic. Like the person who knows nothing of art but knows only what he likes, Freud has no great feel for the 'formal and technical' – that is, *aesthetic* – qualities of a work of art; but rather, when he finds himself moved, it is by the *content* of the work. For Freud, this indicates that what matters is the extent to which an artwork succeeds in communicating 'the artist's intention', this being understood not merely as an intellectual exercise, but as the capacity 'to awaken in us the same emotional attitude, the same mental constellation as that which in him produced the impetus to create' (Freud, 1914, p.254). It is therefore this element of the art object that needs to be understood, and hence turned into words; yet, until the advent of psychoanalysis, it is precisely this aspect of art that has proved so recalcitrant. If it is the case that the 'meaning' of a work of art, or at least its effect, depends on the mobilisation of emotions in the viewer that reflect the intention of the artist, then one needs a vocabulary of the emotions that is adequate for the articulation of this process in order to make sense of it. This is particularly so if one is, like Freud, so devoutly rationalistic that one always needs to produce an intellectual understanding of what one is going through. Freud writes (p.254): 'It is possible, therefore, that a work of art of this kind needs interpretation, and that until I have accomplished that interpretation I cannot come to know why I have been so powerfully affected.' And it is only with the emergence of psychoanalysis, with its clear and extensive explication of (unconscious) mental life, that such a vocabulary and interpretive scheme are available.

In the specific case of Michelangelo's *Moses*, Freud uses a detailed analysis of the position of the statue's hands, beard and tablets to argue that, contrary to the biblical story, Moses is *refraining* from enacting his anger and smashing the tablets. This reading probably has more to do with Freud's specific biographical circumstances at the time (his response to the final break with Jung and the near-disintegration of the psychoanalytic movement) than with any legitimate rendering of Michelangelo's intentions. That aside, the key point here is that psychoanalysis is being used to make sense of the art object not in order to advance understanding of psychological processes (though this may happen as a consequence), nor of psychoanalytic theory, but rather as a mode of art criticism. Without psychoanalysis, Freud argues, no full understanding of a work of art is possible, because it is only through identifying the emotional intention and impact of the work (awakening 'in us the same emotional attitude, the same mental constellation as that which in [the artist] produced the impetus to create') that its 'meaning and content' can be fully known. And only psychoanalysis, which is the specialist study of such emotional attitudes and mental constellations, can provide the tools required to do this. This is, in some ways, a scandalous claim, displacing specialist art criticism, with its focus on genre, history and aesthetics, in favour of a speculative 'reading into /out of' the art object in terms of the possible psychological intentions of the artist. The intentions in question, of course, are particularly those that are *unconscious* and hence can only be revealed by what Freud (p.265) refers to in passing as psychoanalysis' capacity 'to divine secret and concealed things from despised or unnoticed features, from the rubbish-heap, as it were, of our observations'. Psychoanalysis allows Freud to see the things that the specialists could not see, and to do so not only in order to advance understanding of psychological processes, which could be taken to be the appropriate subject matter of psychoanalysis, but also to provide a fuller and more truthful understanding of what Ehrenzweig (1967) later termed 'the hidden order of art'. It can legitimately be argued that Freud's move here, in *The Moses of Michelangelo*, founds a particularly imperialist strand of applied psychoanalysis. This sets aside disciplinary traditions of criticism in favour of speculative psychologistic readings that shimmer with emotional and intellectual excitement, but are perhaps unbound by respect for, or at times even knowledge of, the specialist tools employed by those who have studied their trade all their lives – something which Freud would never have allowed in relation to critics of psychoanalysis itself.

Biographical psychobabble: Leonardo's sexuality

More characteristically and in principle perhaps more appropriately, given psychoanalysis' concern with individual lives, Freud published studies of creative artists in which he used psychoanalysis to bring to light aspects of their psychology. That is, he practiced psychoanalysis on the artist, on the basis of the traces left in the artist's work and on incidental biographical information. As Freud himself knew, this was an inherently problematic procedure. His notorious paper, on *Leonardo Da Vinci and a Memory of his Childhood* (1910a), is an instance of what can be gained by such an approach, but also shows just how highly risky the strategy could be. The editors of the *Standard Edition of the Complete Psychological Works of Sigmund Freud* note that this was Freud's first full-length application of the methods of clinical psychoanalysis to the life of a historical figure and that it 'seems to have been greeted with more than the usual amount of disapproval' (p.146). The paper itself is a deeply engaged investigation of the sexual issues that might have been at the source of Leonardo's creativity, an investigation which seems to have been sparked off not only by Freud's admiration for the combination of artistic and scientific genius that so marked Leonardo, but also with an identification with him – though the nature of this identification is open to speculation. For some, the emotional intensity of the piece has to do with the employment of mythological elements in the argument: the supposed 'vulture' that swoops down on the infant Leonardo, opens his mouth, and strikes him many times with its tail against his lips, permanently affecting his imagination, is held by Freud to have links with 'hieroglyphics of the ancient Egyptians' (Freud, 1910a, p.178). Once again, it is exactly at this time that Freud is most engaged with the father–son elements in his relationship with Jung (who reacted very enthusiastically to *Leonardo*, despite – or perhaps because of – the hostility it engendered in other quarters), and the terrain of mythology was one on which this relationship was being worked out. But *Leonardo Da Vinci and a Memory of his Childhood* has much more to it than being merely another exercise in mythological speculation. It is very clearly an attempt at psychobiography, using extremely sparse materials and hence totally at variance with the usual psychoanalytic procedure of careful examination of the rich and idiosyncratic details of a person's autobiographical narrative. It also develops an account of creativity which draws out in great detail the sexual components at its root, and in so doing enunciates a theory of homosexuality and also of sublimation, understood as the expression of sexuality in a socially valued form, this being here the work of art. That Freud should have chosen for this a dead, idealised figure rather than a potentially intractable, but nevertheless responsive, live patient is itself an issue of some interest. Might it be that his pyrotechnics could only be safely achieved with material like this, held at arm's length, *especially* in the light of the ongoing biographical circumstances – the 'homosexual' investment in Jung?

Freud claims that Leonardo's curiosity and creativity were both inhibited and mobilised by his sexual history. The argument about inhibition comes in the form of Freud's objection to the conventional belief that Leonardo was exceptionally speedy in his artistic productions, and that the unfinished nature of so many of them signifies his impatience:

> On the contrary, it is possible to observe a quite extraordinary profundity, a wealth of possibilities between which a decision can only be reached with hesitation, demands which can hardly be satisfied, and an inhibition in the actual execution which is not in fact to be explained even by the artist inevitably falling short of his ideal. The slowness which had all along been conspicuous in Leonardo's work is seen to be a symptom of this inhibition and to be the forerunner of his subsequent withdrawal from painting. (p.156)

Freud uses the early part of his paper to establish that Leonardo's chief psychological characteristic was a search for knowledge, and that the profound and utterly dominating strength of this was directly connected to his 'cool repudiation of sexuality' (p.158). Leonardo's sexuality, he holds, was evident only in an apparently inactive homosexuality expressed mainly by surrounding himself 'with handsome boys and youths'. Using a routine but nevertheless powerfully sexualised metaphor, Freud argues that the energy behind Leonardo's thirst for knowledge was the replacement for sexual activity; that is, the mental mechanism at play here, as in all creativity, is sublimation:

> In reality Leonardo was not devoid of passion ... He had merely converted his passion into a thirst for knowledge; he then applied himself to investigation with the persistence, constancy and penetration which is derived from passion, and at the climax of intellectual labour, when knowledge had been won, he allowed the long restrained affect to break loose and to flow away freely, as a stream of water drawn from a river is allowed to flow away when its work is done. (p.164)

Why should Leonardo have been constituted in this way? Drawing on the memory of the 'vulture' that had so roughed him up in childhood, and on a totally speculative reconstruction, from barely any documentary evidence, of the eroticisation of the young Leonardo by his single mother, Freud constructs a theory of the origins of one form of homosexuality in an identificatory love for a mother who must not be abandoned or betrayed through loving another woman. Calling upon some of his psychoanalytic cases for corroboration, Freud writes:

> In all our homosexual cases the subjects had had a very intense erotic attachment to a female person, as a rule their mother, during the first period of childhood, which is afterwards forgotten; this attachment was evoked or encouraged by too much tenderness on the part of the mother herself, and further reinforced by the small part played by the father during their childhood ... Indeed it almost seems as though the presence of a strong father would ensure that the son made the correct decision in his choice of object, namely someone of the opposite sex ... The child's love for his mother cannot continue to develop consciously any further; it succumbs to repression. The boy represses his love for his mother; he puts himself in her place, identifies with her, and takes his own person as a model in whose likeness he chooses the new objects of his love. In this way he has become a homosexual. What he has in fact done is slip back into auto-erotism: for the boys who he now loves as he grows up are after all only substitutive figures and revivals of himself in childhood – boys whom he loves in the way in which his mother loved *him* when he was a child. He finds the objects of his love along the path of *narcissism*. (pp.190–1)

By repressing his love for his mother he unconsciously preserves it and from now on remains faithful to her. 'While he seems to pursue boys and to be their lover,' writes Freud (p.192), 'he is in reality running away from the other women, who might cause him to be unfaithful.' The relative absence of a paternal figure is not only made responsible for the lack of a heterosexual object choice (as in the quotation above), but is also drawn on to explain Leonardo's neglect of his finished compositions – he discarded them as his father had discarded him – and his capacity to break with established authority, his relentless curiosity about science and his inventive flourishes. Unlike most people, who remain tied to it, Leonardo had no need for the authority of the father. On the other hand, his 'two mothers' (his actual mother and his stepmother) appear in some of his great works, either separately (*St Anne with Two Others*) or together in the famously ambiguous smile of the *Mona Lisa* ('the contrast between reserve and seduction, and between the most devoted tenderness and a sensuality that is ruthlessly demanding' – p.200). For Freud, what is happening here is that the sexual researches of Leonardo's childhood had been transformed into the search for knowledge (fantasies of flight, for example, being expressions of a desire for sexual potency), and in turn this sublimated energy fuelled the intense creativity of this most profound and productive of artists. This also explains the *effect* of Leonardo's art on others: 'Kindly nature has given the artist the ability to express his most secret mental impulses, which are hidden even from himself, by means of the works he creates; and these works have a powerful effect on others who are strangers to the artist, and who are themselves unaware of the source of their emotion' (p.199).

There is much in *Leonardo* that is of great contemporary interest, not least the sympathetic account Freud gives of homosexuality, his attempt to construct a convincing sexual history out of biographical materials, and his analysis of Leonardo's 'inhibition'. But here the main issue concerns what it says about the application of psychoanalysis to art. Freud's classical view of 'great art' led him to look for the exemplar of sublimation in a dead (male) artist rather than in one of the struggling real patients of his day, where it is possible that the *complexity* of sublimation as a way of dealing with sexual urges might have been more apparent. In *Leonardo*, however, what we get is a relatively simple account. The boy's sexual history, in this case belaboured with a frustrated mother and an absent father, who then confusingly moves in to take over from the mother and finds a substitute for her, leads to an imperative to make sexual researches. These are theorised as too painful to be integrated into the artist's personality. Instead, he becomes notionally desexualised, and in Leonardo's case this became a 'peaceableness' that seems to have dominated his personality. Yet, in his art he was restless, striving, ambitious, patient whilst at times wilful, and of course immensely original. The sexual energy has not dried up, but rather has been channelled into scientific and artistic curiosity, this being a psychic mechanism which has general significance for art. But how convincing is this? Freud's main worry seems to have been that in analysing Leonardo he would be thought of as somehow denigrating him, which was not in the least his intention or indeed the effect of his work. However, other doubts remain. Apart from the total inadequacy of the historical record on which Freud based his ideas, alongside the clumsiness of some of the detailed aesthetic work in the piece, there is also a problem with his use of mythology to support some of his interpretive claims – the 'vulture' of Leonardo's early memory turns out actually to have been a 'kite', which does not warrant the Egyptian resonances that Freud gives it (Editor's note to Freud, 1910a, p.62). What has been especially criticised, however, is the reductive nature of Freud's reading of the links between creativity and sexuality. Despite his own tolerance and in some ways admirably nuanced account of homosexuality, the mother is at the source of sexual inhibition, the lack of an appropriate father blocks the way to heterosexuality, and the block on sexuality is the source for creativity. Is this *always* so (Freud refers to 'all our homosexual cases' in offering his account)? Does it mean that such blockages are *required* for creativity to occur? There seem to be plenty of examples of creative individuals, both heterosexual and homosexual, who have not had problems with expressing their sexuality more directly; indeed there is really no lack of examples of people who seem to be *exceptionally* sexualised and yet still manage to be profoundly creative. If the sexual drive does not need to be sublimated, by what means do they produce their art? And what of Leonardo's artistic *facility*, the traditions upon which he drew and those which he consciously subverted? Are these peripheral issues next to the emotional features of the work, or do they have their own connections with his creativity, independently of anything that might have derived from his sexually fuelled curiosity? This is not to say that Freud had it completely wrong, but he certainly had it incomplete, and while it is unfair to accuse him of pathologising Leonardo, the tradition which this study institutes both in psychobiography and art criticism is deeply problematic for all the plausible, pressing questions that it leaves unaddressed. In some ways it instances the worst excesses of psychoanalytic arrogance – of psychoanalysis when 'applied' non-reflexively in the non-clinical sphere. It takes as incontestable a set of knowledge claims that are in fact dubious (psychoanalysis' *clinical* account of homosexuality is one of its most controversial areas – see Frosh, 2006), asserts them as facts which are established by clinical work (and hence lying within the area of specialist knowledge of psychoanalysis, so unchallengeable by mere art critics) and then imposes them on material that meets none of psychoanalysis' own usual requirements for 'data'. This trail of speculative claims and ungrounded reasoning then hardens into 'reality' and becomes *the* psychoanalytic explanation of a phenomenon that is complex and multifarious, and irreducible to simple, linearly causal psychological factors. In this process, despite the characteristically illuminating and suggestive potency of Freud's text, the artist, the traditions of art criticism and appreciation, and psychoanalysis itself, become devalued.

Using literature to validate psychoanalysis: the example of Jensen's Gradiva

So far, a few different uses of psychoanalysis by Freud in the realm of art and literature have been outlined: to explain the creative process; to identify other psychological processes that might be at work generally in people; to elaborate on the impact of an artistic work; and to reveal the biographical sources of a particular artist's activities, thereby also developing a fuller understanding of the relationship between sexuality and sublimation. All these elements have something useful to offer and have led to further research, but all have problems, particularly in their neglect of the aesthetic domain so central to most artistic and literary criticism – that is, their neglect of the *specificity* of the artistic terrain – as well as their general reductionism and false certainty. These features of this work, particularly the kind of biographical character analysis evident in *Leonardo*, have given a bad name to much psychoanalytic literary and artistic criticism. However, in many other instances Freud was cautious in his approach to art and in particular wary of pronouncing too definitively upon it. Instead, he used literature and art in order to demonstrate the utility of psychoanalytic thinking, whilst remaining highly respectful about the artwork itself. Freud does not always sustain this, for instance slipping into making unsustainable generalisations based on treating fictional characters as real, but he is usually aware when this happens and steps back from the brink. The principle seems to have been that the creative artist (especially the writer) is closer to the mainsprings of phantasy life than most, and has privileged intuition of mental processes that psychoanalysis more laboriously reveals. Creative work consequently can be a source of validation for psychoanalytic ideas. *The Uncanny*, for example (Freud, 1919), with its analysis of Hoffman's *Sandman*, presents a remarkable examination of experiences of doubling, alienness and unsettledness that both increases appreciation of the impact of the literary original and also draws from it some insightful and influential psychological ideas. But is this more than the generation of speculative thought, valuable in itself but still ungrounded, open to a million interpretations?

Freud was a subtle writer and his awareness of the dubiousness of his own claims is never far away, even though he usually both submits to it and wriggles out of it at the same time. The relatively early 'case study' of Jensen's *Gradiva* (Freud, 1907) is perhaps the clearest extended example of this duality. The story, which Freud lovingly describes, or even rewrites, concerns a young archaeologist's pursuit of a girl he believes to be the reincarnation of a young woman portrayed in a Pompeiian sculpture ('Gradiva'), only to find that she is in fact his childhood love. *Gradiva* seems to have appealed to Freud for numerous reasons, including its setting (Pompeii), its imagery (archaeology, the preferred metaphor which Freud used for his own investigative practices), the presence of dreams in it (which he analyses according to the rules used with his patients), and its presentation of a 'treatment by love' (which enabled him to make some useful technical statements about the activities of the psychoanalyst). *Gradiva* may also have been a kind of gift to Jung (although Kerr (1993) states that it was written before Freud and Jung started corresponding in earnest), who introduced Freud to the book and who also proved to be one of the most receptive readers of Freud's paper: the 'Jungian' realm of the imaginative and mythic is not far off at any time in this piece. The central appeal, however, is that it enabled Freud to indulge in his romantic attitude towards creative writers as the source of intuitive knowledge of the unconscious. This stems, he thought, from their supposed facility with psychological thinking and is a kind of spontaneously generated understanding of the psychological processes that psychoanalysis had inched towards through a more systematic, but also humbler path:

> [C]reative writers are valuable allies and their evidence is to be prized highly, for they are apt to know a whole host of things between heaven and earth of which our philosophy has not yet let us dream. In their knowledge of the mind they are far in advance of us everyday people, for they draw upon sources which we have not yet opened up for science. (p.34)

Freud goes on from this to argue that *Gradiva* can be given the status of a 'psychiatric study', because its representation of psychological processes is so accurate ('all [Jensen's] descriptions are so faithfully copied from reality', p.66), and furthermore that this is a general condition of good writing. Of the creative writer, Freud states: 'The description of the human mind is indeed the domain which is most his own; he has from time immemorial been the precursor of science, and so too of scientific psychology' (p.68).

These claims about the perspicacity and realism of the creative writer allow Freud to do two things in *Gradiva*: first, to interpret the actions, thoughts and dreams of the characters in the story as if they were those of real people; and secondly, to treat the representation of psychological processes in this fiction as if it is true and hence can act as a test of the veracity of psychoanalytic theories. In the former case, for example, Freud provides interpretations of the character Hanold's dreams, discusses his personality and the infantile and sexual sources of his behaviour, and treats the interpretations and actions given by the female protagonist Zoe as if they are genuine interventions that produce a cure. In the course of his commentary, Freud acknowledges the potential difficulties of using fictional characters in this way, showing a sophisticated grasp of the problem of his method:

> My readers will no doubt have been puzzled to notice that so far I have treated Norbert Hanold and Zoe Bertgang, in all their mental manifestations and activities, as though they were real people and not the author's creations, as though the author's mind were an absolutely transparent medium and not a refractive or obscuring one. (p.66)

The neglect of the productive, artistic work carried out by the author is indeed a major problem here, and on the face of it makes Freud's approach in *Gradiva* even more unruly than that in *Leonardo*, where at least the artist's work was taken as expressing something about the artist himself, not as 'real' in its own right. But Freud dismisses this problem on the grounds of the truthfulness of Jensen's psychological understanding, and then cheerfully moves on to contaminate his material still further by making himself the 'patient' in the case. This happens in a peculiar way. Given the absence of a real person who can be asked to free associate and whose psychic structure can be probed, Freud substitutes himself into the equation and uses his *own* mental processes as the model for what must be happening in the minds of these fictitious characters. There are two moments where this is explicit. The first occurs when Freud quotes 'a doctor's' experience of having mistaken a patient for the ghost of her dead sister: 'The doctor to whom this occurred was, however, none other than myself; so I have a personal reason for not disputing the clinical possibility of Norbert Hanold's temporary delusion that Gradiva had come back to life' (p.95). The second such occasion is when Freud is faced with the impossibility of analysing Hanold's dream because of the unfortunate absence of the dreamer from the couch; so instead of using Hanold's associations, he uses his own:

> We are able to apply to this dream the technique which may be described as the regular procedure for interpreting dreams. It consists in paying no attention to the apparent connections in the manifest dream but in fixing our eyes upon each portion of its content independently, and in looking for its origin in the dreamer's impressions, memories and free associations. Since, however, we cannot question Hanold, we shall have to content ourselves with referring to his impressions, and we may very tentatively put our own associations in place of his. (pp.96–7)

Revealingly, this is rather like Freud's (1905, p.134) approach to the analysis of the second dream of 'Dora': 'I shall present the material produced during the analysis of this dream in the somewhat haphazard order in which it recurs to my mind.' That is, faced with recalcitrant material, Freud is happy enough to use his own mental processes and associations and then present them as evidence, without methodological apology. Treating himself as what one might call a 'normal neurotic', his own psychological imaginings can substitute for those of anyone else. This rather extraordinary slippage from the mind of the other to the mind of the analyst is a methodological strategy used extensively in early psychoanalysis; given that one of the discipline's founding texts, *The Interpretation of Dreams*, is based largely on the analysis of Freud's own dreams, it can perhaps even be cited as *characteristically* Freudian.

This has both positive and negative consequences. On the former, it establishes psychoanalysis as a discipline that from the start takes seriously the relevance of personal issues to supposedly 'scientific' practices, and asserts the importance of reflexivity and of intersubjectivity. On the latter, it allows speculative overgeneralisations derived from personal whims and prejudices a place centre stage in analytic activity.

The treatment of *Gradiva* as providing confirming evidence for psychoanalytic theory in general is equally problematic, but also much more interesting. Again, Freud is aware of the methodological pitfalls, and especially of the charge that could be laid against him that he is simply reading the story in line with psychoanalysis' assumptions – that is, that his method of verification is circular:

> It may be that we have produced a complete caricature of an interpretation by introducing into an innocent work of art purposes of which its creator had no notion, and by so doing have shown once more how easy it is to find what one is looking for and what is occupying one's own mind. (p.114)

But he is quick to dismiss this rather serious problem, both on the grounds of the realism of the author's approach (the 'psychiatric case' argument) and of what is sometimes (Grünbaum, 1984) termed 'consilience' of converging lines of independent evidence. Freud argues that psychoanalysis and creative writing are completely separate activities, so that if they produce the same findings, then this is support for the claims each of them might make about the truthfulness of their representations of life. 'We probably draw from the same source and work upon the same object,' he writes (pp.114–15), 'each of us by another method. And the agreement of our results seems to guarantee that we have both worked correctly.' The psychoanalyst consciously observes mental processes in patients and others so as to be able to state their laws; the author 'directs attention to the unconscious in his own mind, he listens to its possible developments and lends them artistic expression instead of suppressing them by conscious criticism' (ibid.). The psychoanalyst can then get at the laws of the unconscious by analysing the writings of the author, which allows for assessment of the degree to which this intuitive mode of understanding supports findings derived from the scientific approach. The end result is that 'either both of us, the writer and the doctor, have misunderstood the unconscious in the same way, or we have both understood it correctly' (ibid.). It takes no great feat of imagination to work out which of these possible conclusions Freud prefers, and which is preferred by his detractors.

Learning from love

It is surely clear that Freud's analysis of *Gradiva* is so riven with mundane methodological difficulties as to make it untenable as a piece of scientific investigation, and certainly to defuse its prospects of offering 'independent' verification of psychoanalytic claims. As well as the standard difficulty of treating fictional characters as if they were real, ignoring the traditions and structures of literary activity (the relationship of *Gradiva* to the conventions of gothic writing, for example), there is the unabashed way in which Freud uses his own associations and imaginative responses in order to find in the story support for his own theory. This is a process of 'reading in' to the text that is routinely part of a response to literature, perhaps, but is in no way testimony to its evidential value. Noting that others have produced the same ideas independently of psychoanalysis is not in itself a way of assessing its scientific or factual value: all sorts of similar ideas might be produced at roughly the same time in a culture, without any of them being 'true'. After all, religious beliefs are widely shared and deeply held by many, yet Freud would not grant them the status of being scientifically true – a point which will be returned to below. The existence of shared perspectives and 'consilient' ideas is indeed bound to occur, as culture is in large part the process of responding to problematics that appear in specific circumstances, in a range of usually closely related ways. That psychoanalysis and literature can be made to agree with one another, if it says more than that the one is being forced into the image of the other, may simply reflect the fact that both are cultural expressions of a particular set of then-contemporary experiences (in this case, these included the growth of individuality, the production of nostalgia and romantic holism, the conflict between 'surface' and 'depth'). Literature has its own dynamic, its own traditions and modes of response to cultural concerns, and analysing the details of this is a legitimate, indeed important, intellectual activity with which it is possible that psychoanalysis might help. But using the imaginative products of one person's mind to measure the accuracy of the possibly equally imaginative products of another's is not going to establish the veracity of either.

Despite all this, *Gradiva* has some significant gains. One relates to the clarifications that Freud is able to bring into his own theory through his thinking about the parallels with the tale of Hanold and Zoe. The clearest example here concerns the process of analysis itself as a therapeutic endeavour. With the appearance of Zoe, writes Freud (p.93), 'So far we have been present at the development of a delusion; now we are to witness its cure.' Zoe engages in the process of 'giving [Hanold] back from outside the repressed memories which he could not set free from inside' (p.111), but according to Freud this in itself would not have been enough – what was important was the addition of an affective component, the elicitation or renewal of feelings, in this case of love. This aspect of the story is, according to Freud, in precise and profound agreement with the tenets of psychoanalysis:

> the similarity between Gradiva's procedure and the analytic method of psychotherapy is not restricted to these two points – the making conscious of what has been repressed and the coinciding of explanation with cure. It also extends to what turns out to be the essence of the whole change – to the awakening of feelings ... The process of cure is accomplished in a relapse into love, if we combine all the many components of the sexual instinct under the term 'love'; and such a relapse is indispensable, for the symptoms on account of which the treatment has been undertaken are nothing other than precipitates of earlier struggles connected with repression and the return of the repressed, and they can only be resolved and washed away by a fresh high tide of the same passion. Every psychoanalytic treatment is an attempt at liberating repressed love which has found a meagre outlet in the compromise of a symptom. Indeed, the agreement between such treatments and the process of cure described by the author of Gradiva reaches its climax in the further fact that in analytic psychotherapy too the reawakened passion, whether it is love or hate, invariably chooses as its object the figure of the doctor. (pp.112–13)

At this time in his writing, this was one of the clearest statements made by Freud concerning the nature of the therapeutic process and in particular the effective component of psychoanalysis as therapy. This demands not just identifying the unconscious conflict at the root of the symptom, which is a process of 'explanation' of its logic to the patient, but also 'what turns out to be the essence of the whole change – to the awakening of feelings', specifically, 'a relapse into love'. Psychoanalytic therapy has to reawaken the love that has been repressed, or more broadly (as in the last sentence of the quotation above) the 'passion' that can be love or hate, and it does this through drawing it onto the person of the psychoanalyst. The psychoanalyst as love object is a poor thing, of course, and very much inferior to Gradiva/Zoe, who can 'in reality' give love to the patient Hanold, and this is one of the factors that places a restriction on the efficacy of psychoanalysis itself: 'The doctor has been a stranger, and must endeavour to become a stranger once more after the cure; he is often at a loss what advice to give the patients he has cured as to how in real life they can use their recovered capacity to love' (p.113). What *Gradiva* shows to Freud is how the lover and the analyst are in the same structural position when it comes to knowledge and cure; and also how they differ, how the abstinence practised by the analyst is problematic – even though later he became clearer that it was itself a necessary part of therapeutic progress.

What has happened here is that the dubious claims to evidencing psychoanalysis through fiction have given away to a reflection on what the nature of the psychoanalytic process might be, and this reflection is both fruitful and well-founded. Without making any truth-claims about what is scientifically necessary, it enables Freud to articulate the way he sees the core effectivity of the analytic process, and to distinguish it from other possible modes – in particular, a 'cure by love' that involves enactment and reciprocation of the patient's desires. This aspect of *Gradiva* is no longer an attempt to use literature to support psychoanalysis, or use psychoanalysis to interpret literature; it is, at its simplest, a trigger for Freud's further examination of how psychoanalysis works. In this lie the seeds of another kind of approach to 'psychoanalysis and literature', in which there is a respectful appreciation of the 'agency' of literature – how it has its effect on the reader, what the imaginative actions of the writer produce – which can be used to reflect back upon psychoanalysis, seeking thereby to clarify its mode of operation and theory. Psychoanalysis is not here as a supplicant, seeking literature's support and guidance. Rather, in investing in an open and intelligent reading of the text, full of curiosity and willing to consider its lessons for his own thinking, Freud shows that it is possible for the engagement between disciplines to be illuminating and respectful, more modest than when in conquistador mode, but also more interesting. Simply by laying bare the comparison – the fictional cure by love, the psychoanalytic transference – Freud manages to address some profound issues about the nature of intersubjectivity, the use of another as a love object, and the avenues through which personal change might occur. There is still plenty of confidence about what psychoanalysis knows in this section of the paper, but there is no particular attempt to impose it on the story, only to meditate on questions raised that might have resonance with, and be clarifying for, psychoanalytic ideas.

Social Freud: the case of religion

The previous sections have argued that whilst there are plenty of occasions on which Freud used psychoanalysis interpretively to make sense of literary or artistic work, so that he was clearly applying psychoanalysis *to* art or literature, he also showed a countervailing tendency which was less colonising and more open to the contribution of creative work to psychoanalysis itself. This was in some instances manifested as an attempt to use art or literature to throw light on psychological processes or as a way of checking and supporting psychoanalytic claims. More enticingly, there are moments in Freud's work where what is enacted is an openness towards artistic forms that allows them to stir up ideas which can then be taken back into psychoanalysis. This even includes the raising of challenges to psychoanalytic assumptions and developments of theory. Sometimes this too falls into the trap of treating the artwork or literary creation as a 'real' character from whose peregrinations universal truths can be gleaned. However, at other times there is a more humble appreciation that what is going on is a mode of dialogue, in which the text suggests things which allow Freud to associate to new psychoanalytic ideas, or to unblock points of theoretical uncertainty. It is on these occasions that 'applied psychoanalysis' begins to hold promise as a way to articulate something new in the humanities and social sciences, breathing subjectivity into them whilst leaving intact their specific disciplinary contribution. In the case of art and literature, this means respecting the aesthetic and historical conventions that give them cultural weight; in the case of the social sciences, it means drawing on notions of the social that can be reflected back into psychoanalysis' primarily psychological mode of thought, shaking it up and producing fissures that might allow both disciplines to gain. Unfortunately, Freud's personal engagement in social scientific thinking, which was extensive and imaginative and immensely productive in setting an agenda particularly for theorising social conflict, shows few instances of this more open and reflexive approach necessary for a respectful encounter with other disciplines. Nevertheless, it immediately offers a number of psychoanalytic concepts that have proved crucial for later attempts to think in a more 'hybrid' way, even if Freud's actual use of them was to present a one-sidedly psychoanalytic theory of social phenomena.

The capacity to pronounce on social issues from the perspective of a psychological sage seems to have been increasingly expected of Freud as his fame grew. This was the origin, for example, of the exchange with Einstein that became the paper *Why War?* (Freud and Einstein, 1933), in which Einstein pre-empted Freud by evoking an inbuilt human destructiveness that paralleled Freud's notion of the death drive. (Freud commented: 'though you have taken the wind out of my sails I shall be glad to follow in your wake' (p.203).) More generally, the contribution of psychoanalysis to theorising on some characteristic early twentieth-century themes, the origins of civilisation and the 'conflict' between society and the individual, seems to have been seen as an important test of the standing of psychoanalysis. If psychoanalysis is an account of the sources of human trouble, then surely it should be able to comment on how and why these troubles are so often inflicted in the social domain. Especially after the First World War, which clearly revealed people's extraordinary capacity for self-deception and destructiveness, any psychology that claimed to explain the depths of human nature must also be able to say something novel about what happens to it in what was increasingly ironically called 'civilisation'.

One major premise of Freudian psychoanalysis is indeed that there is a clash between what the individual might wish for and what society might allow. This is implicit in the relations between the pleasure principle and the reality principle and also in Freud's early distinction between 'sexual drives' and 'ego preservative drives'. This version of his drive or 'instinct' theory proposed that the sexual wishes of the individual always have to be moderated, because let loose they would undermine the capacity of the subject to function rationally in a peopled world. As a consequence, Freud had to think about how the conditions of society impinge on the individual, what is necessary by way of constraint and what unnecessary, and what restrictions are both painful and essential. From an early view that the social repression of sexuality produces neurosis, he gradually moved to a more subtle account of the connections between social forces and psychological structure (or, more crudely, between society and unhappiness), culminating in a reappraisal of his drive theory and some great 'social' texts in the wake of the war. The development of his more refined views about the processes through which repression operates, and in particular the emergence of the concept of the superego, described briefly in Chapter 1 (see also Frosh, 1999), led to a variegated understanding of how certain social processes might find their way 'into' the mind of the individual. The key idea here is that the internalisation of authority as a response to the outcome of the Oedipus complex results in there being a kind of 'state' within the mind, with the superego acting as a sort of proxy for the repressive activities of the external social world. Just as unbounded infantile sexuality is channelled through developmental processes into genitality, so aggression is mastered by incorporation into the punitive superego; civilisation advances at the expense of individual happiness. This also means that what is usually seen as 'internal' has external sources and resonance: 'We have also learned how the severity of the super-ego – the demands of conscience – is to be understood', writes Freud (1930, p.127). 'It is simply a continuation of the severity of the external authority, to which it has succeeded and which it has in part replaced.' Freud's narrative focuses on the manner in which impulses or feelings that seem so much part of our 'selves' that one assumes they are basic, inborn consequences of being human, are actually products of our immersion in the social world.

Whilst this might be an important description of how social forces operate at the level of the individual, what is also present in Freud's thinking is a more sociological urge to make sense of 'civilisation' itself. This is clearest in his accounts of religion (Freud, 1927) and society generally (Freud, 1930), and also in his poignant study of Judaism and anti-Semitism, in one of his last works, *Moses and Monotheism* (Freud, 1939). This raises the question of whether psychoanalysis really is a social theory, or whether it is illegitimate to extend what is actually a psychological, individualistic way of thinking to the social and cultural level. There are various ways into this, but perhaps a useful one is to take up an area in which Freud was always interested yet stood outside of, and which continues to be of importance in contemporary times: that of religion. For Freud, rationalist, committed atheist and 'godless Jew' as he was, religion was an opponent of scientific advancement; but he recognised its significance and devoted a good deal of attention to understanding it, particularly in his later years. One major fruit of this was his 1927 work, *The Future of an Illusion*, part of a series of late texts that all reveal Freud's moralising inclination – not the kind of moralism that preaches 'good' behaviour, but rather the kind that attempts to develop an *ethics*, an approach to human life that focuses on what he clearly regarded as the 'truth'. Put more sparingly, Freud believed strongly in the necessity of seeing through 'illusions', defined in *The Future of an Illusion* as beliefs 'derived from human wishes' (p.30). 'We call a belief an illusion', writes Freud (ibid.), 'when a wish-fulfilment is a prominent factor in its motivation, and in doing so we disregard its relations to reality, just as the illusion itself sets no store by verification.' Exposing the wish at the heart of an illusion was for Freud a way of making humanity own up to the truth, of making people face reality free of the 'consolations' that might indeed buffer them against the worst storms, but only at too high a price – the price of an escalating irrationality that does them no service. Rather disingenuously, in fact, Freud takes up the criticism that in removing the illusion of religion he is damaging civilisation, which of necessity has to allow people to live with defences against anxiety. Maybe so, he allows, but this is not the whole story:

> Religion has clearly performed great services for human civilization. It has contributed much towards the taming of the asocial instincts. But not enough. It has ruled human society for many thousands of years and has had time to show what it can achieve. If it had succeeded in making the majority of mankind happy, in comforting them, in reconciling them to life and in making them into vehicles of civilization, no one would dream of attempting to alter the existing conditions. But what do we see instead? We see that an appallingly large number of people are dissatisfied with civilization and unhappy in it, and feel it as a yoke which must be shaken off; and that these

> people either do everything in their power to change that civilization, or else go so far in their hostility to it that they will have nothing to do with civilization or with a restriction of instinct. (Freud, 1927, p.36)

The task of psychoanalysis in exposing the roots of religion is completely parallel to its task when faced with neurotic patients: *of course* their symptoms have developed for good reason, to protect the ego against what might seem to be something worse; but these defences have turned destructive, they cause too much further unhappiness and they need to be outgrown.

Freud sees the analogy between the religious illusions of society and the neurotic illusions of the individual patient as being pretty direct, even though he is careful to maintain the vocabulary of parallelism rather than identity (i.e. he does not explicitly make society a 'patient', even though his argument tends strongly that way). Religions come about because societies need ways to appease their members, who might otherwise panic in the face of the overwhelmingly destructive potential of nature; and also as a way of inculcating moral laws that prevent people from being at each other's throats as they give full vent to the ambitions of their drives. After various discussions of the way in which authority is internalised (through the superego), of the limitations of ordinary people (the 'masses') and their need for leaders, and of how ideals serve as narcissistic gratifications which bind people into the social order, Freud picks up particularly on the theme of the helplessness people experience when confronted with nature, and of how deeply analogous this is to the helplessness of the infant confronted with a world that seems too big, too arbitrary and too dangerous. Under these circumstances, the infant takes refuge in the parent, a figure who is worryingly fierce but who nevertheless presents the infant with the promise of special protection. Maintaining this protection depends on the infant's wishes being constrained and psychic energy being mobilised in the service of the preservation of the relationship itself, much as the gods have to be appeased through prayer or sacrifice. This process starts early, with the mother, but is soon taken over in what Freud calls 'white Christian civilization', by the Oedipal father:

> In this function [of protection] the mother is soon replaced by the stronger father, who retains that position for the rest of childhood. But the child's attitude to its father is coloured by a peculiar ambivalence. The father himself constitutes a danger for the child, perhaps because of its earlier relation to its mother. Thus it fears him no less than it longs for him and admires him. The indications of this ambivalence in the attitude to the father are deeply imprinted in every religion, as was shown in *Totem and Taboo*. When the

> growing individual finds that he is destined to remain a child for ever, that he can never do without protection against strange superior powers, he lends those powers the features belonging to the figure of his father; he creates for himself the gods whom he dreads, whom he seeks to propitiate, and whom he nevertheless entrusts with his own protection. Thus his longing for a father is a motive identical with his need for protection against the consequences of his human weakness. The defence against childish helplessness is what lends its characteristic features to the adult's reaction to the helplessness which he has to acknowledge – a reaction which is precisely the formation of religion. (p.23)

Religion is thus not just built on the *model* of infantile dependence; it is produced by the *same processes* – the need for protection and the wish that this will be offered by a powerful, superior being who has sought one out. The infantile history of the individual is an exact replica of the infantile history of civilisation: religious ideas, 'which are given out as teachings, are not precipitates of experience or end-results of thinking: they are illusions, fulfilments of the oldest, strongest and most urgent wishes of mankind' (p.29). Moreover, the generalisation of the defensive strategies adopted by each individual into a defence adopted by the whole culture is of great help to all concerned: 'It is an enormous relief to the individual psyche if the conflicts of its childhood arising from the father-complex – conflicts which it has never wholly overcome – are removed from it and brought to a solution which is universally accepted' (ibid.). Thus the generation of religion on the social level supports the well-being of citizens by bolstering the individual's own defensive wish-fulfilments, and the conditions for a neurotic, illusion-preoccupied social world are laid.

There are many issues that could be taken up here, not least the vexed question of the extent to which 'civilisation' can be treated as a person, or as a collection of individuals who all have the same need and consequently project their father-images into the heavens. Freud is not very clear about the specificity of the social in his work, perhaps understandably so: as he states, 'My work is a good example of the strict isolation of the particular contribution which psycho-analytic discussion can make to the solution of the problem of religion' (p.22). In some ways it is fair enough to take the line that Freud's sociopolitical texts are attempts to explore what the psychological insights derived from psychoanalysis might have to add to the sociological perspectives that even in his day were fairly advanced. Marxism, after all, was a well developed theory, instantiated in the Soviet Union, as Freud acknowledges in *The Future of an Illusion;* and Durkheim and Weber had very much established the discipline of sociology on its own feet. Freud shows some awareness of this with his reference to the infantile model as an 'analogy' (p.41), and he also allows for what might be termed the primacy of the social in arguing that in the life of an individual, society offers religious beliefs ready-made as vehicles for each person's defensive structure. Nevertheless, the explanations given for these social processes are not themselves social: they treat 'civilisation' as a collection of individuals with the same basic psychic structure and existential dilemmas.

A more interesting issue here is the use to which Freud puts his argument, or perhaps the motivation for it. This can best be labelled 'therapeutic'. Just as the individual neurotic needs to shed her or his illusions in order to find a more truthful way of encountering reality, so civilisation as a whole needs to grow up – pretty literally in this case: 'surely infantilism is destined to be surmounted. Men cannot remain children for ever; they must in the end go out into "hostile life". We may call this "education to reality". Need I confess to you that the sole purpose of my book is to point out the necessity for this forward step?' (1927, p.48). Religion does not solve the problem of unhappiness in society, and indeed adds to it by its direct assault on rationality, which is the only hope for humankind. 'Think of the depressing contrast between the radiant intelligence of a healthy child and the feeble intellectual powers of the average adult,' writes Freud (p.46): 'Can we be quite certain that it is not precisely religious education which bears a large share of the blame for this relative atrophy?' In Freud's view, the only reliable instrument that people have with which to deal with the demands of reality is the mind ('we have no other means of controlling our instinctual nature but our intelligence' – p.47), and to use the mind productively requires freedom from ridiculous, irrational constraints that stunt the intellect. Relinquishing illusions may be a painful process, but it is also liberating to encounter this kind of truth – *scientific* truth, drawing on Freud's idealising view of science. In fact it is essential, if humankind is to develop, that the neurotic aberrations and infantile beliefs of the past, such as religion, are set aside.

The contrast between the analysis of religion in *The Future of an Illusion* and the applications of psychoanalysis in the field of art and literature is quite strong. Whereas Freud often seeks to learn from creative artists and writers, in the realm of social issues he is in very strong pedagogic mode, showing what psychoanalysis can teach, and with the exception of anthropology he barely draws on other social scientific work at all. His approach is analytic, but even more noticeably it is strongly *moral* in what it is trying to offer. Through the development of psychoanalysis, he argues, the gains in rationality that derive from the scientific world view have become available to individuals and to social groups – to 'civilisation' as a whole. The self-reflective understanding that people can now have of their position is radically different from what came before. We can now see the operation of false beliefs in action, how they function as the product of wishes, how they prevent a full engagement with reality, and how this applies to groups as well as individuals, to whole societies and their dominant beliefs. Just as psychoanalysis is evangelical in the field of individual development, interested in setting aside unnecessary sexual inhibitions, for example, and in particular in finding more reality-oriented substitutes for neurotic symptoms; so it operates on the sociopolitical level, able to preach about what is required to make a good society that works. Despite Freud's ironic impulse and his pessimism about what humanity can achieve, this can be described as a kind of utopian project: the insights of psychoanalysis, which themselves are the insights of the rational, scientific world view, can be applied both to make sense of the social order and to offer a programme, however vague it may initially be, for progressive social improvement.

In developing this social analysis, critique and programme, Freud is certainly applying psychoanalysis. Fundamentally, what happens is that his discoveries in relation to patients are being used as templates for understanding what he takes to be the parallel processes that can be observed at work in society as a whole. Additionally, the procedure for reconstructing lost infancy that comes from work on the couch is being extended into a mode of historical reconstruction from the observation of current social behaviour – particularly in religious beliefs and practices, seen as infantilism and neurosis, and in the actions and beliefs of 'savages', taken to be the equivalent of the infant in relation to the adult individual. Along the way, some very powerful observations are made, and some provocative conceptualisations of social processes that integrate understanding of the unconscious with accounts of mass phenomena are provided, a point that will be developed more fully in Chapter 6. But it also exposes a degree of reductive thinking that is untenable in more contemporary times, when the complexity of social processes is – or at least should be – better appreciated. For Freud, whilst there is awareness of how 'society' regulates the wishes of individuals, there is a constant tendency either to theorise society as if it is the same as a person, or to see it as no entity at all, but as simply the accumulation of individual subjects who each express their unconscious wishes in predictable ways. The consequence of this is that the 'application' can only be in one direction: psychoanalysts discover their truths when working with patients; they then observe processes that look like neurosis going on in the social world (e.g. belief in the existence of things that are not there, or ridiculous hopes for protection from imaginary figures, or self-destructive violence); and they account for these with the same explanations that they would use in the clinic. What is missed here is the *autonomy of the social*, the way features of the social world have causal properties and impact. This is true at the level of the individual, where 'race', gender and class have formative consequences for certain modes of subjecthood. Equally relevantly, it is true at the level of the social itself, which is structured according to its own principles, however much it might also be 'infected' by the unconscious wishes of its subjects. For Freud, there often seems to be no 'social' at all, only the individual writ large; this means that his application of psychoanalysis can only be very limited in its capacity to offer an explanatory account of social events and of what he terms 'culture', 'civilisation' or society. It also misses an opportunity: if the social is entwined with the psychological, then just as psychoanalysis might indeed add something important to the depth of analysis of social events, so appreciation of how the social world operates might fill out psychoanalysis' own thinking. This might refer particularly to how drives come to be articulated or object relations formed, but also to the limits of therapeutic efficacy and the way subjecthood can be disrupted and disturbed by forces that come from outside. It is these mutual encounters that one seeks when advancing 'applied' psychoanalysis, and it is examples of instances in which they take place that will be examined in later chapters.

Conclusion

Freud's forays into art, literature and sociology flag up some of the issues that have recurred throughout the history of applied psychoanalysis, revealing some of its promise and some more of its limitations. Much of his work was in 'conquistador' mode, aiming to colonise areas outside the clinical homeland of psychoanalysis. The motivation for this was partly the appeal of grand theory – psychoanalysis as a kind of 'theory of everything', not dissimilar in this respect from Einsteinian physics. Additionally, applied psychoanalysis was a way of validating psychoanalysis in general, its lines of evidence used to offer supposedly 'independent' support for some of the key claims that had been derived from the consulting room. In the case of applications to social theory, Freud seems also to have been driven by a moralising impulse in which he saw commentary on the disturbances of society as necessary in order to show what might need to be done to protect the well-being of individuals. In this area, psychoanalysis has enough in it of the social to contest other more explicitly sociological theories. Most particularly, its rich account of unconscious processes inserts an appreciation of the 'irrational' into theories that otherwise find the unexpected, self-destructive or fanatical eruptions of social disorder hard to fathom.

The strengths and weaknesses of this work can be summarised briefly in the question of how well it articulates a specific contribution of psychoanalysis to broader intellectual activity that nevertheless respects the non-psychological elements of the fields into which it strays, and indeed learns from them. Freud certainly provokes something important, notably a set of enquiries about how the unconscious seeps into social and cultural events, and what it might mean to recognise this as a fact. He also sets up a one-sided attitude in which psychoanalysis already knows the answers to its questions before it investigates them. How surprised can one be, for instance, that it reveals God as a projection of infantile wishes, given its commitment to Oedipal theory? What kind of analysis or evidence could have produced a different Freudian account of religion? The problem here is of how psychoanalysis can hold onto its capacity for radical deconstruction of the material with which it deals – this being what one might very generally term the 'analytic attitude' (Rieff, 1966) – whilst retaining a reflexive ability to do the same to itself. In the next chapter, which again deals with some historical debates, an attempt will be made to start to describe a way in which this difficult balance might be achieved.

Chapter 3

Psychoanalysis as/of Literature

The previous chapter provided an account of some of the history of 'applied' psychoanalysis in the humanities and social sciences through an examination of Freud's work in this area. At the end, it raised a set of questions about what might be meant by a genuinely open encounter between psychoanalysis and other fields of study, in which a two-way influence is possible. This involves not simply imposing psychoanalytic interpretations on the other discipline, so that psychoanalysis plays the role of an 'expert' system that can force literary criticism or sociology, for example, to take account of unconscious features in their landscape of concern. It also asks for a reciprocal openness of psychoanalysis itself to what might emerge from the movement 'outside the clinic', in particular to anything that might challenge its concepts and assumptions. Additionally, it requires some respect on the part of psychoanalysis for the specific disciplinary terrain in which it is treading, for example in appreciating the aesthetic traditions that might govern the form taken by a work of art, or the political investments reflected in a social event. Put at its strongest, if psychoanalysis is to retain its capacity to disrupt and provoke the research traditions with which it comes into contact, it also has to be ready to face such disruption itself.

Freud provides some hints of such reciprocal openness, particularly in his writings on literature, where his respect for creative authors meant that he was willing to forego some of his authority as the 'master' of the unconscious. In the current chapter, a second historical example is used to try to tease out some more elements required for productive uses of psychoanalysis outside the clinic, focusing especially on some debates around psychoanalysis and literature in the 1980s. This was a particularly interesting moment, as the growing influence of Lacanian theory and the general poststructuralist 'turn' in the arts and social sciences meant that questions of meaning and representation were being avidly reconsidered in academic work. In the field of literary studies, which was rapidly developing many new theoretical perspectives, psychoanalysis came under scrutiny for two opposed reasons. On the one hand, its 'colonial' embrace of literature, in which it claimed to be able to supply to texts the 'real' meaning that would otherwise escape notice, was made problematic by an appreciation of how reading is performed *contingently.* The 'meaning' of a text could no longer be regarded as fixed for all time, with the task of the critic being to identify it accurately. Instead, it was appreciated that readings are always multiple and partial, linked to very particular perspectives (for example, governed by class or gender). On the other hand, it also came to be understood that literary texts reveal 'traces' of their own history and of the many other texts from which they derive, with which they might be in a kind of 'dialogue'. Sometimes, this is reflected in direct citational practices, but in all cases texts are part of a community of writings that can only be read in conjunction with one another. This recognition of what is termed 'intertextuality' suggests a need for a vocabulary that could track such 'unconscious' traces. As psychoanalysis, mainly but not solely in its Lacanian form, had had its own 'linguistic turn', it could be seen as offering precisely such a vocabulary, so long as one was careful not to assume that the 'unconscious' of a text would be the same as the 'unconscious' of a person. This meant that it could be considered sympathetically even by literary critics who bridled at its actions when in its more colonial mode of action. Finally, some literary scholars were also reading Freud not as a scientist, but as a writer of profound literary works. The attention they paid to the characteristics of these works followed the lines of their usual scholarly activity, meaning that psychoanalysis itself could be treated as a literary endeavour. This offered something back to psychoanalysis: an understanding of its own characteristics, its own textual unconscious, which might otherwise have escaped *psychoanalysis'* notice.

It is such backwards and forwards movements that promote the kinds of open encounters being pursued here. This chapter therefore takes up this debate over psychoanalysis and literature in order to outline a kind of 'model' of what is required to sustain such openness. This will lay some further groundwork for the interventions in subsequent chapters, which explore some exemplary psychoanalytically informed debates in contemporary social and psychosocial studies.

Problems of character and interpretation

Psychoanalysis has always been controversial as a method of literary analysis, particularly amongst writers and critics who regard it as a colonising discipline trying to tell the 'truth' of literature without necessarily appreciating its specificity, including its aesthetic properties. There is certainly much for such critics to get their teeth into, as psychoanalysts have not been coy about applying their clinical insights to literature. Sometimes, as with Freud, this is because they admire creative writing and wish to understand it better; but often they seem simply unable to resist the temptation to speculate freely about literary characters or their authors, perhaps rejoicing in them as 'patients' who cannot answer back. The most outrageous instances of psychoanalytic 'reading in' to literary productions treat them as somehow transparent indicators of the mental state and psychobiographical attributes of the author. Examples here include Marie Bonaparte's (1933) early study of Edgar Allan Poe, which identified necrophilia as a pathological personality state underpinning Poe's writing, or Ernest Jones' (1910) study of *Hamlet* as Oedipal drama. The limitations of this approach and of the parallel tendency to treat literary characters as real have been well recognised for a long time. As noted in Chapter 2, Freud himself showed anxiety at realising that he was attributing mental processes to the fictional protagonists of Jensen's *Gradiva*. Virginia Woolf firmly opposed psychoanalytic criticism on the grounds of its reduction of characters to 'cases' (Abel, 1989, p.17). Interestingly, however, Woolf also had some sympathy for the idea that literature might be the writer's equivalent of psychoanalytic treatment. Writing about the composition of her novel *To the Lighthouse*, she said, 'I suppose that I did for myself what psycho-analysts do for their patients. I expressed some very long felt and deeply felt emotion. And in expressing it I explained it and then laid it to rest' (Stonebridge, 1998, p.63). Perhaps this relates to the reason Woolf would not countenance psychoanalytic treatment for her own psychological distress; in the version given by Alix Strachey, this was because of the fear (which Strachey endorsed) that psychoanalysis might endanger Woolf's creativity, that is, that unpicking her madness might destroy her work (Appignanesi and Forrester, 1992, p.370; Abel, 1989).

Whatever the 'therapeutic' possibilities of *writing*, many of the classical strategies of *reading* found in psychoanalytic approaches to literature are clearly wrong-headed. As in Bonaparte's and Jones' studies, there is a tradition of treating literary texts as equivalent to dreams, offering a 'royal road' through to the neurosis of their authors. There are numerous problems with this. For one thing, the biographical detail needed to inform psychoanalytic formulations and the opportunity for testing interpretations in the context of clinical transference relationships are not available even if one accepts the premise that a literary work might be akin to a dream. In the case of the dream, each element might open out associations *in the dreamer* that can be subjected to psychoanalytic work; in the literary example, no such associations are available, with the consequence that (as in the example of *Gradiva*) it is commonly the *analyst's* associations that are substituted for the author's. Moreover, whilst an author might well 'inhabit' her or his writing in ways that give rise to biographical curiosity, any interpretive account of a text in terms of the character or psychopathology of the author is undermined by the *intentional* opacity of textual surfaces employed by writers. Put simply, they *craft* their work in ways that are significantly different from the work of self-presentation and defence that goes on in the psychoanalytic consulting room. This does not belie the existence of some apparent similarities: patients, like writers, use certain cultural conventions in order to express themselves. Suffering and free association both have their genres, and these vary across time and place, as is indicated by the withering away of the once dominant psychoanalytic entities of 'hysteria' and 'neurasthenia' and their replacement by clinical presentations regarded as 'narcissistic' or 'borderline'. The consulting room is a space with its own expectations and traditions, just as the broader self-presentational actions of people in encounters with others have their own traditions and aesthetic properties, and are themselves dramaturgically crafted (Goffman's *The Presentation of Self in Everyday Life* (1969) is the seminal text here). However, this seeming similarity is in fact a difference, and part of the point. The conventions built on to make meaning in the consulting room are not the same as those used by writers to construct their literary pieces. These have their own specificity, lay down their own routines and boundaries, and provoke their own modes of artistic resistance. Writers work with their material in ways that are derived from the history of their profession; even when they challenge and depart from this history (and even, one might say, if they are influenced by psychoanalysis in doing so), it is in relation to the practice of writing that this happens, not the practice of (to use a shorthand) free association. One might be able to read 'through' a literary text to the traditions that inform it, just as one might in principle read 'through' a patient's speech to the unconscious; but these are not the same things.

What happens when such methods are used is that the significance of the text is bypassed in favour of a supposed 'true' meaning that lies behind it in the character of the author – a meaning which is actually unavailable and indeed probably factitious. Lionel Trilling, in his classic mid-twentieth-century book *The Liberal Imagination* (1951), which is by no means unsympathetic to psychoanalysis, notes the key defect of Jones' approach to *Hamlet* along these lines:

> Dr Jones's study of Hamlet search[es] for a 'hidden motive' and a 'deeper working', which implies that there is a reality to which the play stands in the relation that a dream stands to the wish that generates it and from which it is separable; it is this reality, this 'deeper working' which, according to Dr Jones, produced the play. But Hamlet is not merely the product of Shakespeare's thought, it is the very instrument of his thought, and if meaning is intention, Shakespeare did not intend the Oedipus motive or anything less than Hamlet; if meaning is effect then it is Hamlet which affects us, not the Oedipus motive. (p.63)

Whilst the effect of a piece of literature might in part be ascribed to the specific psychological complexes that it calls up in the reader (which is part of Jones' argument as well as Freud's explanation of the continuing hold of the Oedipus story), the idea that that is what the work is *about* is misguided. The literary work exists in its own terms, linked in with its culture and making sense in the context of various modes of intertextuality, including the sophistication of readers in psychoanalytic perspectives. It is produced by the play of textual meanings, from which psychoanalytic narratives might be read out – but not as diagnostic categories, rather as associations. Hence Maud Ellmann's (1994) indictment of traditional psychoanalytic criticism:

> the stories psychoanalyse their own interpreters: the scenes of sexual possession discovered in the texts tell us less about the authors than about the critics, and less about eroticism than about the will to power over literary ambiguity. Only by attending to the rhetoric of texts, to the echoes and recesses of the words themselves, can we recognise the otherness of literature, its recalcitrance as well as its susceptibility to theorisation. Without this vigilance to language, psychoanalysis is doomed to rediscover its own myths grotesquely multiplied throughout the course of literature. (p.3)

This notion of the *otherness* of literature and its link with 'vigilance to language' has become increasingly important in more recent psychoanalytic criticism, which echoes to the footsteps of Lacan, however ambivalently; and it will be returned to below. But it is also worth noting that interpreting the characters in a literary work is just as problematic as reading through the text to the personality of the author or the universal mythological complexes that are seen as the 'truth' of any tale, however entertaining the speculations might be that are thereby produced. The tendency to understand characters as if they were real is a very strong one, even without the psychoanalytic gloss to which Woolf objected, presumably because of the dominance of narrative structures in western culture that pull one towards making a causal story out of even quite fragmentary material. Psychoanalysis' own assumptions (its understanding of how the mind works) are in any case highly influential culturally and are drawn upon strongly by people to make sense of their experiences, giving them enormous purchase and plausibility when mobilised in literary contexts. However, the application of such assumptions to literary characters is illicit for some very obvious reasons. Ellmann, having noted that the tendency to view the character as a 'person' to be analysed is heavily aligned with American ego-psychology's focus on individualism, makes the key point. 'Hamlet', she writes, 'has the disadvantage that he can never contradict his psychoanalyst. Unlike a real analysand, he cannot lie down on the couch and free associate about his dreams or recapitulate the trauma of his infancy. Amusing as it is to speculate about his early history, Hamlet *never had a childhood*' (p.3). In *Wild Analysis*, Freud (1910b) notes, 'psychoanalytical treatment absolutely presupposes prolonged contact with the patient' (p.7). Even psychoanalytic *interpretation* requires as much – and this is simply not possible with a patient who does not actually exist.

Psychoanalysis 'and' ...

All this is preliminary to an interesting set of issues surrounding the relationship of psychoanalysis with literature, which has some useful implications for the broader question of what it might mean to develop non-clinical applications of psychoanalysis, including in the social sciences. A way in here is presented by Shoshana Felman's (1982a) examination of the 'and' in the phrase 'psychoanalysis *and* literature'. Felman points out that psychoanalysis' approach to literature has been one of attempted mastery, with literature being called on to take a subservient or 'slave' position, in which psychoanalytic interpretation is the key to unlock what literature 'really' has to say. The effect of this approach is to present literature as blind to itself; that is, just like the analyst in relation to the neurotic patient, psychoanalysis knows literature better than literature knows itself.

> Although 'and' is grammatically defined as a 'coordinate conjunction' in the context of the relationship between 'literature and psychoanalysis' it is usually interpreted, paradoxically enough, as implying not so much a relation of coordination as one of *subordination*, a relation in which literature is submitted to the authority, to the prestige of psychoanalysis. While literature is considered as a body of *language* – to *be interpreted* – psychoanalysis is considered as a body of *knowledge*, whose competence is called upon *to interpret*. Psychoanalysis, in other words, occupies the place of a *subject*, literature that of an *object*; the relation of an interpretation is structured as a relation of master to slave, according to the Hegelian definition: the dynamic encounter between the two areas is in effect, in Hegel's terms, a 'fight for recognition,' whose outcome is the sole recognition of the master – of (the truth of) psychoanalytical theory; literature's function, like that of the slave, is to *serve* precisely the *desire* of psychoanalytical theory – its desire for recognition; exercising its authority and *power* over the literary field, holding a discourse of masterly competence, psychoanalysis in literature, thus seems to seek above all its own *satisfaction*. (pp.5–6)

Expressed like this, it is pretty clear why literary critics might object to psychoanalysis, which comes in from the outside as a master discourse that can sweep everything else away: it *knows*, and in demonstrating its knowledge, it serves the good not of literature, but of psychoanalysis itself. From Freud's appropriation of the Oedipus story, through many of his acolytes as they apply the mighty cudgel of psychoanalytic interpretation, psychoanalysis uses literature in order to demonstrate its own authority, its own capacity to make sense, to be true. This is in some ways simply disrespectful, reducing the long history of literature to that of a patient waiting for the doctor to arrive to pronounce the actual name of the illness; literature takes the position of the hysteric whose lock is picked only by the Freudian key. It is also, as Felman expresses it, a *misrecognition*: 'the psychoanalytical reading of literary texts precisely *misrecognizes* (overlooks, leaves out) their literary specificity; ... literature could perhaps even be defined as that which remains in a text precisely *unaccounted for* by the traditional psychoanalytical approach to literature' (ibid.). This last point marks the beginning of an alternative approach, in which the capacity both of literature and of psychoanalysis to promote openness to what is 'unaccounted for' is given priority. But for the moment the point is merely that in promoting its own interests, psychoanalytic criticism can miss what is specific to its interlocutor – whether this is the patient in the clinic or, as here, the massive and complex body of thought and writing known as literature.

Despite these cautions, criticisms and caveats, the various commentators quoted so far all see psychoanalysis as having something to say to literature, albeit it only once it has escaped from its own masterful tendencies, its own position as what Lacan (1991, p.29) calls the 'discourse of the Master', the subject actually in possession of the truth. Much of the discussion here centres on what might be called style or *process*, in which the issue is to interrogate literature in ways that open out new modes of reading and understanding – not to find a truth, but to produce more effects. Indeed, it is in demonstrating the impossibility of any one true reading that the productivity of an interpretive account can be found, and there are ways in which psychoanalysis can contribute to this by unsettling obvious renderings of a text so long as this is not in order to replace them with what purport to be 'deeper' ones. In addition, there are possibilities produced by the realisation that psychoanalysis is a literary exercise itself, inscribed in writing and publication but also drawing brilliantly on the tropes and conventions of literature – a point again made early on by Lionel Trilling and developed more fully in the wake of Lacan.

The struggle to develop psychoanalysis, usually coded as an attempt to find a scientific basis for this complex depth psychology, is also a development within the broad disciplinary nexus known as the 'humanities'. This recognises it as an attempt to refine consciousness in relation to human motivation and desire, and to express this refinement in recognisable terms within its own literary genre. In this context, psychoanalysts who recommend the development of literary capacities as a way of mastering technique have something useful to say, not only because of what there is to be learnt from the practice of literature, but also because working *reflexively* in this way leaves psychoanalysis itself open to challenge and change. For example, the leading psychoanalyst Thomas Ogden (1999) describes powerfully (using a Robert Frost poem as an example) how there may be parallels between 'the way he listens to the language of the poem and the way he and his patient speak with and listen to one another' (p.49). For Ogden, the lesson of poetry for the consulting room is not to use language 'poetically' (he describes this as a kind of 'narcissistic countertransference acting in' – p.66), but rather to cultivate a mode of listening and speaking that is attuned to the question of 'what it is "that's going on here" in the intrapsychic and intersubjective life of the analysis, the "music of what happens" in the analytic relationship' (p.50). Ogden argues that both poetry and psychoanalysis make possible forms of 'human aliveness', and the discipline of listening to one can enhance that of listening to the other. In this account the task of the analyst is no longer to unearth the truth of what lies behind the patient's or the poem's words; it is simply to find a way to listen and respond that brings 'feelings and ideas to life in words that will advance the analytic process' (p.66). This moves the discipline towards more of a focus on intersubjectivity, with responsiveness rather than knowingness being a core attribute of the analyst. This too has its direct parallel with the encounter of psychoanalysis with literature. When practised as an expert discipline, interpreting the subservient discipline of literature, psychoanalysis cannot discover anything new. It literally applies its already-existent body of knowledge to make sense of something else, and at best will refine its theories or specific interpretations in the light of problems it might encounter on the way. Its knowledge is demonstrative rather than open and discovering: it knows, and literature must learn. When, however, the encounter is two-way, and psychoanalysis itself is interrogated as a mode of literary discourse, then its doubts and confusions, its unmeant expressions and unresolved conflicts, come into play and can be examined. This produces an aura of uncertainty which might be conducive to change: that is, psychoanalysis can become experimental again, open to feedback. So whilst psychoanalysis becomes rigid when it sets itself up as an expert approach to literature, when understood as literature itself it becomes a more ambiguous and also more productive entity.

The destructive element: Kleinianism and its literary resonances

Before turning more fully to the questions of psychoanalysis *as* literature and of how seeing it this way helps in considering its contribution to literary studies, it is important also to acknowledge that despite all the criticisms of the 'expert' status of psychoanalysis mentioned above, there are ideas that flow from the content of psychoanalytic theory that may add to appreciation of literary works. An example here is the impact of Kleinian theories of destructiveness, particularly in elaborating some of the concerns to be found in interwar British literature. The extraordinary viciousness of the Kleinian world has few counterparts anywhere, except perhaps in twentieth-century external reality. Here, famously, is Joan Riviere (1936), describing the fully Kleinian infant in the mid-1930s:

> Limbs shall trample, kick and hit; lips, fingers and hands shall suck, twist, pinch; teeth shall bite, gnaw, mangle and cut; mouth shall devour, swallow and 'kill' (annihilate), eyes kill by a look, pierce and penetrate; breath and mouth hurt by noise, as the child's own sensitive ears have experienced. One may suppose that before an infant is many months old it will not only *feel* itself performing these actions, but will have some kind of *ideas* of doing so. All these sadistic activities in phantasy are felt not only to expel the danger from the self but to transfer it into the object (projection). (p.286)

Right from the start, Klein's work focused on the conflictual and complex phantasy life of children, uncovering brutalities and hates which fully put paid to any idealised notion of childhood innocence. What Freud had started with the notion of infantile sexuality was developed by Klein to portray infancy as characterised by an inner battle in which good (love) could only precariously triumph over bad (hate), and was always teetering on the edge of destruction. Even though her notions of paranoid-schizoid splitting and envy were not fully worked out until the 1940s and 1950s (e.g. Klein, 1957), from early in her psychoanalytic career, analysing the play of young children in the same way as others analysed adults, Klein emphasised the punitiveness of the infantile psyche and addressed the need for the analyst to pay it due heed. In contrast to Anna Freud, who argued the necessity for a careful nurturing of the treatment alliance and placed value on the 'educative' potential of psychoanalysis, Klein was unstinting in her assertion that analysis is about revelation of the deepest layers of the mind – that only thus could the terrors of unconscious impulses be faced and overcome. 'Analysis is not in itself a gentle method: it cannot spare the patient *any suffering* and this applies equally to children', she wrote (Klein, 1927, p.344). Riviere (1927) was even clearer: 'analysis ... is not concerned with the real world, nor with the child's or the adult's adaptation to the real world, nor with sickness or health, nor virtue or vice. It is concerned simply and solely with the imaginings of the childish mind, the phantasised pleasures and the dreaded retributions' (p.377). The Oedipus complex and superego formation, dated by Freud to about the fifth year of life, are brought right forward by Klein, so the infantile superego becomes 'pre-Oedipal', present in the obscure pre-history of the human subject, the period which Freud largely forgot. The intensity of this is overwhelming: the biting, needy, hating, desiring infant is an exploding cannon of emotional turmoil.

In the mid-1930s, Klein added a further gloss to this with a major innovation which, according to Segal (1979) amongst others, marked the real beginning of a Kleinian 'school'. This was the introduction of the concept of the depressive position, adumbrated in her 1935 paper, *A Contribution to the Psychogenesis of Manic-Depressive States*. This is a profoundly integrative concept, in which what is stressed is the complexity of the process whereby an infant puts together her or his feelings of love and hate and owns them both. The depressive position is constituted by the movement from feelings of rage to those of loss, carried along by recognition of the reality of ambivalence and the necessity, as well as possibility, of making something reparative out of the impulses towards destruction. Taking hold of hate, recognising its existence, ameliorating it through the containment which a benevolent environment (such as the analyst) can offer, owning one's destructiveness, creatively repairing the damage one has done to self and other – these are now the tendencies and aspirations of the Kleinian psyche. Abel (1989) comments, thinking of Virginia Woolf, 'For Kleinians, culture, opposed not as (paternal) law to instinct but as creativity to inner chaos, emerges from the impulse to make reparation to the mother' (p.11).

The context for all this in post-First World War culture is self-evident, and in many ways was shared by Freud with his announcement of the death drive in *Beyond the Pleasure Principle* and his acerbic cultural commentary in *Civilisation and its Discontents* (Freud, 1920b, 1930). Schwartz (1999) summarises:

> The psychoanalysts of Europe were responding to the same events as was everyone else. Theory in psychoanalysis, in its own way, had to cope with turmoil, uncertainty and death. Melanie Klein's vision of the child's inner world was as situated in the uncertainties and brutalities of the aftermath of the First World War as was the literature, the movies and the architecture. (p.199)

For writers, too, the concern with tragedy and the fragmentation of the past was overwhelming. By the mid- to late 1920s, the nature of the First World War was very well known and its devastating consequences had been felt across an entire generation. Everything had changed and had to change. T.S. Eliot's *The Waste Land* (1922), despite or perhaps alongside its misogyny and reactionary class bias, grabbed hold of this feeling and represented it with appalling precision, in a manner congruent with Freud's later versions of psychoanalysis and especially with the fascination with destructiveness which was Klein's specific contribution. Ellmann (1990), in a marvellous examination of the poem's 'abjection' (a concept taken from Kristeva, 1983, itself inspired in part by Klein, and referring to what is degraded and cast out), comments on the wiping out of a history which then returns, plaguing the text, like the return of the repressed which in Freud is the prototype of death. 'Whereas Freud discovers the death drive in the compulsion to repeat,' she writes (p.188), '*The Waste Land* stages it in the compulsion to citation.' Biographically,

> written in the aftermath of the First World War, and in the midst of a disastrous marriage, the poem has so much to forget: madness, feminism, sexuality, the slaughtered millions, and the rattle of its own exhausted idioms. Yet ... *The Waste Land* works like an obsessive ceremonial, because it re-inscribes the horrors it is trying to repress. For Freud argues that obsessive rituals repeat the very acts that they are thought to neutralize: the ritual, he says, is ostensibly a protection against the prohibited act; 'but *actually* ... a repetition of it'. (pp.179–80)

The 'waste' in *The Waste Land* is what constantly returns, the living dead; the ghosts and fragments, of people and particularly of writing. Obsessed by death, both literature and psychoanalysis have to ask what it is in the modern consciousness that can create such vicious fragmentation, such a violent spell:

> The speaker of *The Waste Land* also stages his own death when he conjures up the writings of the dead, sacrificing voice and face to their ventriloquy. In this sense he resembles the child in *Beyond the Pleasure Principle*, who stages his extinction in the mirror. Freud compares his grandchild to the victims of shell-shock, who relive their terrors in their dreams, repeating death as if it were desire. This is the game *The Waste Land* plays, and the nightmare that it cannot lay to rest, as it stages the ritual of its own destruction. (Ellmann, 1990, p.198)

'Limbs shall trample, kick and hit', writes Riviere (1936), and Klein (1932) describes a vast range of destructive impulses in the young child, for example, 'an early stage of development which is governed by the child's aggressive trends against its mother's body and in which its predominant wish is to rob her body of its contents and destroy it' (p.128). *The Waste Land*, too, 'stages the ritual of its own destruction', as did, in the First World War, the whole of European society. It is not surprising, then, that Kleinian ideas should have been attractive in Britain and that the growth of fascism and Nazism in the 1930s should simply augment that attraction, as explanations had to be sought for the continued eruption of the bestial tumour out of the body of the modern world.

Kleinianism, in this account, does not simply offer an explanation for, or interpretation of, literature (*The Waste Land* as devouring destructiveness), but rather shares in the culture of destruction which makes sense of its products, whether psychoanalytic or literary. In this regard, the very specific resonance of some Kleinian ideas in the wake of the First World War does not attest to their truth value so much as to their cultural congruence, which again makes them useful in a dialogue with literature. Stonebridge (1998) shows this very powerfully in relation to the notion of reparation, a core Kleinian idea referring to 'the variety of processes by which the ego feels it undoes harm done in phantasy, restores, preserves and revives objects' (Klein, 1955, p.133). Reparation rebuilds the world after destruction; yet, it is only in its cultural context that one can get the full feel of the ambiguities involved. Stonebridge (1998) notes that in the immediate aftermath of the war, 'reparations' not only meant making good the damage done, but – because of the disastrous failure of political imagination accompanying the Versailles Treaty – it also had connotations of being unfair and unduly punitive, hence continuing in the destructive mode. Indexing the literary critic William Empson's (1956) famous book on ambiguity, she explains:

> Like redemption, reparation carries with it both the spiritual sense of salvation and atonement and economic connotations of compensation and dues collected. When in 1919 reparation entered the European vocabulary with a new political charge, it also took on two more meanings: first, as the OED puts it, 'compensation for war damage owed by the aggressor' and second, as a direct result of the former, reparation, in an Empsonian manner, began to haemorrhage into almost the opposite of the rightful justice it was supposed to connote. For vocal if not ultimately influential sections of the European intelligentsia as well as for those suffering under the terms of the treaty, reparation came to mean something exorbitant, excessive and punitive, in short, an invitation to more aggression ... In the period between the wars, reparation, in a Kleinian as well as Empsonian sense, is pregnant with the destructive element. (p.32)

The importance of work like this is that it indicates the problems that both psychoanalysts and literary figures were working on. In this instance, these concerned the ambivalence entailed in 'making good' the destruction of the war in an environment in which nothing had been worked through or resolved, and in which the dynamics of anxiety and hatred released in and by the war had not been owned or understood. It is not that the Kleinian notion of reparation offers the key to understanding the literature of the time, though it does give some useful leverage for exploring its nuances. It is rather that the trope of reparation runs through a range of cultural products, including Kleinian psychoanalysis, giving them resonance and appeal, and filling them with the meaning-effects that make them warrantable at that time and place. Psychoanalysis is in dialogue with literature here because both are infected with the problematics of their period; this is not absolute, masterful 'knowledge', but an encounter that makes meaning more subtle and rich.

Psychoanalysis as literature

Recognition of the way in which psychoanalysis draws on literature, and the possibilities this gives for a creative encounter between the two disciplines, has been spurred on particularly by the Lacanian emphasis on language. However, it has not depended on this development. As noted earlier, Lionel Trilling (1951) very clearly articulated an irony of psychoanalysis: that whilst its direct attempts to 'interpret' literature too often produced crass and patronising interpretations that fail to understand the openness of artistic meanings, when one turns to the decidedly non-literary elements of psychoanalytic theory, useful concepts and parallels immediately stand out. For Trilling, these lie in the way psychoanalysis 'makes poetry indigenous to the very constitution of the mind' (p.64). Indeed, he writes, 'the mind, as Freud sees it, is in the greater part of its tendency exactly a poetry-making organ'. This 'poetry' is not to be found in any romantic notion of, for example, the unfathomable depths of unconscious mental life; rather, it lies in the very specific mechanisms proposed by Freud to explain how the mind works.

> In the eighteenth century Vico spoke of the metaphorical, imagistic language of the early stages of culture; it was left to Freud to discover how, in a scientific age, we still feel and think in figurative formations, and to create, what psychoanalysis is, a science of tropes, of metaphor and its variants, synecdoche and metonymy. (ibid.)

Just as Lacan was led to draw on the work of structural linguistics to explain the functioning of the mind in terms of metaphor and metonymy, so Trilling, writing in a very different tradition, saw the essential literary humanism of Freud as residing in his discovery of mental mechanisms such as displacement and condensation. This was additional to a more general humanistic sympathy that, according to Trilling, Freud had with the great literary traditions, one characterised by openness to suffering and an essentially tragic vision that was without cynicism even when it was characterised by irony. Freud himself is an artist, in this sense, or at least his view of the world has much to offer the artist: 'the poetic qualities of Freud's own principles, which are so clearly in the line of the classic tragic realism, suggest that this is a view which does not narrow and simplify the human world for the artist but on the contrary opens and complicates it' (p.68). There are thus two ways in which Freudian psychoanalysis can contribute to the literary imagination: as a general, tragic vision of human nature out of which a moral system can be welded together; and as a specific, 'scientific' approach that shows how the mind itself obeys literary laws, and is thus open to the reception and expression of poetic modes of being. This approach, it might be noted, to some extent reverses the master–slave dynamic of traditional psychoanalytic criticism. This time, it is literature that is being used to make sense of psychoanalysis. It is literature that has the interpretive and technical facility available to it, and psychoanalysis that draws on literary tropes to theorise its own object of study, the mind. On the other hand, what Trilling is pointing to here is an essential sympathy between psychoanalysis and literature that might be used to the advantage of both, without the struggle for dominance that had thitherto characterised the field.

Two 'classic' accounts of the literary nature of Freudian psychoanalysis are worth noting here. The first is Steven Marcus' (1975) exploration of the 'Dora' case study (Freud, 1905). His title, *Freud and Dora: Story, History, Case History*, captures the way in which his reading proceeds, as a highly sympathetic rendering of it as if it were a novel. Marcus is explicit here, seeing Freud as the master of a new literary form, the case history. As a genre this is directly related to other modernist forms, sharing with them particular attributes such as that of the 'unreliable narrator' who is in many ways at odds with her or his material, and who challenges the reader to make something out of the fragmentary nature of what is presented:

> The general form of what Freud has written bears certain suggestive resemblances to a modern experimental novel. Its narrative and expository course, for example, is neither linear nor rectilinear; instead its organization is plas-

> tic, involuted, and heterogeneous and follows spontaneously an inner logic that seems frequently to be at odds with itself; it often loops around itself and is multidimensional in its representation of both its material and itself. Its continuous innovations in formal structure seem unavoidably to be dictated by its substance, by the dangerous, audacious, disreputable, and problematical character of the experiences being represented and dealt with, and by the equally scandalous intentions of the author and the outrageous character of the role he has had the presumption to assume. In content, however, what Freud has written is in parts rather like a play by Ibsen, or more precisely like a series of Ibsen's plays. (p.64)

Marcus tracks the various literary techniques Freud uses, from the framing device in the Prefatory Remarks to the case, which draws the reader's attention to the fragmentary nature of the work and also positions both Freud and Dora as protagonists, through the analysis of Dora's dreams and the way in which the plot line at the end (on transference) calls into question most of what has gone before. Marcus is deeply admiring of Freud's skill even as he speculates that the case history reveals Freud's own blind spots – this too being characteristic of much modernist literature. Freud announces the problematic status of his writing and the 'dubious' character of its achievement, and opens up to the reader the chance of *interpreting him* over and beyond his own work. That is, despite appearances, he is not in command, instructing the reader (and patient) authoritatively in ways that cannot be challenged. Instead, through the very fragmentary nature of the case history and the way in which alternative voices (Freud's own self-doubt being one, but Dora's clearly being another) are allowed to speak, readers can fill in their own narratives, as indeed has been done many times (Bernheimer and Kahane, 1985). Marcus notes:

> the work is also fragmentary or incomplete in the sense of Freud's self-knowledge, both at the time of the actual case and at the time of his writing it. And he communicates in this piece of writing a less than complete understanding of himself, although like any great writer he provides us with the material for understanding some things that have escaped his own understanding, for filling in some gaps, for restoring certain fragments into wholes. (p.67)

By the end, as he shows, Freud has converted everything into writing – transference is *defined* as 'new editions or facsimiles of the impulses and phantasies which are aroused during the progress of the analysis; but they have this peculiarity, which is characteristic of their species, that they replace some earlier person by the person of the physician' (Freud, 1905, pp.157–8). That is, 'The patient does not merely provide the text;

he also *is* the text, the writing to be read, the language to be interpreted' (Marcus, 1975, p.81).

What is happening here, as Marcus explicitly notes, is that psychoanalysis is being forged through the medium of literary expression, and stamps its authority not only (or maybe not at all) through its scientific claims, but also through its capacity to use literary means to articulate the problems facing modern human subjects. The simple bourgeois forms of narrative retained their appeal in Freud's time, but they were also breaking down, and psychoanalysis is a product of a precise moment in western cultural history in which new, often revolutionary forms of expression are coming into view, in politics, art, music and literature. Freud's self-expression is marked by this, his struggle to find a mode of writing that will both persuade and also do justice to the lacunae in his theory that are produced by the real complexities of human psychology. His own multi-layered self-consciousness also comes into play, at times dazzlingly insightful, at others patently defensive; and as this happens, so it is transformed into literature. Even the topic of his study and his way of understanding it are deeply literary: the patient may have bodily symptoms, as hysterics such as Dora in particular do, but these are versions of words, written on the body rather than in sound or on paper. For example, Dora's cough is traced eventually by Freud to an unconscious awareness of the oral sex going on between her father and Frau K. Freud (1905) comments: 'But the conclusion was inevitable that with her spasmodic cough, which, as is usual, was referred for its exciting stimulus to a tickling in her throat, she pictured to herself a scene of sexual gratification per os between the two people whose love-affair occupied her mind so incessantly' (p.48). *Naming* it in this way leads to the cough vanishing. The task of psychoanalysis is in large part to restore words that have become lost and embedded in the 'wrong' places to their linguistic and literary origins, to make narratives of them that are more potent than the broken narratives that produce symptoms. Psychoanalysis is not therefore literary only because it has to be expressed in narrative form; it also treats its patients as literary beings, characters in search of stories that make sense; and it struggles with language as a way to achieve this.

If Marcus shows definitively the connection between Freud and modernist literary forms, Peter Brooks' (1982) essay on *Beyond the Pleasure Principle* (Freud, 1920b) looks at Freud's attempt to create a 'masterplot' that will make life itself narratable. *Beyond the Pleasure Principle* is the moment in Freud's writing when the whole of his drive theory is recast in the light of the work he had previously done on narcissism and, especially, of the encounter with trauma and destructiveness in the First World War. This was a war which he had at first welcomed, like so many who saw it as an opportunity for the listless stagnation of pre-war society to be overcome; but gradually, again like so many others, he understood it as a devastating assault on the assumption of inevitable human progress. Where previously the drive model had proposed an opposition between sexual and ego-preservative drives, with an appropriate compromise between 'pleasure' and 'reality' being the key to individual and social mental health, *Beyond the Pleasure Principle* invents a new metapsychology, in which what governs human activity is a more fundamental opposition between 'life' and 'death'. A postulate of psychoanalysis had been that the aim of the drives was satisfaction experienced in the form of pleasure. Yet, in neurotic behaviour and dreams and even in the childhood play of Freud's own grandson (the famous game in which the mother's disappearance is symbolised by throwing away a cotton reel), the apparently willed re-emergence of disturbing material could be observed again and again. This was not just temporary pain caused to the ego in the service of later drive satisfaction (for instance, the pleasure of the mother's return); it represented a 'remarkable fact', namely, that the compulsion to repeat often brings up material which can never have been pleasurable, and which 'can never, even long ago, have brought satisfaction even to instinctual impulses which have since been repressed' (Freud, 1920b, p.20). Traumatic dreams, of the kind characteristic of war neuroses, are an example of this phenomenon and apparently contradict the well-known formulation that dreams are wish-fulfilments, making it necessary to consider whether there may be another force at work other than the achievement of happiness. Instead, there must be something in human psychology more basic than pleasurable satisfaction, that is, something 'beyond' the pleasure principle. For Freud, oppressed by the legacy of death all around, perhaps by his own emerging cancer and the tired irascibility of what was already becoming his 'late style' (Said, 2007), this 'beyond' would not contradict the idea of a drive achieving satisfaction by restoring the organism to rest, but would exaggerate it, or follow it through to its logical conclusion. Observation of the sexual life of humans had revealed that there exists a drive which aims at preserving living substances and joining them together into larger units. Now it was also clear that there must be 'another, contrary instinct seeking to dissolve those units and to bring them back to their primaeval, inorganic state' (Freud, 1930, p.118). And what could this be, but a state of perfect rest and nothingness, a relief from all tension and unwanted stimulation? 'The aim of all life is death', wrote Freud (1920b, p.38).

Laplanche and Pontalis (1967) suggest that the death drive is not simply a balancing force opposing the life drive, but is better understood as a basic postulate grounding Freud's motivational theory. 'What is designated here,' they write (p.102), 'is more than any particular *type* of instinct – it is rather that factor which determines the actual *principle* of all instincts', this principle being that of movement away (life) and then return. For Brooks (1982), reading *Beyond the Pleasure Principle* with a literary eye, Freud's reconfiguration of his drive theory was more than just a scientific one; it also constitutes what he calls Freud's 'masterplot', 'the text in which he most fully lays out a total scheme of how life proceeds from beginning to end, and how each individual life in its own way repeats the masterplot' (p.285). Moreover, embedded deeply in this masterplot, in Brooks' rewriting of it, is *narrative structure*, and this is what gives it its literary feel and relevance. There are two main elements to this. The first lies in the idea of the 'compulsion to repeat' itself: repetition has always been core to psychoanalysis, for example in the way neuroses are forged out of 'memories', and how transference is a repetition, in the presence of the analyst, of earlier relationships. In *Beyond the Pleasure Principle*, repetition becomes the defining motif of life itself, both in the sense of the death drive's 'desire' to return to an earlier state of inorganic inactivity, and in the way traumatic moments plague the mind and drive it to actions aimed at mastery or self-defence. For Brooks, repetition is also a defining feature of narrative: 'Narrative must ever present itself as a repetition of events that have already happened, and within this postulate of a generalized repetition it must make use of specific, perceptible repetitions in order to create plot, that is, to show us a significant interconnection of events' (p.288). More than just interconnection is at work here: repetition in psychoanalysis and in literature is a matter of the 'baseline of plot, its basic "pulsation", sensible or audible through the repetitions which take us back to the text' (p.291). The parallel between Freud's account of the psychic centrality of the compulsion to repeat and the way narratives are built out of replicable materials to be found scattered around the plots of literature is hardened by Brooks in the further rendering he gives of the way Freud's postulation of the 'journey' of life away from and back to death is itself a model of how narrative works. This holds the implication that this is in some way intrinsic to (perhaps 'hard-wired into', as might be said in the wake of the neuroscientific revolution) human consciousness. For the Freud of *Beyond the Pleasure Principle*, life is a deviation from death, what Brooks calls an 'arabesque' the aim of which is not to avoid death, but to allow each organism to return to death *in its own way.* 'What we are left with is the fact that the organism wishes to die only in its own fashion', writes Freud (1920b, p.39) – to find the death that is fitting for it. In narrative, tension is similarly produced by a process of 'detour', a middle that embellishes and delays the progress from beginning to end, a kind of arc that deliberately takes up more space and time than would the straight line that is the shortest connection between these two points. In life, too, according to Freud, the arc of activity has precisely the same function. It defends against death, but it also brings the subject back to death, albeit in its own way: the right death, the appropriate end or dénouement; this is what is required. Brooks comments: 'The complication of the *detour* is related to the danger of short-circuit: the danger of reaching the end too quickly, of achieving the im-proper death' (p.292). Both narrative development and Eros work to counteract this threat. Brooks continues:

> We emerge from reading *Beyond the Pleasure Principle* with a dynamic model which effectively structures ends (death, quiescence, non-narratability) against beginnings (Eros, stimulation into tension, the desire of narrative) in a manner that necessitates the middle as *detour*, as struggle toward the end under the compulsion of imposed delay, as arabesque in the dilatory space of the text. (p.295)

Much of Brooks' argument involves drawing parallels between the death drive and narrative, which offers some intriguing insights into how narrative works and also suggests that in inventing his model of life and death drives, Freud might have been drawing implicitly, perhaps unconsciously, on familiar and cogent western thought structures and cultural repertoires. Perhaps this is more specific than Brooks suggests: rather than being a universal characteristic of human plot lines, the particular cultural assumptions of modernism are organised around the idea of narrative as 'beginning, middle, end' in ways which may not be true of all cultures, nor even (totally) of postmodern western times. Indeed, Brooks wants to go further here, using Freud's 'masterplot' to make sense of all literary endeavour, arguing that in identifying the basic structure of psychic life, Freud is also offering an interpretive account that can be applied to all texts. In contrast to the traditional psychoanalytic strategy of imposing readings of the author's, reader's or character's 'unconscious' on the text, Brooks argues that

> It is rather the superimposition of the model of the mental apparatus on the functioning of the text that offers the possibility of a psychoanalytic criticism. And here the superimposition of Freud's psychic masterplot on the plots of fiction seems a valid and useful maneuver. Plot mediates meanings with the contradictory human world of the eternal and the mortal. Freud's masterplot speaks of the temporality of desire, and speaks to our very desire for fictional plots. (pp.299–300)

Freud's account of the tension between life and death drives is used here as an explanation of the psychic appeal of fiction, not just as a parallel account – the 'temporality of desire' *explains* the pull of narrative. Yet despite Brooks' assertion that this avoids the reductionism of traditional psychoanalytic criticism 'applied to' literature, it is hard to see how exactly this can be the case. Clearly, literary understanding may be enriched by the parallel with the 'detour' postulated by Freud, but we are still faced with an idea that originates in psychoanalysis and is then applied to literature to explain why narrative has such a profound appeal, why western readers constantly push for satisfaction, for completion, for the 'right' end, and feel frustrated and challenged – sometimes still outraged – when this is not provided. This is 'because' the mind is built that way, as a detour between death and a satisfactory return to death; what else can 'the superimposition of the model of the mental apparatus on the functioning of the text' signify? To that extent, it is difficult to see this kind of analysis moving things forward.

On the other hand, returning to the parallelism between narrative and Freudian theory has its own productivity. What it suggests is that in developing his theory of drives, Freud was not (or not just) building on careful observation and clinical and scientific knowledge, but was ordering those in terms of culturally given narrative structures. The pattern of origin, tension, resolution that is so embedded in 'beginning, middle, end' in literature, as in everyday personal accounts of events, was one that underpinned his model from the start. For Freud, the idea of tension pushing for relief was built on a sexual analogy, and maybe this is one source of the power of the narrative model anyway: that it recapitulates or brings to mind a basic psycho-physiological experience. But more significantly, this reading produces psychoanalysis once again as a literary activity with something to say to other literary activities. It is a *narrative*, for the very good reason that narrative of this kind structures psychology under the conditions of western modernity.

Signs and signifiers

Much contemporary engagement of psychoanalysis with literature has taken place under the sign, one might say, of Lacanianism. This is not a simple procedure, not only because of the famous opacity of Lacanian theory, but also because Lacan himself did not really mark out an approach to literature that solves the problems of psychoanalytic 'mastery' discussed above. Even his most famous literary diversion, the seminar on Edgar Allan Poe's story *The Purloined Letter* (Lacan, 1954–55), 'cannot possibly constitute a model for [psychoanalytic literary] criticism, since on the contrary the literary work is in it a mere pretext for a dazzling illustration of a non-literary thesis', as Jameson (1982, p.375) notes. Indeed, Lacan follows in one strand of Freud's tradition by using literature to show a certain kind of 'truth' of psychoanalysis, specifically to indicate ways in which meaning is produced through the flow of signifiers rather than being the product of 'character', a reading which also articulates the mode of operation of sexual difference in the discursive field (Frosh, 2006). What this does not do, however, is offer any *literary* analysis of Poe's text. Rather, it uses the text to make a point about psychic structure, not about literature itself. Despite this, Lacan's general approach has given leverage on textual analysis, for two related reasons. The first is simply the Lacanian focus on language: whereas the literary and linguistic origins of Freudian psychoanalysis have had to be uncovered philosophically and historically, Lacan was always explicit about language as the core phenomenon of psychoanalysis. His rather misleading slogan, 'the unconscious is structured like a language', is the most famous illustration of this, but more broadly the Lacanian understanding of psychoanalysis as a linguistic endeavour focuses attention on the movement of textual elements as they work across the speech of patient and analyst. This has the important result of shifting analytic attention away from a 'depth' reading of what lies hidden beneath the surface of the text, and more towards an examination and provocation of the 'disruptive' elements of textual play – towards the *effects* of language as they appear in the analytic situation. In comparison with traditional psychoanalytic attempts to find the 'real' meaning of a symptom or text in terms of the unconscious impulses and conflicts that lie behind it, the Lacanian push is on the whole towards tracking the effect of signifiers as they work in speech itself. This gives rise to some promising parallels between the analysis of the discourse of patients and the analysis of other kinds of text, including literary ones. In particular, Lacanian psychoanalysis refutes what it regards as the 'imaginary' task of producing full readings or explanations of unconscious meaning. Meaning for Lacan is a 'retroactive' phenomenon, produced after the event as a way of closing it down; for example, the meaning of a sentence is determined only at its end. In psychoanalytic practice, Lacan (1954–55) gives the following rule for literature, dreams and analysis:

> You must start from the text, start by treating it, as Freud does and as he recommends, as Holy Writ. The author, the scribe, is only a pen-pusher, and he comes second ... Similarly, when it comes to our patients, please give more attention to the text than to the psychology of the author – the entire orientation of my teaching is that. (p.153)

Meaning has to emerge from the play of the text – the movement of signifiers, in the linguistic terms preferred by Lacan; it is not something fixed and definite. Lacan (1973) is insistent that this does not result in arbitrary interpretations, but that interpretation 'has the effect of bringing out irreducible, *non-sensical* – composed of non-meanings – signifying elements' (p.250), with the aim ('what is essential') being that the subject should 'see, beyond this signification, to what signifier – to what irreducible, traumatic, non-meaning – he is as a subject, subjected' (ibid., p.251). Although this is a confusing and difficult idea, implying that there might indeed be a 'meta-meaning' (the 'irreducible' one) lurking 'beyond' the text, the literary attraction of Lacanian psychoanalysis is that it is not devoted to the exercise of interpretation, as are most other psychoanalytic schools, nor to a meaningful intersubjective encounter. Rather, it holds what is in some ways a more modest aim, that of surprising the patient – and, if possible, the analyst – with the appearance of unexpected links or associations that open out new signifying chains, but which do not in themselves present a particular truth or final knowledge. Nobus and Quinn (2005) lay down their version of this right at the beginning of their book on *Knowing Nothing, Staying Stupid*:

> Rather than reintegrating the analysand's stupidities within a consistent body of knowledge, or replacing them with a more adequate, adapted and competent knowledge whose market value is recognised by the authoritative discursive ideologies, the analyst fully exposes the formations of the unconscious as headless pieces of knowledge, disruptive eruptions of meaninglessness against the comfortable backdrop of established reason. (p.4)

The notion that literature might engage in an encounter with psychoanalysis that offers such 'surprises' to each is quite close to the position adopted by some post-Lacanian literary critics. The most influential example here is Shoshana Felman, whose contribution to her own edited collection *Literature and Psychoanalysis* (1982b) is a study of Henry James' story *The Turn of the Screw* prefaced by a penetrating account of what an open dialogue between psychoanalysis and literature might do. Felman's search is for a way in which psychoanalysis and literature can genuinely invest in each other as equals – not one mastering the other, either as psychoanalysis speaking the truth of literature or literature exposing the narrative assumptions of psychoanalysis, even though both disciplines do have something to say to the other from these 'expert' positions. For Felman, the important thing is to expose the fictional nature of psychoanalytic authority (hence exposing the unconscious underside of psychoanalysis) and the dubious authority to be claimed by fiction (hence exposing the unconscious traces within literature itself). Each is deeply entwined in the other, and through this intense face-off, something unexpected can be called on that keeps open the possibility of surprise, refuting the claims of either literary studies or psychoanalysis to have an answer to the question of meaning. Felman (1982b) writes:

> In view of this shift of emphasis, the traditional method of *application* of psychoanalysis to literature would here be in principle ruled out. The notion of *application* would be replaced by the radically different notion of *implication*: bringing analytical questions to bear upon literary questions, *involving* psychoanalysis in the scene of literary analysis, the interpreter's role would here be, not to *apply* to the text an acquired science, a preconceived knowledge, but to act as a go-between, to *generate implications* between literature and psychoanalysis – to explore, bring to light and articulate the various (indirect) ways in which the two domains do indeed *implicate each other*, each one finding itself enlightened, informed, but also affected, displaced by the other. (pp.8–9)

As already noted, literature is deeply embedded in the origins and structure of psychoanalysis, and the congruence between literary and psychoanalytic thinking was one source of 'evidence' used by Freud to support his developing ideas. Equally, as shown in Brooks' (1982) examination of how psychoanalysis throws light on the appeal of, and desire for, narrative, it is almost impossible to undertake literary studies in the post-Freudian world, without also engaging with psychoanalysis, for better or worse. What Felman pushes for in this quotation is recognition of this mutual implication and the teasing out of its effects – what each does to the other, how the strategies of reading involved in textual and clinical work draw on one another and produce new ideas. And it is this question of *reading* that is perhaps central. This concerns not just the masterful analyst reading the patient's discourse for its unconscious significance or the sophisticated literary critic reading the text for its nuances and resonances, but the awareness present in both disciplines that reading is a process of involvement that draws the reader in. Reading is a productive process that changes the reader/analyst as much as it explores any text. Ellmann (1994) comments:

> For Lacan, this complicity between the subject reading and the object read represents the crux of Freud's discoveries ... In other words, it is impossible to understand analysands or literary texts without participating in their dreams or their delusions. The critic necessarily conspires in the text's imaginings; the act of reading is a process of mutual seduction, whereby the reader and the read arouse each other's fantasies, expose each other's

> dreams. It is when we think we penetrate the text's disguises that we are usually most deluded and most ignorant, for what we see is nothing but our unknown selves. (p.10)

The question structuring Felman's (1982b) account of *The Turn of the Screw* is '*What* is Freudian in a Freudian reading, and in what way can it be defined and measured?' (p.103). She rapidly deals with the 'classic' psychoanalytic reading of this text, that of Edmund Wilson (1934), arguing that its rendering of James' ghost story as a product of the governess' fevered sexual imagination is a way of doing Freud that takes sexuality as the pre-given answer to all questions, and then unfailingly finds it in the text. The problem here is not only the importation of a preconceived psychological motivation from the clinical arena, where it might be established as part of the specific, hidden story of an individual, to the fictional one in which this is impossible. It is also that this is what Felman, echoing James himself, calls a 'vulgar' reading of the text, one that 'blocks and interrupts the endless process of metaphorical substitution':

> The vulgar, therefore, is anything which misses, or falls short of, the dimension of the symbolic, anything which rules out, or excludes, meaning as a loss and as a flight – anything which strives, in other words, to eliminate from language its inherent silence, anything which misses the specific way in which a text *actively* 'won't tell'. (p.107)

The problem with 'vulgar' Freudian readings is precisely their *lack* of ambiguity, their capacity to tie the text up too neatly, so nothing new can occur. Felman opposes this through a reading very different from that offered by Wilson, even though she also takes sexuality as the core psychoanalytic concern. In her case, sexuality is understood as that which always problematises meaning, as that which will not let things alone. Sexuality, in the general Lacanian view, always fails, because it can never be fully satisfied except in the 'imaginary'. Felman explains: 'If, far from implying the simplicity of a self-present literal meaning, sexuality points rather to a multiplicity of conflicting forces, to the complexity of its own divisiveness and contradiction, its meaning can by no means be univocal or unified, but must necessarily be *ambiguous*' (p.112; original emphasis). This produces an opposite mode of reading to the one which makes sexuality the source of a text's 'real' meaning. Instead, sexuality (and, one might add, the whole notion of an unconscious) constantly undermines any chance of fixing a single meaning to any text, whether that of a patient or an author, because it signifies something that always fails, a gap that can never be fully overcome, 'that through which meaning in the text *does not come off*, that which in the text, and through which the text, *fails to mean*, that which can engender but a *conflict of interpretations*' (p.112; original emphasis). A Freudian reading is consequently not one that gives Freudian 'answers', but rather one that opens out a text for questioning. It recognises that every text has areas of ambiguity and silence that can only produce more questioning; it demands a reading strategy, therefore, that is shuttered off from interpretive certainty. When psychoanalysis misses this, when readings are presented that 'master' the text, what is at work is not the creative use of Freudian interpretive tactics, but rather a mode of repression in which the 'desire' of the text – its potential for subversion, or for the proliferation of meanings that makes literature rich – is denied. Felman addresses this as precisely a repression of the unconscious:

> To *master*, then (to become the Master) is, here as elsewhere, to *refuse to read* the letters; here as elsewhere, to 'see it all' is in effect to 'shut one's eyes as tight as possible to the truth'; once more, 'to see it all' is in reality to *exclude*; and to exclude, specifically, the unconscious. (pp.193–4)

Samuel Beckett's (1984) famous line comes to mind: 'Ever tried. Ever failed. No matter. Try again. Fail again. Fail better.'

One can see a further example of the potential fertility of an 'open' psychoanalytic engagement with literature in Barbara Johnson's (1996) exploration of the triangular encounter between Poe, Lacan and Derrida over the *Purloined Letter*. Poe's tale is told by a narrator who is foil to the investigator/analyst Dupin and who extracts from him his philosophical musings and his account of how he outwitted the Minister who had stolen a potentially compromising letter from the Queen. The police fail to find the stolen letter because their ludicrously exact investigation is couched at the wrong level: they can only act according to their own beliefs about how a thief might behave. Dupin, on the other hand, imagines himself inside the mind of the Minister, identifies with him, and thus comprehends what his course of action is likely to have been. He understands that the thief's actions will have been determined not by reason alone, but by something more imaginative and compelling – something constituting *enjoyment* in the sense of an excessive and unnecessary involvement – which Dupin suggests is made possible by the Minister being not just a mathematician, but also a poet. Dupin himself also writes verse, giving him a capacity to transcend the simple logic of those who just follow the rules and to enter into the mind of the other, to understand his rational irrationalities, eventually to trick him and recover the lost object.

One of the key components of Poe's tale as recognised by Lacan is that the *content* of the letter, its exact conventional 'meaning', is never revealed. Instead, it is the *lack* of meaning that is suggestive, and the way that the letter acts in a chain of signifiers that produces the story's effect. For Lacan, the letter represents the 'pure state' of the symbol, the 'original, radical subject'. 'One can say that, when the characters get a hold of this letter, something gets a hold of them and carries them along and this something clearly has dominion over their individual idiosyncrasies' (Lacan, 1954–55, p.196). This lack is itself interpretable as a mode of castration; lack becomes the core of the story, as the empty signifier is passed around, positioning the subjects as it moves. It is the position of the letter that is crucial – who has it and to what use it might be put. For Derrida (1975), however, there is a problem with Lacan's reading of the story in terms of castration: rather than appreciating the continual slipperiness of language and text, so that meanings are only ever provisional and partial, Derrida sees Lacan as having alighted on castration as the 'truth' of the tale. Thus, although the Lacanian reading appears to promote the abstract movement of symbols as the mode of operation of textuality, in the certainty and mastery with which this happens a 'truth' of the text – that of castration – is established, which in a sense makes lack 'full', gives it a positive meaning from which all else follows. 'The displacement of the signifier is analysed as a signified, as the recounted object in a short story' (Derrida, 1975, p.48). Derrida's case here is that in operating within a certain psychoanalytic frame, Lacan finds in the text what already exists in the theory, which positions castration and lack as the core of meaning. Lacan, that is, does not analyse the analytic frame itself, does not, for example, see himself in the analytic process – any more than does the Minister in the story. He takes what he knows as a psychoanalyst to be the baseline for his rendering of the truth. Once again, it seems, psychoanalysis finds itself in what it reads, is unable to enter into a truly open dialogue with its texts.

Johnson (1996), however, problematises this once more. She queries the looseness with which Derrida reads *Lacan's* text, for example his readiness to find castration at the heart of the account, when it is not actually mentioned by Lacan (though it is hard not to see its implicit functioning, as described above). For Johnson, Derrida is not actually engaged in the kind of close reading here for which he was famous; rather, it is something about the authority or 'effect' of Lacan with which he is taking issue:

> Derrida's consistent forcing of Lacan's statements into systems and patterns from which they are actually trying to escape must correspond to some

> strategic necessity different from the attentiveness to the letter that characterizes Derrida's way of reading Poe. And in fact, the more one works with Derrida's analysis, the more convinced one becomes that although the critique of what Derrida calls psychoanalysis is entirely justified, it does not quite apply to what Lacan's text is actually saying. What Derrida is in fact arguing against is therefore not Lacan's text but Lacan's power, or rather, 'Lacan' as the apparent cause of certain effects of power in French discourse today. Whatever Lacan's text may say, it functions, according to Derrida, as if it says what he says it says. The statement [by Lacan in the Seminar] that a letter always reaches its destination may be totally undecipherable, but its assertive force is taken all the more seriously as a sign that Lacan himself has everything all figured out. (p.91)

There are many complexities in Johnson's (and of course Derrida's and Lacan's) accounts of the reading of the Poe story, but a couple of issues stand out here as summations of this chapter's argument. First, Derrida's critique of psychoanalysis and indeed of all interpretive approaches that do not interrogate their own interpretive frames as they work, points firmly both to a major difficulty with 'psychoanalysis and literature' and to a way through it. The difficulty is that without self-interrogation or reflection any interpretive method becomes an expert one, which can do no more than display its mastery by revealing precisely but solely what its concepts make it possible to reveal. Whilst clever puzzle-solving might well result, surprise does not; and in the course of this a kind of mis-recognition of the otherness of the text (for instance, its specifically literary qualities) occurs. The potential way through this is to reveal the workings of the frame itself. One contribution made by the *Purloined Letter* debate is that it does this by showing how on top of each interpretation of the story, another one can be made – Lacan can be read by Derrida, whose reading has its own lacunae and polemical cause. The second point builds on this: as each reading displaces the apparent truth of the previous one, raising doubts and elaborating associations, so the richness of both literature and psychoanalysis can increase. Meanings proliferate, not exactly randomly, but provocatively, shading each other as different features of the cultural environment come into play. Feminism, for example, has radically changed the terms of the 'Dora' debate; it is doubtful whether many people read *The Purloined Letter* at all now except as a way of reading Lacan. This proliferation of meanings allows the 'unconscious' traces that can be found in any kind of text to bubble up for acknowledgement and enjoyment, for instance in the way in which repetition occurs – including, perhaps especially, repetition of a fantasy. Psychoanalysis contributes to this not as an exercise in mastery, but as a particularly well-attuned literary endeavour itself. When its questions are not pitched as a way of producing unassailable truth, they can be the kinds of intervention that make new links, or enrich the associative power of what one might find on the page. Conversely, literature challenges psychoanalysis to examine its own tropes and narrative assumptions, its own cultural indices and modes of expression, and in doing so it can at times produce an enriched psychoanalysis, more able to listen analytically to what it might itself be saying.

Conclusion

This rendering of the 'implication' of psychoanalysis in literature, as Felman (1982a) has it, has its own implications for the 'application' of psychoanalysis in the social as well as the literary sphere. As noted in the previous chapter, Freud's tendency was to use psychoanalysis to 'explain' social phenomena, not just observing how unconscious factors feature in the behaviour of social groups, but also theorising them either as if the social itself has 'an unconscious', or simply in terms of the unconscious impulses of the individuals that make up any society. Ironically, rather than construct psychoanalysis as an effective new master discipline, which is the aim of such an application, this *reduces* its significance to one of many competing social psychological theories, with some useful and provocative concepts but limited theoretical and empirical reach. This is also the situation when psychoanalysis is applied in a heavy-handed way to literature. However, as this chapter has shown, the alternative trend amongst cultural critics to counterpose psychoanalysis and literature more equally grants new opportunities for an open engagement that provokes each discipline and subverts their assumptive worlds. Much of this can be drawn together under the general heading of enhancing 'reflexivity', as each discipline reflects on itself in the light of the impact of the other. So, literature is opened up by psychoanalytic querying of the way linguistic and affective traces appear and repeat; and questions such as why narrative should be such a 'draw' are exposed to psychological as well as literary examination. Conversely, psychoanalysis becomes situated as a specific cultural project which is built on literary as well as scientific tropes, having its own rhetorical investments in certain modes of intellectual mastery. The effect of this is, at best, to catalyse practices of renewal in which disciplinary assumptions become unsettled and new thoughts generated, producing new insights – however fragmentary these might be.

Generalising this 'method' outside that of literature, one might now ask whether such an openness of encounter, such an 'inmixing of subjects' (Lacan, 1954–55, p.193), or 'implication' of one with another, provides a basis for a creative involvement of psychoanalysis with those disciplines that try actively to theorise the social world. There are of course highly significant differences between social theory and literature, for example in relation to evidence, the space given to imagination, and the way language is used. Literary studies often seek to 'expand' readings of texts, exploring associations and creating multiple narratives in order to suggest new meanings, an approach congruent with the kind of psychoanalytic strategies advocated here. Social theory, and particularly social scientific research, tends by contrast to try to 'compress' meanings, seeking out carefully grounded, minimal, clear and specific explanations. This is more compatible with ways of approaching knowledge that value linear, causal accounts and hence are susceptible to 'expert' claims. On the other hand, one legacy of the post-structuralist turn in the social sciences and humanities is to broaden the notion of 'text' away from simply literary products to include social actions and cultural and political materials – anything, that is, that can be treated as a symbolic form. This has allowed interpretive ('hermeneutic') strategies to be adopted throughout the social sciences, resulting in a growth in the use of qualitative research methods. Many of these, such as ethnography, are taken from anthropology, but others draw on clinical interviewing techniques derived indirectly from psychoanalysis (e.g. Hollway and Jefferson, 2000; Frosh and Saville Young, 2008). The textual move has also allowed social theory more generally to benefit from the 'expansive' reading strategies previously associated with literature. One consequence of this is to make the debates outlined here – debates about how to hold meaning open rather than close it down – relevant throughout the field of social research.

The rest of this book takes up this argument through a series of examples from, or interventions in, the social field. These examples concern spaces of encounter between psychoanalysis and social research: social psychology, ethics, political philosophy and psychosocial studies. In each instance, the focus is on how psychoanalysis has and can be used not as a 'master narrative' to trump the claims of the 'host' discipline, but rather as a provocative interlocutor that can shake things up, and also be stirred itself.

Chapter 4

Psychoanalysis as Social Psychology: The Case of Identity

The interventions of psychoanalysis in social theory and research described in the next three chapters are characterised by a kind of open interdisciplinarity in which the influences are two-way. In each case, what is being presented is an area of debate in which an existing discipline (social psychology, social theory and political theory) is augmented by psychoanalysis, but also offers a reciprocal challenge *to* psychoanalysis. This challenge is not only to provide grounds for its claims, though this is in each case part of what happens. It also addresses the need for psychoanalysis to reflect on its own theoretical assumptions and to combat its 'regressive' tendencies, in the sense of those that pull thinking back into a conformist, moralising mode. The fourth chapter in this sequence, on psychosocial studies, is slightly different in that the area concerned is not yet a well-established discipline, but is seeking to establish its vocabulary, methodology and focus and is looking to psychoanalysis as an aid in doing so. However, the issues are similar: how psychoanalysis can contribute to the emergence of psychosocial studies in ways which advance rather than close down its innovations, and which also promote the critical capacity of psychoanalysis itself.

In this chapter, the focus is on an area of social psychological research that has spread across the social sciences to be a rather amorphous and all-embracing concern, that of identity. As will become apparent, this is a key notion for much social theory and research, and it recurs in the topics to be presented in the rest of this book. Identity is obviously not a new topic of research, but interest in it has grown remarkably since the late 1990s. Margaret Wetherell (2010), who led a major British research initiative into 'social identities', comments that it has become 'one of the most widely used terms in the social sciences and humanities, appearing in the titles of many thousands, if not hundreds of thousands, of books and articles. Very few concepts can have been as generative' (p.3). The source of this interest is perhaps a convergence of social studies on the location of the human subject in culture. This can be partly understood as one of the legacies of poststructuralism and also of postmodernism, and includes a move within social and political theory towards identity studies as a development of a previous concern with *ideology*. In brief, this means that whereas earlier generations of critical theorists were impressed by the way certain social beliefs came to govern the consciousness of subjects, becoming 'internalised' by them in a manner that always tended to be seen as *passive* (Frosh, 1999, ch. 6), the more recent trajectory has been to examine how each subject is actively constructed in and through culture, and comes to locate her or himself in certain specific identity positions. These identity positions may be quite fluid and even mutually contradictory, but they have the power to draw subjects into social locations or 'positions' in which they become heavily invested.

One of the interesting points about this 'identity turn' in the social sciences is that it brings together a range of sociological, political and psychological considerations and therefore demands a high level of interdisciplinarity. Is identity a primarily psychological phenomenon, referencing the feelings and actively chosen self-definitions of individuals? Is it more sociological, relating to the patterns of group membership and divisions between 'insiders and 'outsiders' that operate in a society? Does it refer to the 'internal' state of subjects or to their observable social positions? It seems obvious that these dichotomising questions simply reveal the complexity of identity issues and the need for approaches that stretch across the conventional distinction between psychological and social, between 'inside' and 'out'. It is perhaps equally obvious that this involves considerations of *affect*, exploring the emotional investment subjects might have in particular identities, and *power*, allowing one to discuss how people accept or resist identity ascriptions placed on them through their social positions. These multiple concerns suggest the likely insufficiency of any one disciplinary approach to identity. They also carve out a specific invitation to psychoanalysis, as a conceptual system that might be particularly well honed to address the kinds of 'intersections' that identity studies demand.

Identity politics

Wetherell (2010) tracks the development of identity studies, noting especially that there has been a historical bifurcation between those that approach identity as referring to a 'subjective individual achievement' (p.3) and those that examine it as a matter of group membership, translating it 'into investigations of social divisions and social solidarities and the practices of marginalization, exclusion, inclusion, resistance, segregation, denigration, etc., linked to belonging' (p.4). In the former case, that of 'personal identity', the focus is on how people construct their sense of themselves, the basis being an assumption of the normativeness and stability of individuality as a developmental achievement. A central task of life is to find an identity within which one can live, which organises one's experiences and allows one to become a 'person'. Identity is *agentic* when thought of this way: it is centred on the human subject as an individual and enables that subject to integrate experience in what Wetherell terms a 'personal project'. It is empowering in its presence and disturbing in its absence, and whilst being an achievement rather than a given, is nevertheless a normative psychological state. This means that the failure to achieve a satisfactory identity is a sign – and maybe a cause – of psychological disturbance. Put this way, it is relatively easy to see how the 'invention' of identity as a social issue corresponds with the emergence of individualism within modernity; that is, it is intimately linked with the idea of separate selves as the core unit of psychosocial analysis. If, for example, one lives in a society in which people are defined totally in terms of their social position (for example, as serfs or slaves), their identity does not have to be sought psychologically – it is given as an aspect of the roles made available by society. If, on the other hand, subjects are seen as individual persons, possessing the capacity for self-actualisation and the potential to change their social position as a consequence of their own actions, then identity is something *achieved*, and it makes sense to ask about the 'fit' between psychological and social identity.

This connects with the second approach to identity, strongly advanced in social psychology and sociology, which sees it as 'social belonging'. Here, group membership is taken to define personhood, and the question of identity becomes that of what determines the group one belongs to, and then of what are the characteristics of that group. On the whole, the effect of adopting this particular lens is to remove agency from the subject and instead grant it to the social group: it is as a consequence of one's class, 'race' or gender position, for example, that one has certain identity attributes. Personal identity then becomes a more or less determined, perhaps even passive, outcome of the social order. A racist society, for example, produces differentiated ethnic divisions and contracts identity positions accordingly; similarly, in a sexually differentiated society gender identity is given from the outside as a condition of the dominant social assumptions about masculinity and femininity. Identity thus becomes a primarily social concept that is to be understood sociologically and politically, rather than as the life project of individuals. Since the 1960s, the more deterministic aspects of this version of identity have been contested by social movements which have reclaimed derogated social identities and given them positive content. This has involved a turn to 'identity politics' in which, for example, the feminist, gay and lesbian and anti-racist movements have enabled their members to adopt newly assertive public positions, buoyed up by social solidarities and coherent political critiques of traditional social norms. This reveals one way in which the 'social belonging' version of identity might be progressive, even though one tends to think of having one's identity fixed by an outside force as somehow constraining and politically reactionary. The idea that it is in social solidarities rather than personal development that people's hopes for freedom might lie is a crucial legacy of this understanding of identity, which one would be loath to abandon.

The notion of *fixed* identities, whether given as personal projects or group membership, has become unsustainable under the weight of evidence that people not only shift their identities over time, but also adopt different identities in different settings. People are heavily influenced in their identity formations by the social situations they are in, yet they can also struggle against these and develop ideas of what might be 'true' for them that are at odds with their social positions. Alongside this, there is equally compelling evidence that identities are often multiple and fragmentary (Phoenix and Rattansi, 2005), plus a corresponding awareness that even apparently fixed social categories breed divergent and sometimes contradictory identities ('masculinity', for example, is much more than one thing, as is 'whiteness'). 'Intersectionality' (Brah, 1996) has become the default position in identity studies; it emphasises the way different identity positions have to be read in conjunction with one another. For example, 'masculinity' is a concept that is heavily racialised, which means that it intersects with categories such as 'blackness' and 'whiteness' and cannot be understood fully without reference to them (Frosh, Phoenix and Pattman, 2002). The idea that identities might be fluid rather than fully achieved is also routine even amongst those who still regard identity as an important psychosocial category and a developmental as well as social achievement. Identity is thus seen more as a *process* than a state. One consequence of this is that *identification*, referring to the active way in which certain identity positions are adopted or invested in, becomes the key social psychological – and in some places sociological (Hall, 1996) – concern.

It is not difficult to argue that psychoanalysis should be a major disciplinary site through which these alternative notions of identities can be explored. The psychoanalytic concept of a dynamic unconscious gives leverage on a number of central issues in the study of identities. These include the tension between an understanding of ident*ity* as something fixed (developmental histories producing stable ways of being that are resistant to change) and of ident*ities* as fluid and multiple (unconscious ideas are variable, contradictory and partial). Both these positions are visible in the psychoanalytic literature itself. For instance, there is a strong though now dated tradition of understanding identity as a process of social adaptation. This sees it as a developmental requirement that unconscious wishes should be brought into line with cultural expectations and possibilities under the guise of 'ego identity' – perhaps understandable as the capacity to know who one is in the context in which one finds oneself. More recently, the vision of a general, overarching personal identity has been displaced by awareness of specific types of identity, particularly sexual, gender, ethnic and racial identities. Nevertheless, the sense of coming to know the 'reality' of oneself in these more circumscribed situations still prevails. Whilst this approach addresses some important phenomenological questions, for example about why people are so often strongly invested in what appear to be self-limiting identity positions, it is arguable that it relies on ideas about character and selfhood that are no longer sustainable in identity studies. On the other hand, there are alternative modes of psychoanalysis that question the stability of identities, preferring to track them as forms of 'masquerade', or as fragile and momentary assemblages of contradictory forces. Lacanian psychoanalysis is particularly cogent here, but relational psychoanalysis offers its own routes to conceptualise how human subjects become invested in particular identities, for example through allegiances or emotional connections with specific groups or social fractions. Its key postulate is perhaps that whilst the original source of identity is based on a relation to body parts, identification with parents and others subsequently leads to more complex and elaborate experiences of identity in a variety of contexts. Identities are constructed through such processes of identification and recognition, and emotional investment by subjects in these processes gives identities their significance, explaining why they can be experienced as constituting psychosocial reality. Because both the constructive processes (such as identification) and the investment are largely or wholly unconscious, identities are lived as if they were 'given' rather than chosen. That is, they are often felt to be fundamental to the subject, as if they have been received whole and constitute the subject's essence. The implication of this is that identities may be lived as real, but are in fact constituted in the flux of contradictory impulses, putting psychoanalysis in line with the generally deconstructive tendency in modern thought.

In summary, if any of the different psychoanalytic approaches are to contribute to identity studies, they have to take account of a contemporary context of fluidity. This is produced by the awareness that the construction of the modern 'self' is a fragile and contingent process, and that the normative assumption that a stable identity is an expectable developmental achievement is hard to sustain. To be compelling, identity theories need not only to show how it is that subjects become located in particular social positions, nor solely how certain ways of being and representing the self become invested in as patterns of belonging and exclusion, though both these things might be necessary. Identity theories also need to convey the shifts that occur as subjects encounter one another and the social formation, including in this the broader context of globalisation in which there is greater awareness than ever before of the multiplicity of identities available to people across the world. That is, they need to engage with the blending of 'identity' with 'subjectivity', understood along with Wetherell (2008) not as opposed categories in which the former refers to group membership and the latter to the 'substantive acting, thinking and feeling being' (Venn, 2006, p.79), but as a site for psycho-discursive practices in which both these things are constantly being negotiated. This brings together questions of agency and ethics as well as of social power, making identity studies an important area for theoretical contestation. The question here is whether psychoanalysis can contribute productively to this contestation, or whether it simply reinforces old 'inside–outside' bipolarities. In what follows, this question will be addressed partly historically, through an account of classical psychoanalytic ideas on identity, and partly through examining how psychoanalytic concepts have infiltrated non-analytic theory.

Classical psychoanalytic formulations of identity

Identity as a term is used only once by Freud in his writings, in a way described by some commentators as 'incidental ... with a psychosocial connotation' (Grinberg and Grinberg, 1974, p.499). In fact, this reference is a very interesting personal one. It is found in a letter by Freud written on the occasion of his seventieth birthday in response to greetings from the Vienna Bnai Brith, the Jewish organisation with which he was deeply involved in the late 1890s, at the time when he was formulating the new psychoanalytic science (Frosh, 2005). Reflecting on the reasons that drew him to the Bnai Brith, Freud (1926/1961) comments on how he had neither religious nor nationalistic (i.e. Zionist) beliefs, but nevertheless, 'there remained enough to make the attraction of Judaism and the Jews irresistible, many dark emotional powers all the stronger the less they could be expressed in words, as well as the clear consciousness of an inner identity, the familiarity of the same psychological structure' (p.368).

Erik Erikson, whose work on identity is the foundation stone for most psychoanalytic – and many other – accounts of the topic, reads this quotation as evidence that identity is necessarily tied up with the social environment. 'It is the identity of something in the individual's core with an essential aspect of a group's inner coherence which is under consideration here', he writes (Erikson, 1956, p.57). Moreover, 'The term identity expresses such a mutual relation in that it connotes both a persistent sameness with oneself (self-sameness) and a persistent sharing of some kind of essential character with others' (ibid.). Certainly, Freud's reference to 'the familiarity of the same psychological structure' that linked him with his Jewish peers supports the idea that he is using identity in this psychosocial sense. However, it should be noted that whilst 'the clear consciousness of an inner identity' is offered by Freud as one element making 'the attraction of Judaism and the Jews irresistible', it is not the one that exercises his *psychoanalytic* interest; that place is given over to the 'many dark emotional powers' to which he refers, but of which he can give no straightforward explanation. The attraction of a shared 'psychological structure' is not mysterious; it is straightforwardly observable and comes largely under the heading of what Freud calls in the same place 'ethical' demands ('I was always an unbeliever, have been brought up without religion, but not without respect for the so-called "ethical" demands of human civilisation.'). The other thing, however, the thing that he calls 'dark', is described elsewhere as the 'essence' of his link with the Jewish people and its culture, and yet as currently inaccessible to science (Freud, 1913a/1930, p.xv). It requires more than simple reflection, more even than the psychoanalytic tools then available, to account for it. This announces a debate that has surrounded the question of identity itself, and Erikson's reading of it in particular: is it really a psychoanalytic concept, or a psychosocial one that goes no further than describing predominantly conscious material? That is, what is it that psychoanalysis adds here to what might be known from more straightforward accounts?

According to Grinberg and Grinberg (1974), the term 'identity' was introduced formally into psychoanalytic literature by Victor Tausk in his classic paper, *On the Origin of the 'Influencing Machine'* (1933), which dealt with the disintegration of selfhood and identity and the manifestation of that identity-loss in paranoia. In the passage in which the term appears (p.543), Tausk discusses early infantile development and specifically differentiates between a stage of identity that is congenital, designated as 'the innate narcissistic one', and a later stage that is 'actively established', which seems to mean that it arises as a consequence of interchanges between the infant and the mother. Tausk's assumption is that the individual 'comes into the world as an organic unity in which libido and ego are not yet separated, and all available libido is related to that organic unity, which does not deserve the name "ego" (i.e., a psychical self-protective organization) any more than does the cell' (p.542). That is, the 'identification' which is the source of narcissistic identity is congenital and relates to oneness with the infant's body. Tausk goes on, discussing innate narcissism:

> In this situation the libido is directed outward, first cathects the subject's own body by the indirect way of projection, and returns by way of self-discovery to the ego. In the meantime, the ego has undergone a decided alteration under the influence of these first psychic stirrings, which one may call experience, and is now again cathected by libido. Let us call this stage, acquired narcissism. (p.543)

The difference between the two types of identity is therefore that one originates with the body and the other with 'experience', but in both cases the notion of 'identity' is being called on to mean narcissistic unity, a mode of psychological functioning *defined* as 'absolute self-satisfaction, no outer world, no objects'. Interestingly, although this formulation of narcissism bears only very indirectly on identity as understood in the broader psychological and sociological literature, it is a reminder of the way in which identity signifies wholeness and singularity, a mode of self-sufficiency that tends to exclude the ongoing functioning of the social world.

It is in the work of Erikson, however, that the most influential psychoanalytic account of identity can be found. Erikson understood identity to be concerned with ego functioning and to connote something like 'social character', the relatively stable sense of oneself in a culture. This approach was consistent with the ego-psychological dominance of the American psychoanalysis of his time. For Erikson, ego analysis was laced with a commitment to a culturally or socially aware psychoanalysis, one that viewed the great task of life as bringing the individual into a constructive relationship with society. However, as was the case within the broader ego-psychological movement, the social aspects of Eriksonian theory seemed to lose their potentially critical bite and drift towards a vision of the task of development as *adapting* the individual so as to ease the potential tension with her or his social environment (Frosh, 1999). This adaptation is required particularly at those developmental points involving transitions between one cultural setting (for instance, the family) and another (society), most notably during adolescence. Erikson (1956) describes his use of the term 'identity' as 'to suggest a social function of the ego which results, in adolescence, in a relative psychosocial equilibrium essential to the tasks of young adulthood' (p.104). Identity is here understood as a long-lasting sense of self as continuous, combined with a feeling of belonging in a community. He comments, 'At one time ... it will appear to refer to a conscious *sense of individual identity*; at another to an unconscious striving for a *continuity of personal character*; and, finally, as a maintenance of an inner *solidarity* with a group's ideals and identity' (p.57; original emphasis). One side point is that this formulation shows awareness of the differing kinds of identity discussed in the literature, specifically identity as personal journey and as social categorisation, with the link between them given by a form of emotional investment, here termed 'solidarity'.

Identity is, crucially and centrally, a developmental achievement of the ego, and one that is necessary for the well-being of each subject. 'I have been using the term *ego identity*', writes Erikson (1956), 'to denote certain comprehensive gains which the individual, at the end of adolescence, must have derived from all of his pre-adult experiences in order to be ready for the tasks of adulthood' (p.56). For Erikson, in language that resonates strongly with Winnicott's roughly contemporaneous writings, the roots of identity 'go back all the way to the first self-recognition: in the baby's earliest exchange of smiles there is something of a *self-realization coupled with a mutual recognition*' (p.69). This experience of having one's reality reflected back to one produces 'tentative crystallizations' that make the child feel known to the other and hence to the self. These crystallisations are disrupted from time to time by the actual 'discontinuities of psychosocial development', but a reasonably reliable family and a supportive community will lead to more integrated development to the degree to which they permit the child 'to orient himself toward a complete "*life plan*" with a hierarchical order of roles as represented by individuals of different age grades' (p.70). 'From a genetic point of view,' states Erikson, 'the process of identity formation emerges as an *evolving configuration* – a configuration which is gradually established by successive ego syntheses and resyntheses throughout childhood; it is a configuration gradually integrating *constitutional givens, idiosyncratic libidinal needs, favored capacities, significant identifications, effective defences, successful sublimations, and consistent roles*' (p.71). It has conscious, preconscious and unconscious components, is never fully finalised (albeit largely focused on the period up to the end of adolescence, with its characteristic 'identity crisis'), but is part of a lifelong developmental unfolding, and is a mixture of dynamic and psychosocial components.

In some ways, Erikson's account of identity formation, and in particular his very detailed description of the 'tasks' of adolescence, have been more influential in social psychology (particularly through their partial parroting in numerous undergraduate textbooks) than in psychoanalysis itself. This may be because of its interactionist flavour, with both sides of what that means. It is relational and links with much contemporary theory (the language of 'recognition' is striking here), but also has problematic psychoanalytic, as opposed to social-psychological, standing. Early on, Edith Jacobson (1964) labelled Erikson's work as not truly psychoanalytic, a description that has often been applied to potentially productive concepts that might disturb psychoanalytic orthodoxies. In Erikson's case, the disturbance may have come from the emphasis he placed on the surrounding social world, although looked at through the lens of critical social theory this does not seem particularly subversive – the community is imagined as essentially benevolent, able to lend its support to the process of identity formation, allowing the individual's life plans to develop and integration to occur. Wallerstein (1998), in a paper that reconsiders Erikson's legacy, suggests that his work is ever more relevant, but that this has been obscured by the language of the new theories of the 'self', which has largely replaced the ego psychological vocabulary of Erikson's time. That is, the ego psychologists rejected him because his concepts were too social, and the self psychologists and relational psychoanalysts have neglected him because they regarded him as too focused on ego structures. Wallerstein comments: 'though the concept of identity, so central to Erikson's conceptualizations over a lifetime, has come in the past two decades to the forefront of psychoanalytic attention, it has done so under the rubric of the self, thereby obscuring the obvious relation of Erikson's earlier theorizing to these new emphases' (p.239). Whilst the ego identity theory of Erikson became peripheral to psychoanalysis, many of the concepts deployed in contemporary intersubjectivist and self theory have connections with it. In particular, the transactional nature of Erikson's approach, in which individual and social components of development support one another, can be traced in the sometimes anodyne psychosocial elements of a fair amount of later work.

Bodies, objects and identifications

In their post-Eriksonian account, Grinberg and Grinberg (1974) emphasise the significance of the integrative function of the sense of identity, the way it registers 'the idea of a self which bears essentially upon the continuity and likeness of unconscious fantasies referring to bodily sensations and emotions experienced by the ego' (p.500) and hence has 'spatial, temporal and social' aspects. These relate to 'self- non-self differentiation', continuity of self-representations over time, and 'the relationship between aspects of the self and aspects of objects by means of the mechanisms of identification' (p.502). This formulation captures a good proportion of the shared ideas of psychoanalysts on this topic.

Identity is a developmental notion and is formed in response to internal and external forces. It has a bodily source that grounds it in a sense of unity or unification. Grinberg and Grinberg claim that

> The idea of the body is essential to the consolidation of the individual's identity ... When Freud pointed out that the 'ego is first and foremost a bodily ego, it is not merely a surface but is itself a projection of a surface' (1923), he was underlining one of the most important factors that form the basis of identity. (p.502)

Revealingly, this claim has the effect of blurring the distinction between identity, self and ego, because as the quotation from Freud reveals, it is not *identity* that is classically thought of in this way, but the *ego itself*. It is the ego that is built up out of perceptions of the body and its functions, from relationships with others that are mediated through the skin and the mouth (Greenacre, 1958), or from the kind of introjective processes based on bodily functions that are so beloved of the Kleinians, a point which will be developed below. Given that the ego is both the site of consciousness and imbued with unconscious features (the defence mechanisms are found within it), and that identity is usually thought of as a 'sense' of being and belonging, this conflation of the two concepts begs a large number of questions. In particular, identity seems to be compressed into 'ego-identity', in the Eriksonian tradition, with attendant assumptions of integration of the ego and its absorption into notions of the 'self'. It seems to suggest a normal outcome for identity formation as fully at one with the subject's self-conceptualisation, understood as reflected in an ego that is not subject to splits or discontinuities in its self-perception. This sets it at odds with many contemporary formulations of the fragmentary and contingent nature of identity as a set of not necessarily reflected-upon lived experiences. Within psychoanalysis, too, the assumption of ego-integrity is contentious. Lacanians, for instance, famously criticise it as a normalising assumption mistaking apparent bodily unity for psychic integrity; for them, recognition of the split nature of the subject is absolutely central to psychoanalytic thought (Frosh, 1999).

Co-option of the notion of identity into that of the ego opens up another strand of psychoanalytic developmental thinking, the idea that the ego is formed through the internalisation of lost objects. Faced with reality, the growing child has to give up desired sexual objects, but doing so leaves it feeling depleted and suffused with loss. To deal with this, the ego takes the objects in (in fantasy), internalising them and in the process altering itself. These forsaken desires and lost objects are absorbed into the ego, along with the psychic energy invested in them, making it possible 'to suppose that the character of the ego is a precipitate of abandoned object cathexes and that it contains the history of those object choices' (Freud, 1923, p.29). This is one Freudian basis for object relations theory and also encompasses a social account of identity formation as something founded on the fantasised relationship with real objects in the interpersonal or intersubjective world. That is, as the ego itself is formed from the internalisation of objects first experienced externally – the mother's breast predominant amongst them – so the formation of identity can be understood to derive from processes of internalisation and identification. In these, what is 'found' externally and related to affectively becomes taken in to provide the model, schema or template for representations of the 'inner world'. Moore and Fine (1990), for example, draw on the concept of identification in their statement of what produces sexual identity:

> Identification with both parents gives a bisexual quality to the self-representations and schemas, and self-concepts of children of both sexes. Eventually, however, an integrated self-organization is created out of the multiple former identifications contributing to its character traits. ...The sense of identity achieves relative stability when bisexual identifications are resolved and adolescence completed. (p.93)

What can be seen in this is both the assumption of a normative heterosexual developmental sequence leading to stable and integrated identity, and the understanding that this might result from a process whereby 'multiple former identifications' based on relationships with parents, are in some way worked on to produce this integrated self.

This type of theory reflects a widely shared perception amongst psychoanalysts that identity, selfhood and even the ego are built up, defensively or not, on the basis of taking in experiences with external 'objects' and combining them with 'internal' factors such as bodily experience or primitive phantasies to create conscious and unconscious representations. This raises the question of how 'external' things – ideas, representations of self and others – get 'into' the subject's 'inner world'. The mind is in constant dialogue with the world, putting into it some of its own contents (through projection, for example) and finding ways of producing internal representations of what it finds there. Without such engagement, it would consist only of what was produced from within; it would be a 'closed system', generating meanings on the basis perhaps of drives or in response to external stimuli, but unable to absorb features of the outside world into itself. What psychoanalysis claims is not only that external stimuli are processed by the perceptual system, but more radically that they are somehow 'internalised', taken in to become part of the mind, infecting its structure and its unconscious contents. That is, psychoanalysis models an 'open system' in which external experiences – encounters with 'objects', relationships, ideas – can become part of the person in a deep way. At its most sophisticated, what this produces is a theory in which 'self' and 'other' are always entwined, so that there is no way of considering any mind in isolation from any other. Thought of that way, identification is a *constructive* process, in that the internalised attributes are not destroyed but are employed in the service of some kind of development (hence, it remains distinct from *incorporation* in the psychoanalytic sense, which devours what it takes in), and it is likely that it is one of the most powerful methods whereby personal change occurs.

Freud (1923) seemed to recognise this with his notion of the ego as the 'precipitate of abandoned object cathexes', even though his theory implies that the first 'thoughts' are representations of the drives, coming from within rather than without. As his work progressed, so identification became seen as more central. This is particularly the case in relation to the Oedipus complex, the outcome of which is theorised as a set of powerful identifications laying the foundations of all later personality development and specifically of sexual and gender identity. As the boy, threatened with the castrating power of the father, represses his desire for the mother, so what emerges for him is a saving identification with the father which creates gender security as well as the promise of later recovery. For the girl too, even though the processes described by Freud are more confused and less potent, there is identification with the mother's position in relation to the father that leads to the gendered construction of identity alongside the channelling of desire. In addition, the construction of the superego as a response to castration anxiety is one big internalising process: what is taken in here is the fantasy of the paternal prohibition, with all its associated aggression. Hinshelwood (1991), writing out of the Kleinian tradition in which there is an emphasis on processes of projection and introjection operating from birth, phrases this about as strongly as could ever be:

> The internal objects are phantasies, but at first phantasies are omnipotent, so through these primitive phantasies involved in identification the object is the self ... Phantasy 'is' reality, and phantasy constructs the reality of the internal world on the basis of these primitive forms of introjective and projective identification. (p.320)

Because the infant is always engaged in a process of 'putting out and taking in', of projecting feelings into the external 'object' and then seeking to absorb properties of these objects, the emerging psyche is filled with representations, however crude, of the object, and it is around these object representations that it becomes structured. Hence, there is no firm division between inside and out, but rather a fluid interchange in which each penetrates the other.

A subtle recent rendering of identifications in the context of gender has been given by Jessica Benjamin (1998). She holds on to the distinction between identification and incorporation, the latter being a kind of cannibalistic taking in of the other until it becomes part of the self and is no longer psychically distinct. She argues that what is precious about identification is that it allows the other to *survive* as a living and appreciated aspect of the self. Identification is consequently built out of an already-existing awareness of the other's existence *as a subject*; that is, it is a loving 'intersubjective' relationship in which aspects of otherness are accepted and used by the self, without destroying the other in the process. It is 'not merely a matter of incorporating the other as ideal, but of loving and having a relationship with the person who embodies the ideal' (p.61). Identification can thus be seen as a form of *relationship*, not just a way in which one person acts upon another. Developmentally, for example, it can be a way in which a boy aspires to be linked to his father rather than to be rivalrous with him. Indeed, in the context of gender development, Benjamin claims that boys and girls both identify with the loving father just as they do with the powerful and loving mother, making multiple identifications along the way. The effect of these multiple identifications is to produce in the child a greater range of possible gender positions, particularly enhancing 'complementarity' rather than the kind of exclusivity which results in the triumph of one gender position over another. On the basis of such complex patterns of identification in which the child incorporates aspects of all her or his loved objects into the self, it is possible to recast development as a process of making increasingly fine internal differentiations which does not necessarily take place at the expense of the valuing of difference, though this depends on the quality of actual object relationships. That is, the classic view of identification, particularly in the Oedipus complex, is that it involves taking in one thing and repudiating another. Benjamin, however, outlines a more mature, post-Oedipal complementarity which brings back together the various 'elements of identification, so that they become less threatening, less diametrically opposite, no longer cancelling out one's identity' (1998, pp.69–70). Multiple identifications forge the basis for identities (including gender identities) which themselves are multiple and fluid, less defensive and hence less caricatured and stereotyped. *Connectedness* is emphasised here, recognising difference but not discounting the other because of it.

This rendering of identification with others as a way of taking in multiple possibilities for development is one important strand in contemporary work. However, the Lacanian critique of the ego and hence of identity applies here, with identification being understood as an 'imaginary' process of taking on an image and 'appropriating' it *as if* it represents the self. That is, identification is primarily a way of losing oneself in the other. More precisely, the fact that identification is at the root of the formation of the ego reveals that the ego is itself 'specious', a false acceptance of an image as real. Identification, psychoanalysis attests, is that process whereby the ego takes the object and makes it *subject*, incorporating each object as part of itself. According to Lacan, this is indeed a formative process, but its effect is specifically to create a kind of radical *misperception*, in which the ego is taken to be the 'truth' of the person when it is actually just 'bric-à-brac' (Lacan, 1954–55, p.155), made up of bits and pieces latched onto from outside. Hence there is a sense in which identification *falsifies*, with the subject 'using' the object to sustain a fantasy of integrity of the self. This is why Lacan was opposed to the idea that psychoanalytic psychotherapy should aim at enabling the patient to identify with the analyst; rather, he suggested, analysis should aim to show the patient how identifications are all impossibly fantastic. No one can become the model for another; instead, suggests Lacan, the 'real' of the subject lies outside what can be organised and known. Identification, therefore, may well be a major mechanism through which what is outside comes to be registered within, but this also makes it a mode of alienation, whereby the human subject is made a stranger to itself. Needless to say, 'identity' as a term does not appear in dictionaries of Lacanian psychoanalysis (e.g. Evans, 1996).

To summarise so far, psychoanalysis has a number of not necessarily compatible ways of understanding the formation of identities. Some of these, following the lead set by Erikson, see identity as a developmental process of the ego through which the subject deals with a set of social experiences and demands (including necessary losses) by adapting her or his internal structures. The end result is, ideally, an ego that is attuned to reality, with positive integration both within the ego itself and of the subject with her or his environment. Sources of identity integration are given as the body and the internalisation of objects that have been emotionally invested in; these become part of the 'self'. Such internalising processes, conceptualised as forms of identification, are central both to Kleinian and relational theory. The latter is also interested in ways in which multiple, non-exclusive identifications can occur (Benjamin's 'post-Oedipal', 'over-inclusive' model), allowing for appreciation of the layered and complex nature of identity formations. Amongst the many attractions of these positions is the way they offer an account of the mechanisms that might be at work in connecting the social version of identity as belonging with the personal version of it as an internal, self-actualising state. On the other hand, this raises questions over whether what is being described is an elaborate form of *alienation*, in which the structures of sociality (for instance, the 'message' given to the subject concerning the kind of person she or he could be) are taken to be the 'truth'. This issue will be returned to below, in the context of a slightly fuller account of Lacanian thinking in this area.

Post-integrative identities

The view of identities as potentially integrated, if multifarious, constructed entities formed through internalising relationships with external objects, connects with broader notions of selfhood to be found in British and more recently American psychoanalytic schools. These posit the self as arising in the crucible of caring (usually maternal) relationships that give rise both to a set of capacities and attributes and a reflexive function that itself constitutes the 'sense of identity'. Winnicott's (1960) description of false and true selves, and in particular his ideas on the formation of secure selfhood in the context of maternal responsiveness, have been very influential in this. Without rehearsing the details of Winnicott's account unnecessarily, it is worth recalling that the 'true self' is understood to be a *potential* for growth that will naturally unfold under the right circumstances, and that can be damaged or hidden in a hostile environment. The mother is supposed to provide her infant with the conditions under which her or his potential for selfhood can be realised. Interference with this function, for instance because of the mother's depression, is experienced by the infant as an 'impingement' on the natural organisation of experience, and leads to anxiety about total disintegration. This results in a defensive hiding away of the child's spontaneous desires in the form of a secret true self, which avoids expression because of the danger that it will be destroyed by the inadequate environment. To enable transactions with reality, a conformist 'false self' is formed, split off from the true self and protecting its integrity. The false self is inauthentic because it is built up on the pattern of the mother's desire, not the child's, hence its conformity. The child is formed in someone else's image of her or him, acting in line with the mother's expectations and wishes so as to win her love. In Phillips' gloss (1988),

> It is part of Winnicott's demand on the mother that she be robust; if she is in any way rejecting, the infant has to comply with her response. It is the strategies of compliance that Winnicott calls the False Self Organization.

> Because of this primary and enforced attentiveness to the needs of the mother, the False Self, he writes, always 'lacks something, and that something is the *essential element of creative originality.*' (p.133)

The true self is the essential creativity of the human subject in action, consisting of a variety of capacities such as the ability to be alone, to be in states of 'disunity' out of which new modes of experience can emerge, to live with risk, and so on. The false self, on the other hand, is something close to what other psychoanalytic authors would call 'narcissistic' – a defensive shutting-down, organised around close scrutiny of the other and an inability to feel real.

The impact of Winnicott's thinking on selfhood has been immense, especially when combined with his seminal notions of transitional objects and transitional spaces – those intermediate, half-imagined, half-material entities used by subjects to establish their relationship with the world, and to manifest their creativity. At its core is, however, a set of assumptions that may be deeply evocative – as much of Winnicott's writing is – but also problematic for a poststructuralist context that refuses to take as given the idea of an easy fit between subjecthood and society. For Winnicott, everything depends on what Phillips calls 'robustness', or perhaps is better coded as 'maternal resilience'. The capacity of the mother (and in therapy, the analyst) to *survive* in the face of her infant's psychic attacks on her allows the child to absorb an experience of her- or himself as real and legitimate, and of loved objects as actually existing, not just as a figment of the child's imagination. This gives the child a firm sense of location in her or his own needs, which are now experienced as legitimate and acceptable, and of a setting that is not going to collapse. From this, the true self can emerge as an integrated, spontaneous, creative entity that can deal with the world on its own terms. Without such early maternal resilience, the self remains fragmentary and takes refuge behind the conforming false self striving desperately to appease a persecutory environment or – in cases where the mother is depressed and unresponsive – to bring it to life. It should be noted that this is a theory of self as an experiencing core, not of identity as a 'sense' of self, but that the latter is implicit in the former: the foundations for a clear sense of continuity, integrity and belonging lie in these early experiences of maternal holding.

In theorising clinical phenomena, many psychoanalysts operate with a loosely similar set of perceptions, understanding psychopathology as a breakdown in selfhood subsequent to failures of maternal holding and psychological recognition. This is roughly true not just of Winnicott and object relations theories, but also of followers of Klein and Bion in the British School and self-theorists and relational psychoanalysts in the

United States. However, there is something troubling about the assumption that there is a normative progression from adequate ('good-enough') recognition of the infant's needs to a secure selfhood and an integrated self-reflexive capacity that can be called a 'sense of identity'. From outside psychoanalysis, postmodernism and poststructuralism emphasise the 'normality' of fragmentary experience; there is also a strong strand within psychoanalysis that questions the idea that psychic integration should be either a developmental or a mental health norm. This leads to a much greater interest in identity as a formation-in-process than as fixed, and also asks about the degree to which the focus on self-representation and egoic knowledge of the self (for example as represented in integrated self-narratives) is an actively defensive process. That is, given that psychoanalysis is in many ways *deconstructive* in that it pursues the analytic decomposition of all the phenomena with which it is faced, is the search for integration, reflected in the views of self and identity to be found in much of the psychoanalytic literature, a way of avoiding psychoanalysis' own most radical insights? Does it represent an abandonment of what Laplanche (2003) refers to as 'the properly "analytic" vector, that of de-translation and the questioning of narrative structures and the ideas connected to them?' (p.29). In other words, the 'analytic attitude' is always suspicious of entities that appear integrated, because it senses that this appearance is likely to be covering over states of contradiction and conflict. That is, after all, the nature of a symptom. Consequently, when psychoanalysis itself advocates integration, one is always liable to wonder whether this too is symptomatic of an unanalysed conflict; it suggests something that is not fully thought through, or perhaps even a motivated state in which the disturbing realities of contradiction are being denied.

In this respect, the Lacanian deconstruction of the ego, mentioned above, is fundamental to much contemporary thought. In Lacanian terms, identity acts in the register of the Imaginary, which is always over-inflated in terms of its claims to mastery and completeness. Identity is thus a narcissistic entity, yet one with great power and significance. In contrast to the way much classical and object relational thinking on identity references a stable ego as the necessary underpinning of a secure sense of self, Lacan's work has as one theme the exposure of the ego as something fabricated *as a defensive structure*, hence embedding an alienation of the subject within its own psychic life. This is famously explicated in Lacan's (1949) notion of the 'mirror phase', which continues to act as a source for theorising the paradoxical fragility and rigidity of selfhood, despite the fact that there are many difficulties with the concept and with his paper on it (Billig, 2006). In contrast to Winnicott (1967), who uses the idea of mirroring to convey the importance of a developmental process in which the child sees her- or himself accurately and thoughtfully reflected back by a concerned mother (that is, who enters into her or his true self/identity through this interpersonal process), Lacan emphasises the impossibility of identity as related to a 'true' self. In his view, the ego is used to create an armour or shell supporting the psyche, which is otherwise experienced as in fragments. The subject thus takes refuge in seeming-security (rigidity) as a bulwark against actual-insecurity (fragility). In a move that is intimately connected with a strand of theorising that makes otherness primary in the formation of subjecthood, Lacan (1949) emphasises the *exteriority* of this process. That which appears to us as our 'self' is in fact given from the outside as a refuge, an ideal ego, a narcissistically invested image that is simplistically thought of as a mode of alienation:

> The fact is that the total form of the body by which the subject anticipates in a mirage the maturation of his power is given to him only as a *Gestalt*, that is to say, in an exteriority in which this form is certainly more constituent than constituted, but in which it appears to him above all in a contrasting size that fixes it and in a symmetry that inverts it, in contrast with the turbulent movements that the subject feels are animating him. (p.2)

Here, Lacan is portraying the subject as gaining relief from the intensity of fragmenting internal impulses through the imposition of boundaries and the apparent stability of the mirror image – something external but connected to the subject, holding a promise of future 'power'. Whereas Winnicott portrays the mirroring function as one which, when accurate, allows the child actually to grow into her or his self – to genuinely find the 'maturation of his power' – for Lacan this is a process in which the subject is hoodwinked into taking on the image as if it were real. The subject becomes a dupe of the external world, lured into the belief that its spectral image reflects an actual psychological integrity; this belies the absence of integrity that really operates in the subject's formation. This can also be read as a statement about the nature of the specific social world into which this mirror-phase subject is being ordained as a 'self'. The message that the ego has integrity and wholeness is a socially constructed one, legible in the reflecting surfaces and faces of an order stressing the autonomy and psychological independence of individuals; that is, it is a social order premised on *individualism*. The society that works in this way hides its power by holding out the promise of individual autonomy to subjects; but behind this lurks an uncanny sensation that something is being denied. The consequence of this is the haunting of the satisfying image of the integrated self by the spectre or memory of something else: despite appearances, each subject knows that it is not really whole, that this seeming-self of 'identity' is a cover for a disturbing dis-integrative pulsation. This produces a paranoid sensation, which it might be argued is one of the characteristics of the triumph of capitalism under late modernity, arising from the sense of being promised something that is always about to be taken away. The mirror is thus a source both of reassurance and of threat, its seemingly smooth surface containing unexpected ripples caused by that which can be seen yet not quite named. Bodily unity is no guarantee of psychic unity, which in fact is disrupted continually by the play of drives.

The mirror stage reflects the impossibility of becoming a self without taking on the meanings of the other – without becoming *identified* with another's gaze, with the pre-existing desire of the other that one should be some one thing and not anything else. The social order is lurking behind the mirror phase as that which offers to the subject the pacifying image of self-integration. In the move to the Symbolic order, which is the next stage of the Lacanian progression and which is built on the classical Freudian understanding of the Oedipus complex, society becomes an explicit figure for the subject. The structures of language interfere with the image-making process, revealing that it is already organised by a law indifferent to the emotions and desires of the individual subject. The importance of this in terms of the existence of an Other that regulates the intersubjective encounters of people will become more evident in the discussion of ethical violence in Chapter 5. In relation to identity, the theory of the Symbolic emphasises that the positioning of the subject with respect to language requires an encounter with otherness in a way that fractures the omnipotence of the mirrored 'I' in the Imaginary, just as the father blocks the incestuous relation of mother and son in classical theory. If the Imaginary celebrates the fictitious identity of subject and ego, it is the tearing of this identity that moves the subject into the Symbolic order and at the same time constructs the unconscious: what is 'left out' becomes repressed. This is the relevance of the familiar statement that Lacan invokes an empty subject, constituted through lack and marked by the impossibility of fulfilment or of recognition of the actuality of the other. The Symbolic order positions the subject in relation to other subjects, marking each as incomplete, only present through its relationship with what lies outside. Claims that identity is fixed and legitimating become understood as defensive manoeuvres protecting the psyche against its own inherent splits. This account, it might be noted, is radically different not only from normative versions of identity that celebrate it as a way of integrating the self, but also from 'social belonging' versions that see it as a consequence of specific features of the social. The Lacanian version of things has the subject always mis-located in a phantasmatic framework that constructs and undermines it at the same time.

Disruption of notions of secure identity is not confined to Lacanian theory, but is engaged in by many who try to weave a poststructuralist and postmodern sensibility into psychoanalysis. Jane Flax (1996), for instance, also sees the defensive structures of stability and integrity at work, in her example when there are claims to stable gender identity. 'A "stable" gender identity', she writes, 'may be partially constituted by, and may serve, multiple defensive purposes, including warding off unwanted aspects of subjectivity or affects, such as aggression' (p.585). The idea that identities form through identifications and introjections that may be multiple and partial is widespread. In addition, the division between external objects and inner worlds is undermined by the way inside and out mutually construct each other. This is an area of general agreement between relational and Lacanian psychoanalysts, theorised for example by Kleinians through the interchanges of projection and introjection, or evoked in Lacan's (1973) use of the image of the Moebius strip to convey subtle processes of interpenetration. The point here is that there is no clear distinction between 'internal' and 'external', but rather there is a pattern of forces that runs through the subject so that wherever one looks, 'inner' and 'outer' are both present. Tracing the path of the apparently internal and individual leads to the social, and vice versa. This needs to be seen as a worm of dissent at the heart of anything that might be thought of as a fixed, stable identity: we always consist of something alien at our core. 'Identity' is consequently not only always fabricated and provisional, but also it *is* the 'social' just as it *is* also the 'personal' or individual – it is not the adaptation of one to the other, but another emanation of the indissolubility of the two. This raises a set of issues that have at their core a certain kind of ethics, questions of what it might mean to live a 'good life' psychoanalytically, that might radically enlarge our current conceptualisation of 'identity politics'.

Relational and diasporic identities

Despite its congruence with poststructuralism, there is an elusiveness to this kind of psychosocial formulation which may not be necessary and which makes it hard to bring it to bear on the practical study of identities (or anything else). It is worth tracking back to see what is being evoked and what responded to in this attempt to wriggle out of too much knowledge and fixedness and instead to focus on the constant disruption that is seen both as a necessary state of knowledge (epistemology) and a paradigm for subjective encounters (ethics). In part, this is a derivative of contemporary events in the 'real' world of technological change, war and terrorism, in the rising consciousness (but neglect of action) over ecological disaster, in the spread of AIDS and the promises of biomedicine and the genome. One might expect that these developments will impact on people's psychological states and their sense of identity and selfhood, now perhaps more panicked than before, but also more technologically mediated through, amongst other things, the explosive growth of the internet. Indeed, the argument that we are biotechnical subjects is well established in certain branches of academia. Examples here include Donna Haraway's (1991) theorisation of 'cyborgs' and Rosi Braidotti's (2006) exuberant evocation of the nomadic subject, fluidly repositioning across a multifarious terrain of non-human life, with any notion of identity well and truly dismembered as a consequence. Social and cultural theory has responded to this by seeking out models of biosociality that emphasise multifariousness and networked connections, displacing the human subject and introducing in its place a sense of productive activity that gives rise to sensations and identities. In Haraway's (2006/2007) work on 'companion species', for instance, the emphasis is on 'knots' of entanglement, a process of 'knott[ing] companion and species together in encounter, in regard and respect' (Haraway, 2006, p.102). This relates to Judith Butler's recent (2008) writing on 'precacity', and on which lives are recognised as 'grievable' – and hence to which people the status of 'human' is granted, whose life is treasured, whose death is named, who therefore has conferred upon them an 'identity'. The point is that in being 'knotted' together, certain subjects (and not others) are made recognisable. Wetherell (2010) notes that this move is in line with the general development of identity studies 'from the already formulated and established individual and the group to the relational constitutive process', the issue being 'how in any particular site nature, culture, subjectivity and matter coalesce along with the divergent histories pulled together in these new figurations' (p.22).

Much of this is relevant to theorising identity, including a resurgence of interest in the work of Gilles Deleuze and the adoption of his metaphor of 'rhizomes' as a model of spreading networks of articulated forces (Deleuze and Guattari, 1988). This lays the foundations for a return to affect as that which gives rise to subjectivity, rather than following on from it. As well as being a political philosophy, this perspective addresses psychological experiences in a way that is antagonistic to the depth perspective of traditional psychoanalysis, emphasising relationality and 'assemblage' (Latour, 2007). Within psychoanalysis, it also has resonances with the Lacanian interest in the de-narrativising encounter between a subject who desires and one who is 'supposed to know', an encounter that is always waiting to be punctured, for example by the famously sudden ending of a 'short' psychoanalytic session or more soberly by the emergence into speech of something completely unexpected. These ideas give priority to disruption over meaning making, to paradox over order, and most importantly to the crisscrossing of bodily and symbolic networks as they create points of coherence that fade away and re-form. In relation to 'identity', they argue for a restless coming-and-going of the subject. Overall, what is celebrated here is not only fluidity, but also a kind of non-human impersonality that runs as a force through subjects, activating them whilst also conferring agency upon them, in networked yet unpredictable ways. All this is at odds with traditional notions of identity formation, though it can be aligned in part with intersectionality, if that is understood broadly as the procedure whereby one category of sociality or experience is disrupted by its exposure to another. At its simplest, what is being described here is the production of the subject as a kind of 'nodal point' in which different lines of force meet. In relation to identity studies, these include the common categories of race, gender and the like – that is, points of difference that fix the subject in certain positions, albeit not as a stable entity, but as one that is constantly on the move.

If one is to root this turn to a theory of intersectional identities in something that can also draw on contemporary psychoanalysis, one way to do it is through the notion of 'diaspora', as a set of material displacements that provoke multifarious, unstable identities that are nevertheless experienced as lived realities. Wetherell (2010) comments that amongst the social changes which have decisively altered identity studies 'are those associated with post colonialism, trans-nationalism, the emergence of new diasporic communities, new complexities in cultural relationships, new mobilities and migratory flows' (p.20). The theoretical stance towards these that has made most difference has been postcolonialism, with its orientation towards 'subaltern studies' as a way of examining the impact of colonial histories on social subjects (e.g. Spivak, 1988). 'Diaspora' itself relates both to the historic uses of the term to refer to Jewish, Greek and Armenian diasporas and also more recently particularly to African and Caribbean ones, but also to those of the Chinese, the South Asian, the Irish, the Italian and others (Quayson, 2007). From the point of view of identity studies, however, what is important is the expansion of diaspora studies away from simply mapping the routes of connection between and within communities, to a comprehensive examination of the way in which these distributed relationships construct subjects. Laying out an agenda for diaspora studies, Quayson (2007) comments:

> The arts of memory, the dialectics of place, the ethnographies of nostalgia, the intersubjectivities of social identity, and the citational practices that ground senses of cultural particularity outside the homeland (names, family photographs, memorializations of the homeland, special community journals, etc.) along with the categories derived from a social typology (village of provenance, race, class, gender, generational differentiations, and degrees of capacity and opportunities or lack thereof for integration into the host land) are all crucial for understanding diasporas (p.589).

Couze Venn (2009) offers a description of the impact of diaspora when he presents it as the defining state of contemporary life, and also as fundamentally disruptive of classical identity claims and politics.

> [T]he analysis of global diasporas has demonstrated the suspect character of the assumption that identities or cultures are basically unchanging, homogenous entities, rather than heterogenous, polyglot, plural, relational, existential and in-process. If subjectivity is relational and metastable by reference to the material, discursive and psychological conditions that constitute it, it would follow that dislocations provoked by displacement occasion mutations in subjectivity and identity. (p.4)

Diasporic identities are *essentially* fluid, produced as unstable by the displacements of massive social forces (colonialism and capitalism, to be brief). They are also, however, concrete and heavily invested in, not thrown on and off as mere fashion statements. In this way, they can be seen as iconic for all contemporary identities and subjectivities. Venn claims that the artworks that explore diasporic identities are 'canonical for interrogating identities today' (p.6). The same could be said for such identities themselves: they define the state of identity as something which can be laid claim to and deployed (so diasporic identities have their political and emotional uses), but can never be reified as secure, permanent or real. 'Deracination', one might say, is the natural state of affairs for human subjects and the topic of core narratives from the Bible and the Odyssey through to today. With this realisation comes the demise of a mode of identity that reflects the classical psychoanalytic idea of a naturally developing path.

Stuart Hall (1990) retains some space for historically rooted notions of identity when he argues that

> There are at least two different ways of thinking about 'cultural identity'. The first position defines 'cultural identity' in terms of one, shared culture, a sort of collective 'one true self', hiding inside the many other, more superficial or artificially imposed 'selves', which people with a shared history and ancestry hold in common. (p.223)

Hall notes the importance of this kind of shared identity for mobilising postcolonial struggles, particularly in bringing to light 'hidden histories' that played a critical role in emancipatory political activity. But, in line with the emphasis on the disruptions produced by diaspora described above, a second, more fluid conceptualisation of diasporic cultural identity also makes itself felt:

> Cultural identity, in this second sense, is a matter of 'becoming' as well as of 'being'. It belongs to the future as much as to the past. It is not something which already exists, transcending place, time, history and culture. Cultural identities come from somewhere, have histories. But, like everything which is historical, they undergo constant transformation. Far from being eternally fixed in some essentialised past, they are subject to the continuous 'play' of history, culture and power. Far from being grounded in a mere 'recovery' of the past, which is waiting to be found, and which, when found, will secure our sense of ourselves into eternity, identities are the names we give to the different ways we are positioned by, and position ourselves within, the narratives of the past. (p.225)

A central trope here is 'becoming'. Cultural identity is something inhabited in a precarious way, what Hall calls 'the unstable points of identification or suture' (p.226); they exist as a reinvention of a past that is real, but which is neither determining nor unequivocal in its effects. In terms of identity studies, what this produces is an interest in specific histories out of which the impact of colonialism and diaspora emerges, as well as a theoretical thrust towards an understanding of identities as unstable registers in which these histories of subjectification and oppression materialise but also are transformed.

For Hall and Venn, as for others, much of the analytic thrust of diaspora studies is given by explorations of art works of various kinds, including music, writing, performance and installations as well as visual arts. The reason for this is that for many such writers, the 'voice' of diaspora has often struggled to be heard in academic work, and instead is expressed through modes of representation that trigger affective rather than 'intellectual' responses. Venn (2009) claims that art is particularly effective here because 'It is in the gap between representation and the un(re)presentable that something dwells which ushers in the question of the "there is" which is the signifier of the "thrownness" as well as the ex-centredness of the subject' (p.11). Despite his own doubts about the place of psychoanalysis, there is already visible in this quotation an inkling of where it might be introduced back in as an explicatory tool. The 'something' that dwells 'between representation and the un(re)presentable' is a common formulation both for the Lacanian Real (that which drops out of the Symbolic) and for the unconscious itself.

Venn goes on to speak more fully of the relationship between this mode of psychoanalytic thinking and the social discourses more characteristic of diaspora studies, as follows:

> [E]xpressive or creative media such as novels, painting, film and so on are themselves the means or vehicles whereby what cannot be presented in the form of critiques or sociological data can be intimated or presented at the affective and emotional levels. The importance from the point of view of transformation in subjectivity and identity is in emphasising the aesthetic-affective labour which is necessary for this to happen, in the form of an anamnesis, that is, a process of working through that produces a rememorisation ... and in the form of self-reflection working at the thresholds between unconscious psychic economy and conscious activity, individual identity and collective identity, the process of individualisation and the trans-subjective domain. (p.15)

What might be meant by this kind of 'aesthetic-affective labour', and how can psychoanalysis contribute to its promotion as well as its comprehension? Venn himself draws on the work of a psychoanalyst who is also an artist, Bracha Ettinger, whose theory of the 'matrixial' as a kind of intrauterine-originated connective network offers a way of thinking about subjectivity and identity that immerses them in a pattern of connectivity and encounter. The passage Venn draws on here comes from Ettinger (2006, p.63) and refers to a conceptual space defined in terms of 'the matrixial stratum of subjectivization proposing a matrixial *subjectivity-as-encounter* as a beyond-the-phallus feminine field related (in both men and women) to plural, partial, and *shared* unconscious, trauma, phantasy, and desire having imaginary and symbolic impact'. The emphasis here on what is *shared*, what links across subjects, will be returned to in the next chapter, but it is characteristic of a mode of psychoanalytic reasoning that has moved away from the classical 'closed' system of mainstream Freudianism and also from its focus on 'depth', and towards issues of relationality and intersubjectivity. What is additionally specific to psychoanalysis is the constitution of affectivity as that which 'fuels' subjectivity, that is, in this context, as a mode of *investment* which promotes the materialisation of identity as linked to specific practices of belonging and becoming. 'Affective labour' does not have to be theorised psychoanalytically: the Deleuzian turn is a major example of an alternative tendency in the social sciences. However, the psychoanalytic apparatus allows it to be conceptualised as a process in which the different specific forces acting in and on the subject – drives, bodily experiences, social positions, ideologies, practices of oppression and emancipation, phantasies and fears – can be brought into contact with one another as the framework for an understanding that is genuinely 'dynamic', in the sense of being 'on the move'. Venn refers to 'a process of working through that produces a rememorisation'; these terms ('working through', 'rememorisation') are saturated with psychoanalytic resonances. Indeed, one might argue that psychoanalysis makes such ideas thinkable.

In relation to the impact of this work on psychoanalysis itself, it is clear that the emergence of theories stressing migrancy, unsettledness, fluidity and networks shifts attention away from drive models and towards relational approaches. However, there is nothing cosy in this. If psychoanalysis allows space for such moves, through its object relations and more recent intersubjectivist traditions, it also maintains an investment in what was earlier called 'pulsations': fields of force that interrogate and disrupt, that puncture even the most carefully maintained relational networks. Many contemporary theorists emphasise the reimagining of identity that is constantly demanded in the light of diasporic movements. In so doing they advance a critique of theories – including psychoanalysis – that seem to neglect the social and historical forces operating on the subject, and also to focus only on loss and lack rather than on the transformative fullness of subjecthood. Psychoanalysis has to respond to this if it is to continue to contribute to identity studies, but it also has something additional in its armoury. This is linked to its understanding of what Lacan (1959–60, p.139) calls 'extimacy', which refers to the problematisation of the distinction between 'inside' and 'out' and the way the 'centre of the subject is outside; the subject is ex-centric' (Evans, 1996, p.59). But more than this, it also resides in psychoanalysis' fascination with what is disruptive and uncertain, so that disturbance in the stability of what is taken to be identity is at the core of its concerns. Psychoanalysis certainly must develop its awareness of how the positioning of the subject in historical and contingent networks of relations produces identities of various kinds, fluid and partial in their nature. If it can do this, it can then offer back to the field its own peculiar expertise, that of a discipline that knows about unsettledness, that has marginality and diaspora as part of its own source (in the historical development of psychoanalysis out of certain Jewish diasporic experiences – see Frosh, 2005); and that is always reminding its acolytes that nothing can be taken for granted, that no self-definition or affective state is ever quite what it seems.

Conclusion

Identity has become a major concern of social studies in recent years, as a result of the interest in culture and in how the human subject is constructed both as subject *to* power and as an agentic subject making sense of itself and of the world. Understood in the various ways outlined in this chapter, identity is a summary term referring to subjects' investments in certain ways of experiencing themselves, and in their affiliations with particular groups and social roles. It stands at a meeting point of processes of self-construction that arise from what are usually seen as 'internal' psychological states and 'external' social forces. Despite the convention of thinking about identity as if it is a fixed and stable developmental achievement, this conceptualisation of it as a nodal point at which various forces meet shows how transitory and elusive it is. Added to now routine observations about the multiplicity and fluidity of contemporary identities, and the input from diaspora studies, this emphasises the need for concepts which can appreciate the general 'intersectionality' of identities. This does not refer so much to places at which apparently fixed social categories such as race and class can meet, but more, echoing Hall's (1990) terminology, to moments of 'becoming'. What this emphasises is the illusory nature of identities as stable entities; they are, rather, momentary snapshots, gathering together a variety of influences and investments before these slip away again and become something else.

Utilisation of psychoanalytic ideas in identity studies has been widespread, if ambivalent. It has often been used as an interpretive categorisation procedure with perhaps too firm a diagnostic subtext. That is, psychoanalysis is called on in its traditional role of making sense of apparently irrational material, or of explaining the investment that subjects might have in discursive positions that in some respects might seem to go against their own rational 'interests' (Frosh et al., 2003; Hollway and Jefferson, 2005). Whilst this role is important in drawing discussions of the unconscious back into the social psychological domain, it also neglects a more recent contribution of psychoanalysis to 'making interpretation stupid' (Nobus and Quinn, 2005, p.186). What this refers to is a mode of reading against the grain in order to track the idea of a subject in process, with no fixed identity however strong the identifications might be. 'Making stupid' involves holding to the provocations of psychoanalysis as an approach that continually deconstructs, without looking out towards eventual fullness of knowledge. Using psychoanalysis to 'explain' identities may miss the point: taken that way, psychoanalysis is just one of many vocabularies for naming the momentary stabilities of subjectivity and trying to pin them down. Instead, the specific contribution of psychoanalysis could be to draw on its understanding of unconscious processes and of the endless cycles of emotional investment, defensive psychic manoeuvre, identification and encounter to keep open awareness of how identity functions as a kind of sticking-plaster over disruption and uncertainty. That is, through its understanding of defence and of imaginary processes, psychoanalysis is well placed to remind the social sciences that there is no integrative psychic system that can draw together all the forces acting upon it to create a stable, fully formed human subject. Once again, however, psychoanalysis itself needs to reflect on this. In its classical forms, it actually buys into the idea of a possibly stable, mature kind of identity. Identity studies themselves, however, talk back to psychoanalysis about this: where ego-identity was, there something fluid, partial and ambiguous must come to be.

Chapter 5

Recognising Others: Towards a Relational Ethics

This chapter traces an engagement between psychoanalysis and 'ethics' pursued by some social theorists who are either psychoanalysts themselves or who draw on psychoanalysis in conjunction with philosophical works. The area is one that is particularly well attuned to the involvement of psychoanalysis because it deals with intersubjective encounters of a kind that, on the face of things, might have links with what goes on in the psychoanalytic consulting room. Psychoanalysis in the clinic trades on the quality of the contact between analyst and patient, and on the subtlety with which the dynamics of this contact can be formulated. In its contemporary forms, psychoanalysis is particularly interested in the transference, which means that it focuses on how fantasy enters into human relations, how one subject can become a loved or hated other for another, on what it means (or feels like) for people to be in close yet troubled connection with each other, and on ways of articulating and ameliorating discontent through the construction of relationships that are open and in important senses truthful. It is therefore always advancing a very practical type of ethics, because it is concerned with the 'right way' to treat people and, specifically, with how to enhance their standing as human subjects. If one can use this loosely as a definition of ethics itself, one can perhaps see immediately how central it is to the interests of much contemporary social theory.

The question of how one relates to others is of special importance in late modernity, perhaps particularly in the wake of the immense destructiveness of the twentieth century and, in the West at least, the 'post-9/11' situation of the construction of an 'other' that is hostile and somehow incomprehensible. It is not that this is a totally new concern, but the *centrality* of questions about how to conceptualise, and forge human relations with, the apparently alien other might be seen as a specifically post-Holocaust phenomenon, fuelled additionally by post-colonial interest in racism and the impingement of global networks of communication. One could possibly argue that the contemporary moral panic over ways in which apparently sovereign boundaries and walls are transgressed by strangers, some of whom constitute 'barbarians' (the kinds of populations that walls are meant to keep out), reveal that the threat of the other is being felt as more immediate. Some theorists (e.g.

Reinhard, 2005) have used this to reconstitute the other as a *neighbour*, drawing attention to the way the issues are no longer just those of how to manage a stranger who is separate from oneself, but rather how to deal with what is experienced as an intruder, as someone who is living right up close. This retains the connotations of promise and intimate exoticism present in the concept of the other, but adds to its already-existing threat a sense of coupling, of dependence on the other/neighbour of whom one is also fearful. But the central question is shared across these different nomenclatures: how does one craft relationships with others that are not colonising (reducing the other to the same, failing to appreciate difference), yet also not premised on the positioning of the other as an alien, with its connotations of hostile threat? And how does one deal with the real threat of the other, which derives both from the other's aggression and from the way in which one's dependence on her or him makes one vulnerable?

Much of the debate here has been in the realm of political philosophy, bordering on a philosophy of ethics. However, key terms drawn on in the debate, such as 'intersubjectivity' and 'recognition', are also staples in the vocabulary of contemporary psychoanalysis, often presented to evoke intense encounters between one person and another. This has resulted in a situation in which, whilst psychoanalysis is not always referenced by philosophers, it is always present at least at the margins of debates on relationality; and in places it is particularly central. In this chapter, the concern is with some psychoanalytic thinking on what it means to 'recognise' others; and beyond that with some ways in which psychoanalysis is being deployed as a critical tool in developing an 'ethics' of otherness. More broadly, this involves identifying the components of a stance towards knowing, singling out, or being in a relationship with an other who in her or his impact on the subject can be a disturbing yet longed-for neighbour. In the course of this, psychoanalysis is being looked to both for 'technical' backing for philosophical ideas (for example, the provision of a developmental account that will support or refute particular philosophical claims about the ontology of otherness) and as generative of new ethical possibilities. This chapter takes up some elements of these debates to ask whether and in what ways psychoanalysis is genuinely such a resource.

Recognising others: lessons from relational psychoanalysis

For Freud, the primary entity of study was the individual, driven by internal forces to seek out others in order to accomplish wishful impulses. Relationality was a kind of secondary phenomenon, in which the individual subject had to negotiate her or his way as a consequence of needing an object to satisfy the drive, especially the sexual drive. That is, sexuality was seen as motivating the formation of relationships with others, rather than being an expression of enjoyment within those relationships. Essentially, biological drives were theorised as the motor of human action. Whilst there was always an 'object-relational' element to Freud's thought, specifically in the formulation of the Oedipus complex as a moment in which the 'cultural' prohibition imposed by the father put paid to the biological possibility of incest, the main thrust of the theory was from inside to out. The problematic, if one can call it that, was the regulation of inner wishes to make it possible to live safely in a peopled environment; relationality was needed, but only for protection or to service one's impulses (Frosh, 1999). This position has changed radically in post-Freudian psychoanalysis, as witnessed particularly in object relations theory but also in post-Kleinian and even contemporary Freudian thought, as well as in much American work. In fact, as noted in my *For and Against Psychoanalysis* (Frosh, 2006), 'To a considerable degree, all the mainstream psychoanalytic schools, including those in the U.S.A., have turned their attention to what is best termed "intersubjectivity" – the ways in which mental representations of relationships are formed and the effects these have on the development and actual social relationships of individuals' (p.18). The language of objects, of representations, of 'inner worlds' in which relational constructs dominate, and of 'intersubjectivity' to reference particularly the interweaving of the 'subjective worlds of child and caregiver or of patient and analyst' (Stolorow, 2006, p.250), is now central to the vocabulary of psychoanalysts of all persuasions. Stolorow comments: 'Recognition of intersubjectivity does not entail adherence to or rejection of any specific psychodynamic theory. In fact, acceptance of the foundational significance of intersubjectivity enables therapists to employ the various psychodynamic concepts with greater discrimination and effectiveness' (ibid.). This might not actually be completely true, with the Lacanians (to whom this chapter will return), as ever, coming in as an exception to this generalisation. Nevertheless, outside Lacanian thought, it is fairly hard to find any contemporary psychoanalyst who does not accord central significance to object relationships, even if they differ on many other aspects of theory (such as the place of drives or the order of developmental accomplishments) or practice (such as the way interpretations should be phrased, or the use of the negative transference). Included in this is the notion that 'bridging' difference is key; that is, that the task is to find ways to link with others, to translate their needs and one's own into something that can form the basis for relationships that can be mutually fulfilling. This is a model both of therapeutic activity and 'ordinary life'; the question of the other thus becomes one of how to draw people together rather than just how to survive.

In much contemporary psychoanalysis, the stance that otherness is something to be bridged is reflected in a relational position which takes the self–other link as constitutive of human subjectivity. From this position relationality does not need to be explained, but is rather the starting point out of which all analysis flows. Jessica Benjamin's take on intersubjectivity, which is rooted in feminist scholarship and critical theory and hence oriented towards emancipatory practice, is an especially significant variant of this general approach. For Benjamin, the intersubjective stance is a specific move within the general domain of relational theorising, one which holds on to a position in which the other is related *to* but is not *appropriated*. It is a stance that understands the appeal of omnipotence (in knowing the other we come to colonise her or him), but works against it. The manner in which omnipotence is contested is through a process that Benjamin calls 'recognition', which acknowledges the other as a source of subjectivity and gives rise to what Benjamin (1998) calls a 'subject–subject' psychology. This stance echoes the 'I–thou' relationship described by Martin Buber (1959), a mode of reciprocity in which there is engagement with the other as a full being, in contrast to the more instrumental 'I–it' relationship in which the other is a means to an end. Similarly, 'subject–subject' recognition is built out of an understanding of the other's continuing otherness, maintaining the subjecthood of both participants in the exchange who are thus autonomous and yet also exist in relation to one another. In 'the intersubjective conception of recognition,' writes Benjamin (1998), 'two active subjects may exchange, may alternate in expressing and receiving, cocreating a mutuality that allows for and presumes separateness' (p.29).

Benjamin's approach seeks a balance between theories that emphasise difference and those visions of subjectivity that implicitly require disappearance in or of the other, either through self-effacement (as in many theories of mothering), or through instrumental use of the other (the main thrust of rationality). Recognition staves off the absorption of self into the other just as it prevents the other being colonised by the self; rather, the possibility is raised of allowing difference yet also appreciating similarity. Benjamin (2000) herself makes explicit the distinction between omnipotence and recognition:

> The tension between recognizing the other and wanting the self to be absolute (omnipotence) is, to my mind, an internal conflict inherent in the psyche; it exists independent of any given interaction – even in the most favourable conditions. It is not interpersonally generated but is, rather, a

> psychic structure that conditions the interpersonal. The problem of whether or not we are able to recognize the other person as outside, not the sum of, our projections or the mere object of need, and still feel recognized by her or him, is defining for intersubjectivity. (p.294)

Recognition of this kind is not a merely cognitive event, nor is it a passive reflection or mirroring of what is already somehow 'in' the other. It is, rather, something actively reaching out that makes what it finds, yet also lets the other be. It is, in this sense, a process of *sanctification*, in which what is found in the other is also cherished specifically for its capacity to be different, and its otherness.

Building on the work of Winnicott, to whom Benjamin (2000) states herself to be deeply indebted, the argument can be restated as privileging the role of respect for the other *as other*, with whom one has connections, but whose inner space cannot be fully known. This is a surprisingly difficult aspiration to realise, even in theory. In many psychoanalytic accounts, for example, the highest point of an intimate relationship is a process of identification or even incorporation, rather than recognition of the otherness of the other. More generally, there is a small space between the liberal urge to understand the other and the wish to remove the other's otherness – as can be seen in recent debates about the limits of 'multiculturalism', in which as soon as the other claims a right to maintain its difference, it is regarded as hostile. Clearly, just seeing the other as different is not the solution: that can be a defence against recognising relatedness where it exists, of noting and experiencing the similarity of human experience. There is plenty of circumstantial evidence, indeed, that this kind of 'othering' can be a source of social hatred, especially when 'different' is cast as 'alien', for example, in ethnic and racist hate (Frosh, 2002). Instead, the idea of recognition embraces the acknowledgement of existence of the other as other in the context of relatedness: there is a real difference, yet this difference is not necessarily marked by preference, it is 'just' difference. There is an other who or which cannot be made 'same', but that does not mean that there is a lack of connection, only that this connection is for the sake of bridging rather than for invasion or incorporation. Benjamin's idea, read this way, suggests that becoming 'real' is premised on the situation in which one's otherness is noted and valued for what it is.

In her analysis of the implications of Benjamin's theory for mothering, Lisa Baraitser (2009) describes how Benjamin's account draws on Winnicott's (1969) ideas about a developmental phase that involves 'object use'. Winnicott's argument is that what he calls the use of an object is made possible through seeing that the (paradigmatically, maternal) object survives unconscious destruction. Assuming that the infant, through frustration and also the expression of 'natural' aggression, attacks the object, Winnicott claims that the infant's perception of the existence of a real external other is enhanced so long as the mother survives and is non-retaliatory in her response. That is, what the infant is supposed to discover is that the mother is not subject to the infant's 'internal' experience of having destroyed her, and hence is an object with more than merely imaginary existence. Benjamin builds on this idea by suggesting that recognition depends on processes of destruction in the form of 'negation' which test the reality of the other by establishing the degree to which it is resilient and hence has a subjective trajectory of its own. Baraitser comments: 'In Benjamin's view there is an ongoing and endless cycle of the establishment of mutual recognition followed by its negation, constituting a never-ending tension between complementarity and mutuality, between relating to the other as object or like subject' (p.30). Further:

> In Benjamin's work, we are not fundamentally constituted through loss, but through processes of separation that are tempered by the pleasures of mutual recognition and the possibilities of shared understanding made possible through surviving destruction. And if we follow this through, difference can then be experienced as something that can be identified with, not just repudiated, negated or controlled. The infant can enjoy the fact that the mother has a life of her own to get on with, as it means that she is like me, with desires of her own. (ibid.)

The idea of 'enjoyment' here is a potentially important one as it conveys the sense of erotic charge existing when the subject confronts the other in its *difference* from the self. Indeed, the threat of the other, which produces the impulse towards omnipotence in the subject, always has erotic components – something reflected in much of the discourse of racism as well as in the attractions of the 'exotic' (Frosh, 2006). Baraitser's use of the term 'enjoy', however, has a less sexual connotation and points to the domination of the relational stance by concepts such as 'holding' and 'containing'; it seems to mean something more akin to 'feeling secure and satisfied' than to feeling excited. This might mark up one of the deficiencies of relational theory in the context of the revelations of psychoanalysis about the passionate feelings so often associated with destructive urges. It sometimes seems as if the humanistic component of relational work trumps its analytic rigour; even the notion of 'destruction' lacks the passion of, for example, the Kleinian concept of envy, with its connotations of greed and murderous violence. Judith Butler (2000) comments on this:

> Although Benjamin clearly makes the point that recognition risks falling into destruction, it seems to me that she still holds out for an ideal of recognition in which destruction is an occasional and lamentable occurrence, one that is reversed and overcome in the therapeutic situation and that does not turn out to constitute recognition essentially. (p.273)

This translation of destruction as a fall from grace that can be overcome by a reparative relationship is perhaps part of the legacy of an object-relations position which assumes the existence of an integrated psyche at birth that then becomes split because of frustration and loss (Frosh, 1999). In contrast, the Kleinian view is that destructiveness is a basic force that always has to be contended with and can never be fully resolved. Without being a Kleinian, Butler (2000) picks up this issue to wonder about the authenticity of an approach that assumes destructiveness can be overcome. Addressing Benjamin's use of negation, she asks:

> And if negation is destruction that is survived, of what does survival consist? Certainly, the formulation implies that destruction is somehow overcome, even overcome once and for all. But is this ever really possible — for humans, that is? And would we trust those who claim to have overcome destructiveness for the harmonious dyad once and for all? I, for one, would be wary. (p.285)

The bridging-across-differences element in Benjamin's work reflects both the strengths and perhaps the dangers of her stance, and can be seen too in her more recent and highly productive concern with 'thirdness'. This is a concept that has a considerable history in psychoanalysis, and in the guise of Oedipal thinking has been the main element in its approach to social theory, from Freud (1930) onwards (see Frosh, 1999). Whilst acknowledging the utility of Oedipal scenarios for understanding aspects of development, however, Benjamin (in line with other relational theorists such as Guntrip, 1968) has long been critical of the Oedipal framework as the overriding element in analytic theory. She sees it as fixing a bipolarity (father *versus* mother; reality *versus* narcissism) that is not only misogynist in its assumptions, but also misses the true 'overdeterminism' of psychic life. Benjamin's critique of Oedipal theory in *The Bonds of Love* (1988), as well as in later texts, has established a line of thought in which the dichotomy of pre-Oedipal (seen as referring to narcissistic relationships) *versus* Oedipal functioning (relationships based on reality) is seen as insinuating itself into a denigration–idealisation dynamic. This dynamic is both heavily gendered (the mother's intimacy versus the father's separateness; the mother's narcissism versus the father's symbolic power) and individualistic. With this kind of approach, she argues, it is inevitable that difference will be marked by repudiation rather than acceptance or linkage; otherwise selfhood cannot be sustained. What Benjamin argues for in its place is recognition built on the subject–subject dynamic, in which new modes of identification are central. The infant is involved in 'over-inclusive identifications' that facilitate absorption of difference and the experience of the other as a separate subject of consciousness (Benjamin, 1998). The question then becomes not that of how to survive the pull to narcissistic disappearance of the self in the other, nor of the acceptance of castration, but rather how to connect in a 'post-Oedipal' way across difference, experiencing the other as one amongst many possible and actual objects for identification and love.

The idea of the 'third' developed here moves psychoanalytic theory away from Oedipal structures. Benjamin formalises her interest in connectedness and relationality through postulating a 'space' in which contact occurs. This space is a dynamic space, 'a principle, relationship or function which is constantly collapsing and needing to be repaired' (Baraitser, 2006). It has two elements, the 'third in the one' and the 'one in the third' (Benjamin, 2004). The 'third in the one' is the capacity of the mother or the analyst to hold in mind what subject and other can create together, a kind of reparative ability to believe that it is possible to comprehend the other even when the other is destructive and alien. The 'one in the third' is a pattern of being that links subject and other and produces something new, a space (for example the projected space of the analytic encounter) for meeting, reflection and creativity, owned by neither party but an aspect of them both. For Benjamin, this links further with the idea of the analyst being actively present in the therapeutic encounter, ready, for example, to acknowledge errors, and hence very much engaged in the process of negotiating the relational dynamics of the session. Thus, building on intersubjectivity as an active nexus of relatedness, Benjamin (2004) rejects the Kleinian tendency to speak from the countertransference but not to become relationally involved with it, to insist 'that the patient is ultimately helped only by understanding rather than by being understood' (p.35). For Benjamin, it is necessary for the analyst who is 'caught in enactment' (ibid.) to find a way to acknowledge it to the patient, a stance or position that Benjamin (2009) refers to as the 'moral third', referring to 'those values, rules, and principles of interaction that we rely upon in our efforts to create and restore the space for each partner in the dyad to engage in thinking, feeling, acting or responding rather than merely reacting' (p.444). It is this that differentiates the relational from the Kleinian perspective. Benjamin (2004) comments: 'The analyst says, in effect, "I'll go first." In orienting to the moral third of responsibility, the analyst is also demonstrating the route out of helplessness' (p.33).

'I'll go first' or 'after you'? Benjamin and Levinas on ethical responsibility

Benjamin's emphasis on responsibility has direct implications for working with others, and indeed governs her thinking on reconciliation work in Israel–Palestine (Altman, Benjamin, Jacobs and Wachtel, 2006). Political involvement in this specific instance is coded as the need for engagement with Palestinian suffering from the perspective of accepting responsibility as a Jew. Benjamin links this with the analyst's realisation that whilst she or he might be the 'activator of old traumas, old pain' rather than their instigator, 'you acknowledge that you have, you know, bumped into the person's bruise, and you acknowledge that there is hurt and pain and that you may have responsibility for that, and in doing this, you alleviate a whole level of tension that makes it possible, then, to talk about, to explore' (p.170). In both the political and the therapeutic context, recognition and responsibility go hand in hand, with each entailing the other. Taking responsibility for others arises from recognition of their existence as genuine centres of subjectivity, not just possessing rights but also having the capacity to be hurt. The analyst 'bruises' the patient merely by being there, though her or his infelicities might make this bruising greater; hence, in the tradition of Winnicott, Benjamin (2009) advocates acknowledging mistakes rather than simply interpreting their effects. For her, this is not a matter of making the patient in some way responsible for the analyst's actions, nor of requiring from the patient forgiveness of the analyst. 'On the contrary,' she writes: 'it should serve to reveal how the analyst takes on the responsibility for forgiving herself and thus being able to transcend the shame of her difficulties enough to talk about and analyze them (without excessive or impulsive self-disclosure)' (p.449–50). Through this means the patient may be helped to contribute reciprocally to the analytic relationship, becoming 'an interpreter of the analyst and a co-creator of dialogue, and so develop her own sense of agency and responsibility' (p.450). The emphasis on mutuality here is strong, but it still relies on the analyst's capacity to start it off. 'Bumping into the person's bruise' is bound to occur; it is a necessary part of therapy, because if one is to look truthfully at what exists, then pain is bound to be felt. But this does not mean it can all be put back onto the other; the subject/analyst has responsibility, even if the damage is unavoidable.

Despite the analytic 'I'll go first', Benjamin is cautious about always making the other's needs primary, always taking responsibility in this way, because she wants to warn against a kind of self-abasement in which the subject gives up her or his agency and indeed her or his rights. That is, taking responsibility is not the same thing as always giving way;

and indeed the analytic situation (characterised by 'analytic abstinence') is precisely one in which not giving way (by avoiding becoming involved in the patient's life or by refusing to allow even small shifts in the time boundaries of the session) is seen as crucial both for the containment of a patient's anxiety and for the exploration of deep trauma. The analyst does not say, 'Tell me what you want and I will meet your need.' A kind of robustness is required, again to match Winnicott's idea that the existence of the other is realised through her or his capacity to survive the subject's destructive attacks. This means that the analyst has to hold firm not only to maintain her or his sanity, but in order to become 'real' for the patient; this must be tempered with acknowledgement of errors and readiness to participate in the intersubjective exchange, but not at the price of obliterating one's own subjectivity.

A comparison can be made here with Emmanuel Levinas' approach to 'ethics as first philosophy', which is one of the most influential areas of work in which the 'face-to-face' encounter has become central to comprehension of human subjectivity. The intensity of his argument for the prior recognition of the other as the foundation of ethics is immense and extraordinarily demanding, taking, if one can think of it this way, the notion of *hospitality* to an extreme. However, many therapeutic and social encounters deal with extreme situations, extreme states of mind and extreme politics. In that context, there is something to be said for starkly presenting the impossible ideal, that towards which one needs continually to gesture:

> In my analysis, ... the relation to the Face is the relation to the absolutely weak ... and there is, consequently, in the Face of the Other always the death of the Other and thus, in some way, an incitement to murder, the temptation to go to the extreme, to completely neglect the other – and at the same time (and this is the paradoxical thing) the Face is also the 'Thou Shalt not Kill'. A Thou-Shalt-not-Kill that can also be explicated much further: it is the fact that I cannot let the other die alone, it is like a calling out to me ... at the outset I hardly care what the other is with respect to me, that is his own business; for me, he is above all the one I am responsible for. (Levinas, 1991, pp.104–5)

The Levinasian primacy of the other has given rise to a great deal of philosophical debate, and it is not clear that all its implications stand up to scrutiny. However, there is something powerful here: nothing contingent is assumed in relation to how the other will treat the self, there is no expectation of there being any pay-off from 'love of one's neighbour', no reciprocity such as is demanded by Buber's I–thou relationship. Being responsible for the other does not mean that a positive response will come back to the subject; it exists simply as an ethical imperative, as that which makes one human.

Levinas (1985) makes it clear that this relationship of responsibility – this ethical relation – is in his view *primary*, rather than following on from something pre-existent. It is not the case that the human subject exists and then engages in ethical relations; rather, ethics is the defining feature of subjectivity itself: 'I understand responsibility as responsibility for the Other, thus as responsibility for what is not my deed, or for what does not even matter to me; or which precisely does matter to me, is met by me as face' (p.95). Levinas insists that responsibility for the other comes before the subject can even know what the other is; it is, consequently, an absolute given, and the recognition which is part of it is as non-contingent as can be. Indeed, the term 'recognition' is inappropriate within the Levinasian domain, because of its implication that somehow, through the act of recognition, the other becomes known. Realising that one 'does not know and has never seen' the other, yet that the other exists, is not the same as recognition in the conventional sense. Rather, it is an absolute refusal of the impulse to believe that the other can ever be brought within the realm of the self. Even more so, Levinas states, 'at the outset I hardly care what the other is with respect to me'. Knowledge of what the other might be, what use or reciprocity might derive from it, is irrelevant; the other is not any *specific* 'person', but that which is outside what can be claimed by the self. Knowing the other would be part of the colonising act of reducing it to the same; in the Levinasian scheme, the otherness of the other is always maintained.

Levinas' ontology here is distinct from Benjamin's in a number of ways that have a bearing on the limitations of an account that assumes the bridgeability of difference. In focusing on the 'third', Benjamin is extending her analysis of complementarity in intersubjective relations into an attempt to think about how recognition and reconciliation go together. The point about the third is that it offers a space in which intersubjective recognition can take place; in demonstrating a capacity to think beyond the dyad, the subject creates a third space in which the other can also move. If the analyst abjures the responsibility to move 'first' into this third, then the *analyst's* fear of losing the safety of distance is blocking the possibility of an encounter of this kind. This is best thought of as a mode of 'practical ethics' in which the route to taking responsibility is to move both participants in the intersubjective exchange into a new domain, making thought and mutual recognition possible.

For Levinas, there is no intersubjective meeting; there is rather the construction of the subject *as an ethical subject* through responsibility for the other, whatever that might be constituted by, whatever strangeness it might imply. Baraitser (2009) glosses this as follows:

> Levinas' argument is in a different register from that of sameness and difference, recognition and reciprocity. Recognition ... is not identical with responsibility. Self-recognition that relies on recognition by another subject will perhaps always run into difficulties with how to prevent an infolding of alterity due to the colonizing impulse that is inherent, not only in 'knowing' another but in recognizing too. In contrast, describing the relationship with the Other as an ethical relationship prior to self, a relationship that establishes the subject as a responsible subject prior to 'being' a subject at all, Levinas redefines both the notion of the subject and the Other, as well as the nature of their relationship and that of recognition itself. (p.37)

In Levinas, this is an assertion of the irrevocable otherness of the other as something that stands over and above us and is best coded as the infinite. It makes demands on the subject which are not necessarily reciprocated; 'responsibility' as an approach to the other institutes the subject as an ethical subject rather than simply an intersubjective one. It raises a question that is central to issues of non-violence and care, which can be phrased as, '*how do we take responsibility for the other through exposure to the other prior to the possibility of recognition by that other?*' (Baraitser, 2009, p.39). In relation to other subjects, this means seeing the infinite in the face of the other, in all its inapproachability. Acknowledgement of this primary mode of being, this 'you go first', irrespective of desire, understanding or contact, makes the subject ethical and – definitionally, it seems, at least for Levinas – in so doing constructs the human being.

Language, murmuring and silence

The vocabulary of recognition and responsibility raises a set of issues about the 'mediation' of subject–other contact through language. Questions such as the degree to which language is expressive or determining of thoughts, and also of the structural characteristics of language, have been central to social science for decades, and to psychoanalysis – the 'talking cure' – since its inception. For Freud (1915), the difference between an unconscious and conscious idea was that the former was restricted to the 'thing-presentation' whilst the latter had the 'word-presentation' attached to it (p.200); for Lacan, the unconscious was structured 'like a language'. The question here, however, is what role language might have in the *relationship* of subject to other, and what psychoanalysis might contribute to elucidating this relationship. It should be noted first that whilst psychoanalysis recognises the potency of words, it is also interested in their underside, the continuing murmur of the non-linguistic, of that which falls out of symbolisation (the Real, in Lacanian terms), those experiences that seem to slip away just when we are about to speak (of) them. Language needs to be differentiated from the non-linguistic to make it language, but this also has structural implications for what can be symbolised and what cannot. That which is silenced underpins speech but is also excluded by it. It is also the *impersonality* of speech that is important here, by which is meant the way language works as a system that is not simply at the disposal of individual speakers, but has its own rules, its own way of doing things. As social theory has long recognised, language is both the product of human speakers and is abstracted from them – there are strict limits on the novelty with which it can be used if communication and meaningfulness are to be retained, despite the fact that completely novel utterances are being made all the time. Language has its own life, independent of its speakers; once the genie of words has been let out of the bottle, it cannot be controlled by any human will. This double-facedness of language contributes to the complex way in which it underpins subject–other relations: it both *enables* them (through communication and symbolisation), and subjects them to a system that stands outside them (the linguistic or symbolic 'order'), hence making direct, unmediated contact impossible.

Whilst concern with language is by no means confined to theorists with psychoanalytic interests, psychoanalysis is often close at hand in these discussions, offering reflections on how language and desire operate in tension and in tandem with one another. In particular, psychoanalysis contributes to conceptualisations of how language both links people and alienates them from each other. It offers a vocabulary to writers whose concern is with the emotional or 'affective' connections between people, and how these are constructed, mediated or 'distorted' by words. Denise Riley (2005), for example, notes how 'the deepest intimacy joins the supposedly linguistic to the supposedly psychic' (p.11), making it clear how these realms are 'scarcely separable'. Instead of opposing the psychic and linguistic, she suggests that we maintain an idea of 'affective words as they indwell', pushing forward an appreciation of how language insinuates itself within people and enforces the impersonality at the heart of each human subject. Riley offers a modest form of this impersonal core, arguing that what she calls 'linguistic will' – fundamentally, a person's ability to choose what to articulate – is restricted to moderating the inward impulse that would otherwise tear things apart. Speech wells up and we can only do what we can to rein it in, a process that demonstrates time and again quite how fragile is our control over our own being. In the light of this, Riley suggests, the most that can be made of a human subject is as something recognising its own contingency, its own status as being-produced rather than producing. For her, this is the project of a lifetime:

> It's only through my meanders and slow detours, perhaps across many decades, towards recognizing language's powerful impersonality – which is always operating despite and within its air of a communicative 'intersubjectivity' – that I can 'become myself.' Yet I become myself only by way of fully accepting my own impersonality, too – as someone who is herself accidentally spoken, not only by violent language, but by any language whatsoever – and who, by means of her own relieved recognition of this very contingency, is in significant part released from the powers of the secretive and unspeakable workings of linguistic harm. (p.27)

This impersonality of language working as the enigmatic other within the subject is a familiar image in contemporary writings, owing much to deconstructionism and to Lacanian psychoanalysis. Riley, like many authors deeply in love with words but troubled by their power to go wrong, points to the paradox of language as something impersonal yet apparently the instrument of human agency. Her solution to the paradox seems to be *insight*, possibly of the psychoanalytic kind, the 'relieved recognition of this very contingency' that then somehow releases the subject from 'the powers of the secretive and unspeakable workings of linguistic harm'. Yet the impulse that she identifies as welling up in the subject is that of words that speak without being willed, that speak, often destructively, through an impersonal force – language itself, autonomously drawing on its own structures to deliver its blows. If what we have to do is accept our own 'impersonality', then maybe this is a source of the feeling of distance in human relationships. How can one feel connected to others if one is merely a language machine, and one full of *bad* words at that?

The more the focus is on language, the more significant seems to be the 'left over', that which remains unsymbolisable and inarticulate. If language forces being into shape, the question of what it is that lies 'beneath' or outside it keeps recurring. On the whole, this thing outside language is presented as a threat. However, there is also a rendering of the non-linguistic 'murmur of the world' that can be cast broadly as 'humanistic', albeit couched in the shadow of an understanding of the human as a being constituted in the flux of affective forces, and hence as a product of something outside it, rather than as the source of meaning. This mode of humanism evokes the possibility of recognition which is not dependent on language, precisely because it acknowledges the existence of this shared experience of an unspoken background 'real' out of which all subjects arise, and the workings of which we can observe, and draw on, in one another. As such, this approach opposes the stance towards communication that sees it as the transfer of information lucidly from a speaker to a hearer. Alphonso Lingis (1994) expresses a variant of this idea most compellingly in his appositely entitled book, *The Community of Those Who Have Nothing in Common.* Writing about the experience of being in the presence of someone who is dying, he shows how some kinds of communion rest not on the belief that it is possible to exchange 'meaning' through the transmission of messages in which each is the recipient of the other's sense, but rather on an acknowledgement that we are all rooted in something elemental. This kind of encounter depends not on reaching agreement between subjects who are similar to each other but of drawing on the other's existence in all its *alien* form, so that one has marked out the vista of a world that is not the same as one's own:

> We do not relate to the light, the earth, the air, and the warmth only with our individual sensibility and sensuality. We communicate to one another the light our eyes know, the ground that sustains our postures, and the air and the warmth with which we speak. We face one another as condensations of earth, light, air, and warmth, and orient one another in the elemental in a primary communication. We appeal to the others to help us be at home in the alien elements into which we stray: in the drifting and nameless light and warmth of infancy, in the nocturnal depths of the erotic, and in the domain of dying where rational discourse has no longer anything to say. (p.122)

The appeal of the other here is less harsh than as represented in Levinas, but it is just as unbridgeable. We are linked in the elemental, not through some mediated communication, but as a response to an appeal. The 'third' is transformed into the light of each other's face, its recognition of the mutual being and enlivening power of subjects who are nevertheless not just distinct, but alien from one another.

We have here, in its austerity, a different model from one that assumes the potential linkage of subjects through shared perspectives, drawing-together of narratives or meta-level transformation of points of view. Lingis (1994) characterises traditional models of communication as a search for rational clarity based on rescuing the specificity of the message from the constant interferences that threaten to submerge it. Rationality needs quiet as an unambiguous and transparent medium; it is opposed to 'interference and confusion' (p.70). Yet, he asks, 'is there not also a communication in the hearing of the noise in one another's voices – the noise of one another's life that accompanies the harkening to the message? What kind of communication would that be?' (p.88). To which he gives the partial answer:

> The one who understands is not extracting the abstract form out of the tone, the rhythm, and the cadences – the noise internal to the utterance, the cacophony internal to the emission of the message. He or she is also listening to that internal noise – the rasping or smouldering breath, the hyperventilating or

> somnolent lungs, the rumblings and internal echoes – in which the message is particularized and materialized and in which the empirical reality of something indefinitely discernible, encountered in the path of one's own life, is referred to and communicated. With this internal noise it is the other, in his or her materiality, that stands forth and stands apart making appeals and demands. The other is not simply the recurrent function of appealing to and contesting me; he or she is an empirically discernible vulnerability and intrusion. (p.91)

The 'noise', when listened to, becomes what marks out the other as *human*, as a being excessive to itself, as more than a 'function' because she or he is a significant presence, marking a 'vulnerability and intrusion'. It is the 'internal noise' that makes the other so; deleting this and holding only on to the abstract form of the message also misses what is peculiar about it, hence what makes it real. This notion links with Slavoj Žižek's (2006b) comment that 'The ultimate lesson of psychoanalysis is that human life is never "just life": humans are not simply alive, they are possessed by the strange drive to enjoy life in excess, passionately attached to a surplus which sticks out and derails the ordinary run of things' (p.62). Human life is just too much; that is its nature and its definition, and losing the background noise, screening out the seemingly desolate murmur that lurks behind spoken language, loses life itself. What links us to one another is *access to the excess*: something is being hinted at here that has to do with a mutual core that does not satisfy our usual notions of human essence at all.

Žižek (2006b) similarly emphasises the intractability of the mystery of the other as what is essential; indeed, he argues that *not* knowing the other is crucial to intersubjectivity itself. He writes:

> If I were to 'really know' the mind of my interlocutor, intersubjectivity proper would disappear; he would lose his subjective status and turn – for me – into a transparent machine. In other words, not-being-knowable to others is a crucial feature of subjectivity, of what we mean when we impute to our interlocutors a 'mind': you 'truly have a mind' only insofar as it is opaque to me. (p.178)

The *solidity* of the other comes over in this, its absolute otherness that links both with Winnicott's (1969) ideas on how the other becomes real to the subject by surviving attack, and with the contrary Lacanian emphasis on how all psychoanalytic knowledge is constituted through language, and hence is characterised by 'mistranslation'. However, whilst this parallels Levinas' ideas in suggesting the unknowability of the other and, alongside this, the importance of that unknowability in resisting acts of colonisation and reduction of the other to the same,

Žižek also differs from Levinas in his reading of what is 'human' in this formulation. For Levinas, the ethical turn is crucial: we give the other primacy ('after you'), and that is the excessive act that defines human subjectivity as such. For Žižek, this omits a key element of the encounter of each subject with the other; precisely, its *inhuman* form. 'What Levinas fails to include in the scope of the "human"', he claims, is 'the *inhuman* itself, a dimension which eludes the face-to-face relationship between humans' (p.111). Here Žižek (2006b) draws on Giorgio Agamben's (2002) use of the figure of the *Muselmann*, the most extreme figure of regressed human suffering in the concentration camps, depicted with unremitting clarity by Primo Levi (1960):

> In a properly dialectical paradox, what Levinas, with all his celebration of Otherness, fails to take into account is not some underlying Sameness of all humans, but the radically 'inhuman' Otherness itself: the Otherness of a human being reduced to inhumanity, the Otherness exemplified by the terrifying figure of the *Muselmann*, the 'living dead' in the concentration camps. (p.112)

The point here is that *Muselmänner* do not respond, which is why, according to Agamben, they are both the true witnesses of the horror of the camps and impossible witnesses, who registered nothing. As such, they manifest the reduction of the human to 'just life', as Žižek terms it, or in Agamben's (1995) famous phrase, the 'bare life' of *homo sacer*.

For Žižek, this lifelessness reveals the limitation of Levinas, whose system depends on there being a 'call' from the other to which the subject has the duty to react. 'When we are confronted with a *Muselmann*,' he writes, 'we precisely cannot discern in his face the trace of the abyss of the Other in his or her vulnerability, addressing us with the infinite call of our responsibility – what we get is a kind of blank wall, a lack of depth' (p.113). However, this raises the next challenge:

> What if, facing a *Muselmann*, we are made aware of our responsibility toward the Other at its most traumatic? In short, what about bringing together Levinas' face and the topic of the 'neighbour' in its strict Freudo-Lacanian sense, as the monstrous, impenetrable Thing that is the *Nebenmensch*, the Thing that hystericizes and provokes me? (p.113)

As will be described more fully below, the *Nebenmensch*, the neighbour, which includes within itself the Freudian 'Thing' as understood by Lacan, embodies essential alienness. Žižek emphasises the challenge of this 'monstrous, impenetrable Thing' as the most traumatic extreme of ethics, because the 'facelessness' of the *Muselmann* still calls on the subject precisely because it asks for nothing. That is, the ultimate challenge is to deal with this inhuman thing, which provokes and hystericises by virtue of its deathliness. What makes it inhuman? Is it perhaps not just because of the loss of agency, the unresponsiveness and impenetrability of the *Muselmann*, but also because this terrifying neighbour invokes precisely the deracinated other who is cut off from the 'elemental', the murmuring deep, its capacity to draw on life – even if only to register horror – drained out of it? Levinas assumes the existence of a question, a demand in the other, to which the subject responds; hence, the other is immersed in the same elemental as the subject. Žižek's example pushes the limit case here, suggesting that the ultimate inhuman thing is the one who cannot draw on the elemental at all; the murmuring deep has been silenced.

There is something slightly distasteful about Žižek's critique of Levinas, embedded as it is in the ground of the Holocaust, and perhaps inaccurate in this portrayal of Levinas as reliant on the activity of the other in 'asking' a question – there is plenty of evidence that the mere being of the other is enough in the Levinasian scheme. For Agamben, too, this does not appear to be the whole point. In the context of his meditation on witnessing, Agamben (2002) examines how the *impossibility* of witnessing by the *Muselmann* is matched by the *insufficiency* of witnessing by the survivor – the one who cannot be the end product of the extermination camp, the absolute bare life. Agamben draws this together through an examination of what it might mean to explore the 'inhuman' core of the human: 'this means that the one who truly bears witness in the human is the inhuman; it means that the human is nothing other than the agent of the inhuman, the one who lends the inhuman a voice' (p.120). This rendering of witnessing, which can perhaps be thought of as a way of maintaining contact with the being of the other, produces an alternative to what Agamben describes as the humanist discourse, 'all human beings are human', and the anti-humanist discourse, 'only some human beings are human'. 'What testimony says', writes Agamben, 'is something completely different, which can be formulated in the following theses: "human beings are human insofar as they are not human" or, more precisely, "human beings are human insofar as they bear witness to the inhuman"' (p.121). This suggests that at the core of the tension around language and silence is a space of potential recognition that is impersonal and in that sense 'inhuman' (its origins are not in the subject); but, paradoxically, access to it sustains the 'inhuman' aspect of human aliveness that makes contact with others, and change, feasible. Without access to this elemental, the inhuman becomes deathly; with it, connection is possible. Being 'in' a relationship with another is also a matter of being outside it, sharing in the impersonality that comes from being lived *through* by the forces that constitute the human subject – perhaps affective elements, acceptance of what Riley (2005) terms 'contingency', or of the 'void', as Badiou (2004) has it, referring to the disappearance of the subject which is always threatening to collapse into 'pure, indistinct being' (p.99). This connects back to the Levinasian possibility that what unites people is not something 'intersubjective' at all, but rather that there is an *inhuman* feature that runs through all things as backdrop and elemental, the ground and deep of human activity and therefore of what is experienced in and of the other. We come close to this at those times when we manage to cease seeking out the 'abstract form' in what the other says, as Lingis puts it, and in which we acknowledge the excess of the other – the other's intrusiveness, perhaps – as what is essential. This is perhaps one of the more subtle yet central discoveries of psychoanalysis: it is not what is *in* the message that is important, but what is *transmitted* by it, however untranslatable that may turn out to be. Seeking this out is what gives rise to intersubjective thought, including those projects of 'thirdness' (such as Benjamin's, 2004, discussed above) that convey the attempt to understand what it might mean to be in some kind of full therapeutic contact with another. But these approaches seem to be hampered by a kind of therapeutic zeal, which translates eventually into an extracting, colonising process. A certain kind of withdrawal is necessary, an acknowledgement that the place in which subjects meet may not be one of human encounter at all, but rather of an apparent emptiness, in which subjectivity is evacuated. This place is fought against but drawn upon, feared and exulted in. It is neither silence nor speech, but the source of both. Indeed, one might call it the void, but one that is full of murmuring.

On ethical violence

The question of what it might mean to single out the other as a human subject is also key to discussions of the nature of 'ethical violence' that have materialised particularly between Judith Butler and Slavoj Žižek. The terminology here is somewhat idiosyncratic, but what is being debated is how the other should be acknowledged as connected to the subject, yet also existing in a terrain of its own subjecthood. Put crudely, this means asking how one can avoid the 'violence' implicit in forcing another subject into a frame not of its own choosing whilst holding on to a concern with relationality and social justice. Butler (2005), staking out the ground in relation to Levinas and the psychoanalyst Jean Laplanche, focuses on the question of recognition, which for her is not a humanistic acceptance of the other, but a rigorous and in some ways impossible process of self- and other-scrutiny built on the impossibility of full knowledge. Her account draws both on the philosophy of ethics and on psychoanalysis, using each to interrogate the other, but particularly employing a psychoanalytic understanding of the 'opacity' of the human subject, its organisation around a point of *unknowability* (the unconscious), to develop an approach to engaging with the other without appropriation. Key here is the idea that acknowledging the opacity of the self is a necessary foundation for ethical appreciation of the other, who must also be opaque to the subject in her or his intrinsic formation. Just as one cannot fully know oneself, so one cannot fully know the other; consequently, the other stands in the same relation to the subject as the subject does to her or himself. Butler (2005) comments: 'we might consider a certain post-Hegelian reading of the scene of recognition in which precisely my own opacity to myself occasions my capacity to confer a certain kind of recognition on others. It would be, perhaps, an ethics based on our shared, invariable, and partial blindness about ourselves' (p.41). For her, this is a possible counter to what she terms 'ethical violence', which seems to be best understood as the promulgation of a version of the other that forces the other to become something it should not be. At the source of this is a demand for a certain mode of narrative integrity that is simply not possible without doing violence to the actuality of the fragmented psyche, itself a fundamental discovery of psychoanalysis.

For Butler (2005), the realisation that one is an opaque subject acts against the demand that the other should be transparent:

> Suspending the demand for self-identity or, more particularly, for complete coherence seems to me to counter a certain ethical violence, which demands that we manifest and maintain self-identity at all times and require that others do the same ... one can give and take recognition only on the condition that one becomes disoriented from oneself by something which is not oneself, that one undergoes a de-centring and 'fails' to achieve self-identity. (p.42)

The ethics of this is a kind of tolerance of the other that recognises it as not fully knowable, and hence resists the temptation to appropriate the other through an act of colonisation. Expressing herself with slight echoes of Žižek's emphasis on the 'excess' of human life, Butler sees the interrupted nature of subjectivity as crucial, the way it cannot ever be fully expressed as a whole:

> By not pursuing satisfaction and by letting the question remain open, even enduring, we let the other live, since life might be understood as precisely that which exceeds any account we may try to give of it. If letting the other

> live is part of any ethical definition of recognition, then this version of recognition will be based less on knowledge than on an apprehension of epistemic limits. (ibid.)

Recognising the other means being aware of the limits of recognition, and this is an ethical act because it 'lets the other live' without forcing her or him to be whole and knowable, without imposing a kind of narrative integrity that 'may be preferring the seamlessness of the story to something we might tentatively call the truth of the person, a truth that, to a certain degree ... might well become more clear in moments of interruption, stoppage, open-endedness – in enigmatic articulations that cannot easily be translated into narrative form' (p.64). This 'tentative truth' is something that can only be glimpsed, never known; it revolves around an interruption that is always present, from well before the subject exists. The subject is grounded in interruption, in opacity, in the unknowability that stems from being at odds with itself. Recognition therefore has to tolerate the otherness of the other and not try to make it 'same'. Butler writes: 'If the other is always there, from the start, in the place of where the ego will be, then a life is constituted through a fundamental interruption, is even *interrupted prior to the possibility of any continuity*' (p.52).

This notion that 'the other is always there, from the start' is an important one in Butler's thought, and it partly explains the use she makes of psychoanalysis to fill out what could otherwise be a purely philosophical argument founded in Levinas. The choice here seems to be between a *static* approach that hypostatises the other and makes it a universal call on the subject, and an ethics that is grounded in actual human practices, particularly the relational practices of infancy out of which the subject is formed. To this end, Butler draws in detail on the psychoanalytic account of the other given by Jean Laplanche, whose focus is on the way the other is *inserted into* the subject, constructing the subject by virtue of a 'message' which is in important ways indecipherable not only because it is beyond the ken of the subject, but because the other – the originator of the message – also does not have control over its unconscious resonance. As John Fletcher (2007) explains, one of the key elements in Laplanche's rereading of Freud is to make the origins of the subject 'extrinsic', a matter of partial translation, failed translation or mistranslation of 'messages' from the adult other to whom the subject is exposed, which are 'implanted' in the subject. Whilst some elements of the parental message are successfully translated by the infant, and hence are 'bound into' the ego and its internal objects so that they can be used (Laplanche's version of sublimation), other elements are untranslatable. They are a 'remainder' that cannot be integrated into the subject but rather inhabit the subject as something alien yet constitutive. Fletcher (2007) describes this untranslatable remainder as

> a *psychical thing* that has become the source of the exciting, traumatizing drives pressing toward absolute discharge, drives that attack the homeostatic body-ego from within ... In particular, the drive is the byproduct of the psychical *work* of the infant, both opening up to and defending against the seductive ministrations of the adult. (pp.1257–8)

This means that there is no paradise of integrity from which the subject falls as a consequence of a failed environment, which is the implication of the Winnicottian and often broader object-relational scheme of things. Using Butler's phrase, the subject is rather '*interrupted prior to the possibility of any continuity*', always inhabited by something from outside that prevents integrity, continuity, wholeness or individuality from proceeding. In contrast to the position that claims each one of us as separate from each other, having to reach out to the other from across an abyss and to negotiate difference as a way of surviving – having to modify our aims and drives, our desires and expectations – we have here an increasing focus on the already-present nature of the supposed other. The immediacy of the other is therefore both an ethical demand and an ontological claim: there is no subject without the other. The subject exists in the space of the other, inhabited by the other, disrupted and interrupted; our life stories are fragmented by the presence of the other 'where the ego will be', our boundaries are always crossed.

Butler (2005) emphasises both the disruptive effect of this primacy of the other and the way it instigates sociality as the first cause, with the ethical implications that follow from that. These two elements – disruption and sociality – are closely linked. On the former, she notes that the impact of finding the other's message at the heart of subjectivity is to realise that the demand for narrative coherence does violence to the subject: there is always something 'too much' at play, and denying this is a way of failing to live with the unconscious:

> To understand the unconscious, however, is to understand what *cannot* belong, properly speaking, to me, precisely because it defies the rhetoric of belonging, is a way of being dispossessed through the address of the other from the start. For Laplanche, I am animated by this call or demand, and I am at first overwhelmed by it. The other is, from the start, too much for me, enigmatic, inscrutable. The 'too-much-ness' must be handled and contained for something called an 'I' to emerge in its separateness. (p.54)

Moreover:

> To hold a person accountable for his or her life in narrative form may even be to require a falsification of that life in order to satisfy the criterion of a certain kind of ethics, one that tends to break with relationality ... To say, as some do, that the self *must* be narrated, that only the narrated self can be intelligible and survive, is to say that we cannot survive with an unconscious. (pp.63, 65)

Because the unconscious is the domain of uninterpretability, founded in response to the untranslated messages of the other, it operates as a site of continued incoherence within the subject, yet also as a site of truth; this truth being that the subject is always open to otherness, always formed in its image. This is the core of the second element of this psychoanalytic ethics, as tuned by Butler. The constitutive presence of the other means that sociality is primary in the formation of the subject, that identity is not 'owned' but is shared, and hence that ethics is always forged in relationality. This is a stance that is closely aligned with that of Levinas, even whilst differing from it on the basis of its tighter understanding both of the disruptive presence of 'infantile' otherness within the adult subject, and of the social. In particular, whilst Levinas gives an account of the 'passivity' of the subject in relation to the impact of the other, he has little to say about the developmental emergence of the subject. He consequently underestimates the impact of the other's message, the way in which it is felt as an impingement producing a range of affective impacts, from anxiety to desire. The psychoanalytic supplement to his philosophy fills out the internal space of the subject as a cauldron of activity which is stirred by the social other; that is, the agency of the subject is itself generated by the other's enigmatic embrace. What Butler calls the 'sociality at the basis of the "I"' (p.75) is an obvious foundation for an ethical relationship with the other: 'I find that my very formation implicates the other in me, that my own foreignness to myself is, paradoxically, the source of my ethical connection with others' (p.84). Insisting on one's own integral identity is a way of doing violence to the self; obliterating the opacity of the other through knowing too well, through, for example, a thirst for absolutely transparent 'communication', also amounts to a mode of violence in which the disturbingly interrupted nature of social subjectivity is overlooked.

As well as utilising Laplanchian psychoanalysis for her model of the formative intrusion of sociality in the subject, Butler also draws on psychoanalysis for an understanding of the significance of the other in an ethical reconstitution of a troubled self. For her, this revolves around psychoanalytic listening, which has the characteristic not of offering a holistic narrative where none should be found, but of giving back a kind of subject in fragments. Psychoanalysis, in this vision, is a mode of necessarily disrupted narrative and failed listening, a kind of witnessing that leaves the subject alone precisely at the moment that it acknowledges relational sociality. It is also, as Butler explicitly notes, a model encounter because it is constructed around the transference.

> The other represents the prospect that the story might be given back in new form, that fragments might be linked in some way, that some part of opacity might be brought to light. The other witnesses and registers what cannot be narrated, functioning as one who might discern a narrative thread, though mainly as one whose practice of listening enacts a receptive relation to the self that the self, in its dire straits of self-beratement, cannot offer itself. And it seems crucial to recognize, not only that the anguish and opacity of the 'I' is witnessed by the other, but that the other can become the name of one's anguish and opacity: '*You* are my anguish, surely. *You* are opaque: who are you? Who is this you that resides in me, from whom I cannot extricate myself?' (p.80)

Transference operates here as a way of breaking into the tendency to narrativise experience. The phantasmatic presence of the other, embodied in the listening analyst but not coincident with the *person* of the analyst, disrupts the sense that one is in communication with an other who can fully understand. Butler draws attention to the way the receptivity of the analyst to 'what cannot be narrated' draws in the subject's 'anguish and opacity'. That is, the opacity of the subject is named, but not resolved: transference dramatises the necessity to be in relation to one who cannot be known, as an outcrop of the impossibility of knowing oneself. This argument has links with the Lacanian idea that the transference operates in the Imaginary as a kind of impossible promise that the analyst will have the remedy for all the patient's suffering; the end of analysis occurs when the subject takes back her or his projections, acknowledging the necessary failure of the analyst to offer a 'solution' to the questions of psychic existence. The *ethical* claim here thus depends on a psychoanalytic rendering of the unknown within – the unconscious – alongside a developmental account of the insertion of this 'unknown' from the outside other. It is coupled with a claim that recognition, as that which gives value to the other, selects the other out, is built on an appreciation of alterity as something which all subjects share.

The use of psychoanalysis here is a powerful one, rooting recognition theory in a concrete developmental account that provides an ontogeny for the subject as something 'always-already' social. In a way, it offers a 'new norm' for ethical relationality, based on developmental considerations (the subject is constituted through its others), which has radically critical effects when counterposed to the traditional developmental sequence of increasing 'maturity' and independence. In terms of social theory, it offers a revised 'master discourse' in which the primacy of relationality is forged as a necessary consequence of the existence of an unconscious populated by otherness, the denial of which is therefore an act of ethical violence. Žižek's response to this is characteristically provocative, from the title of his chapter on the topic ('Neighbours and Other Monsters: A Plea for Ethical Violence' – Žižek, 2005) to its content. There are a number of significant dimensions to his argument. For Žižek, drawing on Lacan rather than Laplanche, psychoanalysis offers no new norm, however radical it might be. Rather, it is used disruptively to accentuate the impossibility of a norm, or at least its undesirability, and the necessary maintenance of a place of emptiness where that norm might be ('The question, however, remains: how, *structurally*, does this new Master differ from the previous, overthrown one ...?' – Žižek, 2006a, p.307). His first move involves conflating the 'monstrosity of the Thing' and the presentation of the neighbour as the embodiment of threat and also of unknowability. He comments (2006b):

> What Levinas obfuscates is the monstrosity of the neighbour, a monstrosity on account of which Lacan applies to the neighbour the term Thing (*das Ding*) ... One should hear in this term all the connotations of horror fiction: the neighbour is the (Evil) Thing that potentially lurks beneath every homely human face' (p.43)

Reinhard (2005) clarifies the nature of this supposedly 'evil' thingness in the neighbour in the context of a careful elaboration of Lacanian claims. Lacan, he writes,

> defines *das Ding* as the encounter with something in the other that is completely alien – an intrusive foreignness that goes beyond the compositions of self and other, and their politicizations as 'friend' and 'enemy'. The Thing materializes the constitutive ambiguity of the primal object, the trauma of its uncertain disposition between excessive presence and radical absence ... the Thing is that part of the other that is 'mute', but the neighbour speaks and thus forms a template for the subject's emergence. (pp.30–1)

The neighbour contains the Thing – it is not the neighbour itself, but rather an area of unassimilable alienness within the other, that both intrudes on the subject and allows it to gather something in, to refine itself, make distinctions, and form. Žižek (2005) captures the mediating role of the neighbour and yet the essential nature of the Thing here, arguing that 'if there is no neighbour to whom I can relate as a human partner, the symbolic Order itself turns into the monstrous Thing which directly parasitizes upon me'; on the other hand, without the Thing, 'we find ourselves in a Habermasian "flat", aseptic universe in which subjects are deprived of their hubris of excessive passion, reduced to lifeless pawns in the regulated game of communication' (p.144). Liveliness, that is, depends on the Thing, however disturbing it is and however much mediation by human presence is required to make it tolerable. What is captured here is the sense of dependence on the neighbour in the process of social subjectification out of which the subject emerges, and the accompanying inbuilt feeling that there is always something else at play, a little piece of the real that cannot be accommodated but still has its effect. Laplanche's (1999) 'enigmatic signifier' again comes to mind, despite the significant differences between his developmental approach and the stance taken by the Lacanians.

The negativity of the other – its horror-inducing, Thing-like status – counterbalances the vulnerability of the other that is emphasised in Butler's account, with her concern for the precariousness of contemporary life and her valorisation of the areas of opacity in both subject and other. Žižek acknowledges Butler's move, but disputes what he calls the 'solidarity of the vulnerable' (p.139) opened up by Butler's insistence on human 'weakness'. In contrast, Žižek proposes two things. The first stresses a kind of radical capacity to take responsibility, a 'negativity of freedom' inherent in the agentic ability of the subject to refuse the blandishments and coercions of the symbolic order. This is no liberal fantasy: Žižek is well aware of the power of the social order, but he holds out for a space in which the subject can nevertheless stage a refusal, find a way to say 'No!':

> This negativity of freedom provides the zero-level from which every positive content can be questioned. Lacan's position is thus that being exposed/overwhelmed, caught in a cobweb of preexisting conditions, is *not* incompatible with radical autonomy. Of course, I cannot undo the substantial weight of the context into which I am thrown; of course, I cannot penetrate the opaque background of my being; but what I can do is, in an act of negativity, 'cleanse the plate,' draw a line, exempt myself, step out of the symbolic in a 'suicidal' gesture of a radical act – what Freud called 'death drive' and what German Idealism called 'radical negativity'. (p.140)

This negativity should not be mistaken for passivity, even though one criticism of Žižek's position is that it promotes a political indifference that does not, as is claimed, have radical effects, but is simply a way of disengaging from struggle. However, here Žižek is proposing that the subject does have access to a way of being that steps out of the constraints of the symbolic – a position perhaps akin to that articulated many years ago in Deleuze and Guattari's (1977) *Anti-Oedipus*, where the 'deterritorialisation' embodied in schizophrenia is taken as a model for revolutionary action. But Žižek offers what might be thought of as an ironic twist here. Foregrounding the Thing in the neighbour, Žižek argues that an ethical act – 'ethical violence' – *breaks up* the encounter with the other by introducing the realm of the third, the very structure of the symbolic order, of sociality:

> In order to render our coexistence with the Thing minimally bearable, the symbolic order qua Third, the pacifying mediator, has to intervene: the 'gentrification' of the Other-Thing into a 'normal human fellow' cannot occur through our direct interaction, but presupposes the third agency to which we both submit ourselves – there is no intersubjectivity (no symmetrical, shared relation between humans) without the impersonal symbolic Order. (pp.143–4)

The opacity of the neighbour, in Žižek's view, is not something to be 'gentrified' and romanticised; it is the arena of threat and horror, and the point of a social ethics is lost if one engages in the 'reduction of the radically ambiguous monstrosity of the Neighbor-Thing into an Other as the abyssal point from which the call of ethical responsibility emanates' (p.163). Recognising the other through the Levinasian dynamic adopted by Butler consequently ameliorates something that has to be kept alive in its forceful destructiveness. A true ethics will be one that breaks into this and usurps it with a commitment to an objective – hence genuinely 'ethical' – justice.

Žižek is here making a crucial distinction between love and justice. The former does indeed separate out the one from the mass: love is an act of choosing, of preferring, of specifying an other who the subject will recognise. Levinas, whose theory is based on this kind of recognition, consequently has problems with the 'Third': what does one do when a third appears on the scene, how does one distribute one's attention, one's recognition and singling-out? For Žižek, the Third is always there, not as a kind of space of encounter as in Benjamin's model, but as an impersonal, inhuman force that acts against preference and is consequently the bearer of justice. The Third is primary (even developmentally so, for Žižek, in that 'the first relationship to an Other is that to a faceless Third' – p.184) and regulates the encounter of subject and other. It is 'a positive condition of ethics' precisely because it does not reduce to understanding, but rather insists on the always-present otherness that provides the backdrop to any loving selectiveness that might occur, that in being selective and preferential is always *un*just. 'In contrast to love,' writes Žižek, 'justice begins when I remember the faceless many left in shadow in this privileging of the One. Justice and love are thus structurally incompatible: justice, not love, has to be blind; it must disregard the privileged One whom I "really understand"' (p.182). If ethics is about truth, then this kind of understanding has to be relinquished, an act which is always a mode of violence.

> This brings us to the radical anti-Levinasian conclusion: the true ethical step is the one *beyond* the face of the other, the one of *suspending* the hold of the face, the one of choosing *against* the face, for the *third*. This coldness is justice at its most elementary... Every preempting of the Other in the guise of his or her face relegates the Third to the faceless background. And the elementary gesture of justice is not to show respect for the face in front of me, to be open to its depth, but to abstract from it and refocus onto the faceless Thirds in the background. (p.183)

This, finally, constitutes a kind of psychoanalytic critique of intersubjectivity, and hence a disputation with those who also talk of the Third, but make it a space for recognition and understanding. For Žižek, the lesson of the Third is precisely that there is no space in which such understanding or communication occurs; rather, the ethical stance is to resist understanding but nevertheless stay alongside the other in so doing. Psychoanalysis here is used in an 'anti-humanist' way to puncture the argument that relationality is primary and that ethics should be based on countering the violence of subject-formation with the non-violence of recognition of the subjectivity of the other. In Žižek's formulation, what psychoanalysis shows is rather the way in which something outside subjectivity and intersubjectivity is always primary: a faceless Third that must of necessity be given priority if justice is to prevail.

But can psychoanalysis, which has its origin in an intersubjective, personal encounter in the clinic, sustain itself in a vision of 'coldness', of ethical violence? There is perhaps a lesson here in what happens when Žižek turns to an image of the consulting room to bolster his thinking about how psychoanalysis might model this anti-humanist turn. Warning against the reduction of psychoanalysis to therapy and human relatedness, he nevertheless gets drawn into a way of speaking that emphasises linkage and a kind of alternative mode of human warmth. The starting point is the Levinasian 'face', which, Žižek argues, is definitely not the subject of psychoanalytic intervention:

> We can clearly see, now, how far psychoanalysis is from any defence of the dignity of the human face. Is the psychoanalytic treatment not the experience of rendering public (to the analyst, who stands for the big Other) one's most intimate fantasies and thus the experience of losing one's face in the most

> radical sense of the term? This is already the lesson of the very material dispositif of the psychoanalytic treatment: no face-to-face between the subject-patient and the analyst; instead, the subject lying and the analyst sitting behind him, both staring into the same void in front of them. There is no 'intersubjectivity' here, only the two without face-to-face, the First and the Third. (p.148)

Ironically, perhaps, this image of the analyst and the analysand 'staring into the same void' does not seem so different from Butler's idea about the ethical significance of shared opacity, nor indeed of the Levinasian 'elemental' evoked by Lingis (1994) as 'the alien elements into which we stray' (p.122). There always seems to be some wish for a kind of shelter in the presence of the other, even amongst those most opposed to the humanistic emphasis on the meaning-producing individual subject. Perhaps the ethical pull here will always be compromised when psychoanalysis is brought into play: the contract between analyst and subject may well be to 'analyse', not cure, but something happens between them, something that locates itself in a relationship which always feels 'personal' and specific and consequently caring and 'unjust'; and revealing its unjustness and ethical ambiguity does not always succeed in wishing it away.

Conclusion

This chapter has explored the way some theorists of what is here called 'relational ethics' have drawn on psychoanalysis to secure and advance their claims. A good deal of the debate revolves around the question of recognition. Derived separately from psychoanalytic theory and from philosophy, recognition gives voice to the aspiration for ways of acknowledging others as subjects with whom one might be able to forge reciprocal relationships. For some writers, this form of full recognition is possible, at least in theory. For others, it is a misleading aspiration, caught up in an imaginary fantasy of completeness that is belied by the existence of the unconscious. Psychoanalysis has also been used to supply a grounded, developmental dimension for some more abstract philosophies of otherness, and to offer a critical understanding of 'thirdness' as that which stands outside the subject–other couple. The more 'optimistic', relational theories read this thirdness as offering an opportunity for meeting and reconciliation; the more structural, Lacanian approaches use it as a way of promoting the concerns of 'justice' over those of 'love'. In each case, the thrust is to deploy psychoanalysis in ways that will clarify thinking on ethical relationality, using its familiarity with intersubjective encounters as a legitimation for believing it has something to say about all subject–other relations.

The quality of much of the work described here is very impressive, and shows the potential for deepening philosophical enquiry in this area by drawing on psychoanalytic concepts and experiences. It also provisionally opens up psychoanalysis itself, for instance by placing questions of thirdness in the context of their ethical implications. In this regard, it is interesting to note how there always seems to be some kind of pull back into relationality whenever one draws on the psychoanalytic clinic as a model, however hard one might struggle against this. Whether this is 'good' or 'bad' seems hardly to be the point; rather, it reveals how psychoanalysis' own ethical grounding is crucial. It functions as a kind of anchor for social debate in which the complex layering of subjectivity is highlighted and revolved. This has a certain kind of austerity embedded in it, as psychoanalysis at its best insists on never looking away from what it confronts; but it also continually reinserts an investment in the significance of subjects into what could otherwise become a more abstract theorisation of social processes. It is a kind of high waterline for contemporary scholarship, insisting that the complex affective and fantasy dimensions of subjectivity should always be included, offsetting the abstractly philosophical tendencies of much social theory.

Chapter 6

The Radical Politics of Psychoanalysis

It will be clear from the previous chapter that applied psychoanalysis is often implicated in politics. To some extent this follows automatically from its adoption of an ethical stance on the conditions necessary for people to lead a good life, something which many writers see as essential to the psychoanalytic outlook (e.g. Lear, 2005). If one is to pronounce on this – if, for example, one is to do as Freud did and criticise standards of sexual morality (e.g. Freud, 1908b) – then this is bound to represent an intervention in a political field, even if one is suspicious of politics, as Freud himself was. A clear separation of psychoanalysis and politics is thus never easy to sustain; psychoanalysis is a 'moral' discipline and this always involves making some kind of commentary on social life.

This indirect involvement of psychoanalysis with politics is complemented by a tradition of direct application that has many sources. There is a rather rich seam of work on the politics *of* psychoanalysis, which includes infighting between its various schools as well as investigations of the sometimes dark history of psychoanalysis' collusion with oppressive regimes (e.g. Frosh, 2005). As noted in Chapter 1, this reveals the difficulty psychoanalysis, like other critical disciplines, has had in maintaining itself as a socially progressive practice. However, there are also many examples of ways in which psychoanalysis has been used as an instrument to advance progressive politics by supplying a theory of the social subject that is compatible with radical critique. This theory has various attributes, depending on how it is drawn upon. Some writers have been interested in what psychoanalysis has to say about 'mass psychology', understood as a form of social psychology that reveals patterns of irrationality and desire that fuel many societal occurrences. Others have focused on the apparent mismatch between 'objective' social conditions and the feelings and beliefs of subjects, which is really to say that psychoanalysis is being looked to in order to flesh out a theory of ideology. Still others have drawn on psychoanalysis as a contributor to a grand theory of the social and political sphere, seeing in some of its ideas (for example, envy, phantasy, narcissism, the lacking subject) concepts that offer leverage for accounts of contemporary society. In each case, psychoanalysis' understanding of subjectivity, fuelled by its clinical work, is being extended to provide material for broad political analysis. In each case again, this extension sometimes seems legitimate, and sometimes seems to push logic almost to breaking point. This chapter takes up some of these claims and considerations, asking about the status of these applications of psychoanalysis, both in terms of their contribution to political theory and their impact on psychoanalysis itself.

Psychic colonialism and political parallels

Psychoanalysis has been engaged with what might be broadly thought of as 'the political' from early on in its formation as a discipline. Freud's paper, *'Civilized' Sexual Morality and Modern Nervous Illness* (1908b), can be understood as an intervention in the social and political mores of his time, with its argument that neurosis is in large part caused by the hypocritical relations governing sexuality in the Europe of the early twentieth century. The memoirs of writers such as Stefan Zweig (1943) attest both to this hypocrisy and to the impact of Freudian thought in freeing sexuality, though perhaps it could be equally well argued that Freudianism itself was a *symptom* rather than cause of the rebellion against this particular mode of repression. Zweig (1943), looking back on the European 'world of yesterday' at the end of the 1930s, notes about the period 40 years earlier: 'It is quite possible that there is no sphere of public life in which a series of factors – the emancipation of women, Freudian psycho-analysis, physical culture, the independence of youth – have brought about so complete a change within one generation as in the relation between the sexes' (p.61). It may actually have been the First World War rather than psychoanalysis that exposed the deathliness of the morality of deference in so compelling a way that these previously repressive norms were bound to be swept away, as they were – temporarily at least. Freud's own political position was at best liberal (he was suspicious of socialism, despite having sympathy for the argument that economic and political equality should be sought) and in many ways conservative, with a liking for order. In line with many other social thinkers, he assumed that the drives and desires of the individual always need constraining by society. As has been described elsewhere (Frosh, 1999), this theory that society is ineluctably opposed to individuality is one of the most pessimistic strands of thought associated with the bourgeois era. For Freud, knowledge of the unconscious did not lead to a celebration of its disruptive actions. The aims of psychoanalysis as a therapy would always be to channel what was formless and dangerous into social usefulness, converting 'id' into 'ego' in the famous words of his 1933 *New Introductory Lectures*, as 'a work of culture – not unlike the draining of the Zuider Zee' (p.79). The point here is that culture consists in making the unconscious passions of the individual into works of social value, and this involves 'draining' them, channelling them into good use; in this way, sublimation is made into the organising principle of sociality. That this is a conservative view is clear: social organisation is not only essential but is also inherently constraining; human society could not survive if the terrors of unconscious life were let loose unregulated, and there is consequently no hope for a perfectly utopian future world in which everyone will be libidinally satisfied. Such politically revolutionary ideas, for Freud (1930), were 'consolations' (p.145), similar in function to the illusions and wish-fulfilments that underlie religion.

However, as with much else in Freudian thought, the social theory explicitly promulgated by Freud in works such as *Totem and Taboo* and *Civilization and its Discontents* may be less productive and interesting than his apparently more technical, 'psychological' model of the mind. This is not to overlook the fecundity of the social texts: in each case, Freud's grand and provocative 'sociological' readings have given rise to an extensive literature, much of it critical but also deeply engaged with the question of the relationship between individual desire and human sociality. Yet the most compelling of these engagements are those which address Freud's conceptualisations not so much on the level of his discussions of how society works, but rather through the lens of his account of 'metapsychology'. This refers to his theory of mental structures and mechanisms and the way they construct subjecthood in the warp and weft of drives and relationality. To give just one recent example, Jacqueline Rose's (2007) introduction to Freud's writing on the 'mass' is a meditation on what can be learnt from 'social' texts such as *Moses and Monotheism* and *Mass Psychology and Analysis of the 'I'* (the version of the title used in the translation to which Rose's piece is an introduction), and involves a subtle illumination of how 'mass formations' operate in relation to its subjects. Rose deploys Freud's understanding of society as a kind of necessary evil, marking out the function of mass formation as 'one of the most effective systems a culture creates to keep its subjects sane', and arguing that particularly in the case of religion, this is done by 'deluding them with the false consolations of belief' (p.69). She points out, again with Freud, that the psychology of the mass reveals what humans might be like in the absence of social constraint. This both underlines the need for the protection that society offers, and also shows up the crudeness with which it fulfils its task, producing unnecessary suffering along the way.

> Ugly, the mass lifts the veil of the night, releasing humans from cultural constraint – in the mass, man is allowed to do what no individual would dare. At moments, it is as if the mass *becomes* the unconscious – without logic, knowing 'neither doubt nor uncertainty', living a type of collective dream. Freud may be repelled, he may be frightened ... but he has also made man in the mass the repository of a universal truth: that human subjects suffer under the weight of repressive cultural imperatives that force them against their nature. (p.65)

This is, exactly, the Freudian mode of social analysis, yet what has to be observed here is that apart from explaining that society or 'culture' is repressive, little is said about the structure of society itself. That is, as a 'psychosocial' approach, Freudian theory remains very much on the 'psycho' rather than the 'social' level. There is nothing, for example, stated directly about class, race or gender, to use (in some ways anachronistically) some of the major axes around which sociological and political analysis is constructed. Nor is there anything about 'interests' in the way familiar from much political theory. However, what we do get is a means of understanding the *irrationality* of the social in a form that owes a great deal to the general psychoanalytic understanding of unconscious irrationality, and which is novel in relation to most political approaches. As Rose notes, 'it is as if the mass *becomes* the unconscious', as if, that is, the processes well understood by psychoanalysis as operating in the mind can also be observed – metaphorically or actually – in the workings of the social world. At the heart of this is Freud's insistence on *conflict*: not just the evident one between the individual and society, but the internal conflict that becomes the driver of irrationality in the public sphere. Rose (2007) articulates this in relation to the construction of the individual subject through its encounters with alterity, which is a modern rendering of Freud's understanding of the formation of the ego and the superego through the internalisation of objects and their values. The context for this is given by Freud's post-First World War examination of the sources of destruction, an examination which led to the reformulation of drive theory to include a 'death drive', and which is at one and the same time an account of what drives people to war with others and of what leaves them at war with themselves:

> From *Mass Psychology* to *Moses the Man*, all Freud's writings on collective life share a question. What drives people to hatred? ... As if Freud had made two utterly interdependent discoveries, that also threaten to cancel or wipe each other out, taking the whole world with them. No man is an island: you are the others who you are. But the mind is also its own worst enemy; and there is no link between individuals, no collective identity, which does not lead to war. (p.63)

'Ambivalence' is one way of conceptualising this, 'the cruel ambivalence lurking within our most cherished forms of allegiance' (p.68), but as will be seen there are other ways too, including those that focus more on 'lack' than on conflict, and those that use psychoanalytic formulations to elaborate a vision of social life in which modes of excess and 'enjoyment' are of central significance.

Amongst the various lines of division here, one that stands out is a comparison between those approaches – loosely speaking, Lacanian and post-Lacanian – that focus on the drive or drive-like components of unconscious life, and those that are object-relational in their primary orientation. Despite her unusually strong grasp of Lacanian thought, Rose emphasises the *relationality* inherent in Freud's work, stressing how certain readings of Freud produce a model that makes others the foundation of what is experienced as the 'self', 'ego' or 'identity'. This means that the personae of each subject's social world are always 'in here' as much as they are 'out there'. Society itself is therefore foundational for what is taken to be individual, removing any meaningful distinction between these two classically opposed categories:

> We only exist through the others who make up the storehouse of the mind: models in our first tentative steps towards identity, objects of our desires, helpers and foes. The mind is a palimpsest in which the traces of these figures will jostle and rearrange themselves for evermore. From the earliest moment of our lives – since without the rudiments of contact, the infant will not survive – we are 'peopled' by others. Our 'psyche' is a social space. (p.62)

Identification is a key mechanism here – at its most active, a process of 'devouring' the other in order to become them, to appropriate them for use by the self. The subject is thus built up as a kind of colonialist project, taking in the others upon which its identity and personal economy is to be based, and then denying or repressing the original source of these riches. This denial is always of necessity specious, because it hides the interdependency upon which all psychic life, not just its overtly social formation, is based. Interestingly, this colonial model can also be read the other way around: not so much the subject as coloniser, but as colonised, as the unknowing, subjugated recipient of the intrusions or 'messages' (as Laplanche [1999] names them) of the other. By a further turn of the screw, the subject believes itself to be an active conqueror of the domain of otherness, consuming its gifts in order to strengthen itself; but it is also at the mercy of the other, dependent on it, unconsciously infiltrated and knocked off course by it, tied to it by processes of desire and need, yet always fighting against this awareness. As mentioned in the previous chapter, Butler (2005) describes this as follows: 'If the other is always there, from the start, in the place of where the ego will be, then a life is constituted through a fundamental interruption, is even *interrupted prior to the possibility of any continuity*' (p.52). Perhaps as a metaphor of colonial and now postcolonial states (of mind as well as of politics), this is as precise as it can be.

Rose (2003, 2005, 2007) uses this understanding of the politics implicit in the psyche as a way into discussing significant issues surrounding oppression and ideology, most notably through explorations of South African literature and examination of what might be termed 'counter-currents' within Zionism. In the latter case in particular, she is interested in ways in which Zionism acts as a fragile container for social identities, and how as an 'excessive' set of beliefs and practices – originally seen as a form of insanity by many of its Jewish critics – it both mobilises aspirations and enthusiasms and creates pressures that have potentially damaging consequences. Rose (2005) notes the contemporaneity of the rise of modern Zionism and the foundation of psychoanalysis, and comments:

> Precisely because Zionism had to make itself out of nothing – create a unity, a language, a homeland where there was none before – it knows itself as a child of the psyche, a dream, a figment of the brain ... he who enters here plumbs the depths of the political mind. This makes Zionism, for better or worse, the most wonderful exemplar of the work of the psyche in the constitution of the modern nation-state. (pp.67–8)

Zionism is a political force built out of dreams, and hence out of the elements of the unconscious that have evaded censorship, but that reflect conflictual, disturbing and dangerous wishes. This idea, that Zionism as a political force is expressive of, and inhabited by, unconscious desires that are parallel to, or *the same as*, those to be found in the psyche of the individual subject, allows Rose to explore different resonances of Zionism for some of its opposed progenitors. In particular she invokes those whose voices might be construed as resisting the development of Zionism as a narrowly nationalistic creed and political practice. These writers include Hannah Arendt, Martin Buber and Ahad Ha'am, all working from within Zionist thought but in a way that was countervailing to what became the dominant, aggressive form of Zionism characteristic of the Israeli state. What is rehearsed here, in Rose's reading, is an opposition between different forms of psychoanalysis. The mainstream is paralleled to ego psychology, that classical approach which dominated particularly in America from the 1950s onwards and is centred on promoting conscious control over unconscious urges and adaptation of the subject to the demands of the social world. This notion is one towards which most radical critics have been hostile (see Frosh, 1999), and here too it is the derogated position, despite being recognisably the way in which much of the world works. Politics, read through this lens, is a process of management whereby what is slippery, subversive and counter-intuitive is converted into something solid, orderly and normative. As in the example of Zionism, priority is given to the security and sovereignty of the nation-state as a homogenous element that stands firm against the internal and external forces threatening to fragment it. As a model of psychic life, this kind of psychoanalysis has a strong affiliation to an image of mental health as rationality, in which managing the unconscious – turning id into ego in the most concrete reading of that formula – is the primary aim. As politics, this is an account of identity as forged through the repudiation of doubts and visions, through the loss of dreams, and, most importantly, through the sloughing-off of alternatives. Rose (2005) identifies Weizmann as a proponent of 'normality' for the Jews in this way, and Buber as one of its critics: 'The ego, like the normal nation, carves out its identity. Buber quite explicitly makes the link: "The typical individual for our times," he wrote in his 1939 lecture "The Spirit of Israel and the World of Today," "holds fast to *his expanded ego, his nation.*" ... The nation should not be normal' (p.74).

The opposed strand to ego psychology within psychoanalysis has taken a number of forms, including most voraciously Lacanianism with its antagonism towards the idea of the 'norm' and of the integrated ego as the measure of mental health. The end point of Lacanian analysis is, amongst other things, a moment of stepping aside from the place of knowledge, in which fantasies of perfect integrity and wholeness give way to an awareness and enjoyment of the fissures of non-knowledge, of 'lack' – a point which will be discussed in more detail below. But it is not only Lacanianism that promotes this kind of 'openness' against the 'closures' of the hermetic system of ego dominance. Relational psychoanalysis, with its interest in how the 'other' is embedded in the 'self', also challenges the idea that any subject can be truly 'individual'. The presence of otherness within the subject creates an experience of contingency, of uncertainty and untranslatability (to use a notion from Laplanche) that contradicts claims for homogeneity and rational self-government. The political analogy is taken up by Rose (2005) in several ways, first using material from Hans Kohn:

> For a brief moment, Zionism had the chance of molding a nation that would be not an 'expanded ego' but something else. At the opening of his essay 'Nationalism', Kohn describes how 'shifts of consciousness' are always

> accompanied by 'deep shocks,' creating a time of 'disquiet, tension, isolation, dissociation'; such processes are 'obscure,' 'ambivalent,' 'uncertain.' He could be describing glimpses of the unconscious, those moments – dreams, slips, symptoms – when the unconscious is allowed to steal past the wires, past the defences of the conscious mind, and makes its presence felt. Precisely because of the tragic peculiarity of Jewish history, because Jews have indeed in some sense been lost to the world ... Zionism, as a unique national movement, had the opportunity to forge a model of nationhood, neither belligerently nor preemptively, but ambivalent, uncertain, obscure, something closer to this disquieting and transformative space. But did not take it. (p.86)

The parallel between psychodynamic processes and the political, nationalist movement of Zionism in this is very striking – indeed, is part of Rose's point when she calls this chapter of her book 'Zionism as Psychoanalysis'. Towards the end of the passage above, Rose precisely compares the two modes of management of the unconscious: 'belligerent and pre-emptive' versus 'ambivalent, uncertain, obscure' – but she does so as modes of understanding Zionism rather than as ways of formulating mental processes. Similarly, she goes on to examine Ahad Ha'Am's writing on 'hypnotic agency', whereby the internalised voices of the past (specifically, biblical voices) ventriloquise the present, so that personal and national identity are understood as always part of someone and something else. 'I like to think', she writes (p.100), 'that Ahad Ha'Am is calling on his forebears to soften or modulate their voice (rather like psychoanalysis aiming to reduce the ferocity of the superego in the mind of the child).' Once again, the paralleling between psychoanalytic and political instances is direct and concrete – in this mode of thought, they are the same thing.

Resistance

There are a set of issues here about the legitimacy with which psychoanalytic categories can be made into political ones. Can a movement like Zionism be understood as the expression of a people's unspoken desires in the way that a person's speech and actions can be understood as an expression of unconscious wishes and conflicts? Is it intellectually viable to bring these together, or should we simply understand the use of psychoanalytic categories here as metaphoric? When a writer as subtle as Rose uses psychoanalysis like this, is she seeking to deploy psychoanalytic ideas in an explanatory way, or as a kind of literary device to open out thinking? Is it a mode of speculative, even poetic, elaboration that is itself a 'disquieting and transformative space' rather than a way of fixing our political understanding? It is obvious that there is a risk here of reading Zionism as a kind of psychic activity close to madness, and neglecting its historical, political, economic and military levels of specific operation; but the gain of introducing the 'irrational' and also the fragmentary, alternative wishes of those involved in the movement might still be worth the candle. Some of this comes into the light still further in relation to another component of political thought in psychoanalysis, of great interest to Rose as well as to others, that of *resistance*. This term has the striking characteristic of referring to a political activity and a psychodynamic one that have the same name, yet in important respects describe opposed practices.

Resistance is a prime category of political thought, and of common political parlance. As 'resistance movements' it has a basically good press, though tainted and made more complex by the label of 'terrorism'. Its key resonance is as a force opposed to a greater force, a liberatory activity set against an oppressive structure – resistance stands firm, as power assaults it. In this sense, resistance is what the *healthy* subject does, refusing to be cowed. Of course, the imagery has to be more complex here: governments resist the will of the people, and so on; but it seems fair to argue that the main thrust of the representation of political resistance is that it comes *from* the people against those who would take away their liberties. As referenced in the immensely influential writings of Michel Foucault, however, the picture is more complicated, and makes of resistance not a single oppositional force to the implementation of unwanted power, but rather as power's symbiotic twin. Each goes along with the other, and as the one (power) is always present in all interactions, so the other (resistance) is equally ubiquitous. Resistance here can be read as a *plurality*, in which power operates in and through subjects, so resistance also occurs as an essential element in the field of force. Foucault (1976) famously presents it as follows, in his *History of Sexuality* – itself a key text for critical (oppositional/resistive) appraisals of psychoanalysis. Asserting the 'strictly relational character of power relationships,' he writes:

> Their existence depends on a multiplicity of points of resistance: these play the role of adversary, target, support, or handle in power relations. These points of resistance are present everywhere in the power network … Are there no great radical ruptures, massive binary divisions, then? Occasionally, yes. But more often one is dealing with mobile and transitory points of resistance, producing cleavages in a society that shift about, fracturing unities and effecting regroupings, furrowing across individuals themselves, cutting them up and remolding them, marking off irreducible regions in them, in their bodies and minds. (pp.95–6)

Despite the radical difference between this model and that familiar from psychoanalysis, which deals with resistance as a mode of psychic activity, the fluidity and omnipresence of resistance is starting to feel familiar. In some ways it sounds like the model of ordinary developmental attunement that can be derived from Winnicott's (1969) idea that what establishes the reality of the world is its capacity to resist – to survive, that is – the attacks of the subject upon it. As noted in the previous chapter, Winnicott's notion here is that the reality and 'usefulness' of the object is established when the object resists the infant's destructive impulses, when, that is, it shows it has a life and solidity of its own, outside the infant's fantasies. The infant may, in fantasy, destroy the mother, but in fact she survives. In the current context, the resistive power of the other is what makes the subject's existence possible, marking out a space which is 'real' in the sense of being beyond the subject's control. This continuous process of assertion and resistance is what constitutes the possibility of a stable kind of life.

There is more to it than this, of course: the Foucauldian reading of the power-resistance nexus has revolutionised understanding of these forces as they play out across the social and political terrain. Still, the psychoanalytic idea is lurking not far behind, itself functioning as a mode of 'resistance', or at least as a shadowy presence. Rose (2007), this time in the context of the relationship between Freud and Arnold Zweig as it responded to the rise of fascism, brings out some of the complexity of the intertwining of political and psychic resistance. Despite awareness of the contrast between these two forms of resistance, she sees them as in fruitful dialogue with each other, with the psychoanalytic reading trumping the political:

> If in political vocabularies, resistance is the passage to freedom, for psychoanalysis, it is repetition, blockage, blind obeisance to crushing internal constraint. For Zweig, only the overcoming of resistance in this psychoanalytic sense will allow the world to be saved. ... In this vocabulary, then, resistance is not the action of the freedom fighter, the struggle against tyranny, the first stirring of the oppressed; it is the mind at war with itself, blocking the path to its own freedom and, with it, its ability to make the world a better, less tyrannical, place. (p.21)

Resistance here is something to be overcome. Echoing Adorno et al.'s (1950) account in *The Authoritarian Personality*, Rose presents the fascist mind as full of resistance to freedom, to the terror produced by deep and truthful thought which does not back away from reality. Fascism is 'a carapace against what the mind should, ideally, be able to do with itself. Something shuts down, closes cruelly into its allotted and unmovable place' (ibid.). The task of psychoanalysis, therefore, is to break down such resistance, which is precisely *not* fluid; rather, it is specifically, rigidly *defensive*, closing off possibilities. It lacks the sense of mobility and cunning to be found in Foucault's evocation of political resistance, it creates walls, not tunnels.

Nevertheless, as with all political as well as psychological barriers, the construction of defences shows where something valuable is being kept; so resistance is both an obstacle to change and an indication of where change is most needed. Rose notes how for Freud, resistance became the key to analytic progress: spot the area of resistance and one knows what is most defended against, and hence not only what is most threatening, but also what is most significant in a person's psychic life. The hiding place of repressed material is given away by what happens in analysis, by how the patient goes quiet at certain points, denies the significance of things she or he does, refuses to accept the analyst's interpretations, or messes around with the analytic boundaries (for example by missing or appearing late to sessions). In particular, resistance denotes the patient's ambivalence, whereby she or he might be genuinely seeking therapeutic help, yet might also be undermining attempts to achieve insight into the unconscious source or meaning of the symptoms which have been causing trouble – hence subverting the therapeutic process. Sometimes even the act of apparently seeking help is a way of resisting it. Going to therapy means one has tried one's best to change, even if nothing actually happens. Resistance, therefore, has general significance as a way of indicating how a person might want something but not want it at the same time.

The politics of this psychoanalytic understanding of resistance are consequently complex and uncertain. On the one hand, resistance is what opposes life – it is the way in which subjects and 'masses' avoid having to come to terms with what they really want, that which they seek and at the same time fear. On the other hand, resistance reveals the existence of an unconscious wish that gives glimpses of a subject's desire, of that element of 'enjoyment' which the subject is defending against. Hence the continuing attraction of the most 'resisted' and loathed objects, for example, the racialised other, commonly both eroticised and despised (Frosh, 2006). Resistance here does begin to look Foucauldian in its protean nature, but also ambiguous in its multiple meanings: both necessary signal of conflict and force to be overcome, both resistance 'to' and resistance 'of', both impulse towards death and towards life. This grafting of the psychoanalytic understanding of the dynamics of resistance onto theorising of *political* resistance certainly deepens both concepts, but at the same time it calls for careful distinctions to be made, between types of resistance and also between the different functions that resistance might have. In particular, whilst the psychoanalytic notion well conveys the dynamic tension in resistance, the way in which it is always soaked in ambivalence and hence can never be taken at face value (so resisting something might also imply desiring it), it nevertheless is more restricted than the political model. It does not really encompass the idea of resistance as a positive liberatory force – as something seeking political freedom and emancipation from oppression. In the end, in psychoanalysis resistance is always something to be overcome if the subject is to be freer than before, more able to express and live with her or his wishes; in politics, one might hope, at least from time to time, that resistance might triumph.

This limitation on the efficacy of psychoanalytic notions of resistance for politics does not, however, mean that there is no gain from engaging with the subtleties of understanding of ambivalence and conflict that these notions contain. Perhaps this reveals itself most powerfully when it comes to questions of 'resistance to change', which act both at the level of the individual subject and of masses and even nations. If one desires the thing one resists, it may be hard to overthrow it completely. In relation to this, Freud himself, as his thinking developed, was led to differentiate between a number of different types, or at least sources, of resistance – a differentiation which has remained influential amongst analysts (see Sandler, Dare and Holder, 1973). These different types include resistances of the ego and of the id, and also those due to 'secondary gain', but the most interesting for political purposes is perhaps that arising from the operation of the superego, the 'part' of the mind in which guilt is held, and which is constantly appealing for punishment. This is a source of one weird reality of psychoanalytic progress: patients can come seeking help, but then reject it when it is offered, because they do not feel they deserve it. For Rose (2007), this type of resistance is the most important one for political analysis, the most 'deadly, because it arises out of the pleasure the mind takes in thwarting itself ... Freud is talking about the superego – the exacting, ruthless and punishing instance of the mind through which the law exerts its pressure on the psyche' (p.31). That is, this kind of resistance is the one which is most embedded in the subject, the one which arises not only out of a fear of change, but also out of the sheer *pleasure* of resistance itself, the enjoyment that comes out of the investment of psychic energy – '*jouissance*' – in destroying the opportunities for progress. Increasingly, this idea has been imported into political thinking to explain why it is that so much, so consistently, goes wrong.

Subjective politics and social repression

The terrorising of the psyche by the superego is an issue that has long concentrated the minds of political thinkers drawing on psychoanalysis, as it offers some kind of an account of the widespread resistance to change and of people's investment in staying in 'punishing' situations – those it might seem obvious that they should escape from. From the emergence of political psychoanalysis after the First World War, when the conditions for revolution in Europe were apparently ripe and when steps were indeed taken towards this – in Germany, most of all – yet when reaction set in quickly and fascism rather than revolutionary socialism emerged, the question of why people are 'chained to their chains' has been thought of as a potentially psychopolitical question. Simply, it seems that people somehow embrace conditions under which they are oppressed, or at least fail to take up opportunities to resist them, and this inertia has always puzzled revolutionaries. This need not mean reducing it to a purely psychological phenomenon, a kind of neurotic fear of change to be addressed through psychiatric treatment, though there are elements of that view to be found in some writers. Rather, the question is how and why the repressive features of the existing bourgeois society come to be 'internalised' to such an extent that the subject believes in them, is emotionally invested in them, unconsciously committed to them, and hence self-sabotaging when it comes to the opportunity for release. This question forces an engagement with the political concept of ideology as something more than a superstructural consequence of economic processes.

There was a small pantheon of early Freudo-Marxists who took this question on, for example the members of the 'Children's Seminar' run in the Berlin Psychoanalytic Institute by Otto Fenichel for the purpose of studying relations between psychoanalysis and politics (Jacoby, 1983). Amongst these, the excessive figure of Wilhelm Reich has come down to later generations as the embodiment of a politically daring thinker, part revolutionary icon, part tragic figure of persecution, part madman. As has been rehearsed in many places, Reich's (literally) energetic account of psychopolitics holds tremendous attractions as an early riposte to linear reductionist thinking in which all psychic trials are understood as the straightforward, unmediated consequence of economic woes, to wither away once the economic structure of society is set aright. For Reich, there is an important intervening process in which the 'character' of the subject is installed as 'armour' through patterns of authoritarianism, operating particularly through the family, and this character holds in check and distorts the natural sexual ebullience of the free subject. *Sexual* revolution is thus as necessary as political revolution if anything is to significantly change. Reich thus articulates the modern notion that political structures enter into the core of individuality, constructing each person's consciousness and creating personality around ideological axes. In so doing, he delineates a broad concept of ideology as something that determines not just a person's perceptions, but her or his character. Thus, he moves rather close to the contemporary notion of ideology as a force that positions, or 'hails' (Althusser, 1971) subjects so that they experience themselves in the world in certain ways which are given by society but upon which they also have some capacity to act. Even though Reich still treats ideology as an error or distortion of reality, denying the individual expression of her or his basic and 'natural' desires, the manner in which he describes the insertion of ideology into this natural core is actually both subtle and helpful, particularly his account of the tendencies central to the patriarchal–authoritarian family.

As argued elsewhere (Frosh, 1999), it is the assertion that there is a fundamentally 'true' and healthy core within the human personality, which is only waiting to recover from the assaults of ideological distortion in order to find its proper expression, that is the major drawback to Reich's theories, at least to contemporary eyes. This idea is always problematic, not only because it implies an unchanging, biological 'human nature', but also because it reduces society's role to inhibiting or facilitating the expression of this natural impulse, rather than giving social forces a role in *constructing* 'human nature' in the first place. In Reich's case, it is sexual energy that is seen as the physically measurable natural driving force of the individual, to be liberated as part of a socialist revolution, thence to achieve satisfaction in ways that are no longer restricted or distorted by repressive authoritarianism. Such sexual essentialism (the irreducible core of humanity is biological sexuality) is always problematic for the attempt to create a genuinely 'Freudo-Marxist' theory that understands 'psychosocially' the merging of apparently individual and social forces. One can argue that even in his early works, where Reich avoids the simple reduction of politics to sexual liberation, it is clear that it is the latter which fascinates him, and which also prevents him from uncovering a path towards a genuinely socialist future. For whereas socialism is concerned with the possibilities of enriched relationships between people that are more egalitarian and less oppressive and limited than those available under capitalism, Reich has virtually nothing to say about relationships as such. His utopia is not concerned with a more developed network of social relationships; rather, it is libertarian in the individualistic sense, a system under which each individual's biological urges are to be played out in complete freedom. This form of politics returns to the individual rather than to the transformation of social structures. Consequently, and whatever the intent, politics is reduced to biology just as mental life is reduced to attempts to achieve orgasm, and society and sex are opposed to one another rather than theorised in their complex interrelations.

Reich's provocative yet problematic theory has acted as a partial springboard for many discussions of psychoanalytic politics. These tend to go on to debate the contribution of Marcuse (1955) and the Frankfurt School in elaborating a more sophisticated model that develops further the idea that society enters the psyche as sedimented orthodoxy, as a mode of 'second nature' that represents itself as truth in order to manage or repress the actual desires of the subject. Key elements in Marcuse's argument (see Frosh, 1999, for a detailed account) include his deployment of a distinction between 'basic' and 'surplus' repression, in which the former is what is required for any social polity to exist – and hence is really an alternative conceptualisation of sublimation, of how basic human drives get converted into usable social energy – and the latter is the intensification of repression by the hierarchical distribution of scarcity and labour. The addition of the concept of surplus repression makes repression a specifically historical notion and one which depends on the organisation of any particular society. The necessity of repression varies with the maturity of civilisation, at least in terms of the extent of achieved mastery over nature through technology; given a constant level of repression, more will be 'surplus' in a culture of plenty than in one of scarcity. Under the conditions of late modernity, the potential for release given by technological advances is counteracted by the creation of an 'administered society' in which repression is sustained through the management of pleasure itself. Repression is therefore not a one-off phenomenon but rather (in a move reminiscent of Foucault's rethinking of the operations of power) creates its own modes of subjectivity. That is, the administered society *manages* pleasure rather than simply places restrictions upon it – it creates certain ways of enjoying, leading its subjects to believe that their needs are being met.

The notion that society is in some way 'administered' to *provide* enjoyment as a way to contain it, is important for some contemporary thinking on how pleasure and lack go together, and on what this has to do with political processes. In both Reich and Marcuse, there is an image of a kind of fullness or 'too-muchness' of the drives that has to be managed in order for society to maintain itself. In the case of Marcuse (as in Freud), there is a level at which this is necessary for society to survive at all, whereas with Reich the issue is one of revolutionary transformation – a society purely of the drives is envisionable as the outcome of genuine sexual revolution. Commenting on Theodor Adorno's version of this, which also employs the idea of 'naturalised' drives to which the subject becomes submitted, Žižek (1994) identifies the paradox that arises. In this, repression is made both essential and oppressive, feeding into a kind of paralysis of psychoanalysis when faced with the question of political liberation:

> According to Adorno, this 'naturalistic' notion introduces into the Freudian edifice an irresolvable contradiction: on the one hand, the entire development of civilization is condemned, at least implicitly, for repressing drive-potentials in the service of social relations of domination and exploitation; on the other hand, repression as the renunciation of the satisfaction of drives is conceived as the necessary and insurmountable condition of the emergence of 'higher' human activities – that is to say, of culture. ... There is thus a radical and constitutive *indecision* which pertains to the fundamental intention of psychoanalytic theory and practice: it is split between the 'liberating' gesture of setting free repressed libidinal potential and the 'resigned conservatism' of accepting repression as the necessary price for the progress of civilization. (p.12)

The 'indecision' to which Žižek refers has indeed characterised the history of psychoanalysis' involvement with radical politics, revolving around the question of whether there is an ineradicable core of anti-social impulse within the individual which has to be managed – 'administered' – for society to survive. The distinction between repression and sublimation, which Žižek describes as being obscured in much theory, including that of the Frankfurt School, becomes important in making it possible to theorise a difference between a society that works solely to keep its subjects' urges in check by instituting an internal, repressive process, and one which allows expression of these urges in socially recognisable ways. The latter is more aligned with social reformist situations, and does two related but politically distinct things. On the one hand, it allows one to conceptualise rebellion as 'resistance' in the political sense, as a non-pathological articulation of wishes that has an impact on the social environment. With no distinction between repression and sublimation, every political act can be written off as motivated by unconscious wishes – after all, the main differentiation between a neurotic symptom and a supposedly healthy sublimation then lies only in the difference of response to, say, public masturbation and artistic expression or political grandstanding. If, however, there is a legitimate distinction between repression as a process that drives wishes 'underground', and a life-enhancing way of expressing these wishes, there is a way of conceptualising political resistance as something more than another form of pathogenic defence, and also a way of thinking about the prospects for change that does not have to adopt the attitude of 'resigned conservatism' described by Žižek above. On the other hand, resistance turned into sublimation is also a good description of much that occurs in the administered society. As this society becomes more complex, so it allows expressions of dissent which then get picked up and used in the service of the social order itself, thus averting radical change. The remarkable ability of late capitalism to deal with its critics by co-opting them is an excellent example of the workings of this kind of sublimation. For instance, the originally anarchic wildness and democratic ebullience of the world-wide web is now enjoyed more as a vehicle for entertainment and online shopping than as political critique.

Relationality and social conflict

The relational turn in psychoanalysis, drawn on previously for the discussion of ethics, has seeded some other useful developments in psychopolitical theorising. The British social context has seen some important thinking on social issues in the work of writers influenced by Kleinian psychoanalysis (e.g. Rustin, 1991), as well as some influential interventions by object relations and Jungian analysts promoting new models of emotional integrity in political contexts (e.g. Samuels, 1993). Internationally, the rise of intersubjectivist and relational psychoanalysis has been very important in the development of a politically committed psychoanalysis, both through the feminist-originated work of Jessica Benjamin, discussed in Chapter 5, and in the writings of a group of American psychoanalysts inspired by both the object-relations and the American relational tradition. The core idea worked on in rather different ways in these approaches is that psychological and political well-being both depend on relational conditions that promote rather than stunt growth. These conditions are seen as entwined with processes of recognition and affirmation that are crucial for the developing human subject, but that are systematically stymied by social inequalities and oppression. Lynne Layton (2008), for example, writing about the 'subject versus object' division argues, like Benjamin (1998), for the importance of being recognised as a subject rather than treated 'like an object'. The latter, she claims, is a description of what it is like to be embedded in social processes of exclusion and derogation.

> Each of us, if we are lucky, grows up with some predictable experiences of mutuality in relating. But each of us as well is vulnerable to the shaming assaults that arise from being treated as objects. One major source of these shaming assaults is cultural hierarchies of classism, racism, sexism, and heterosexism – the power structures that establish norms of recognition. Such hierarchies tend not only to idealize certain subject positions and

> devalue others, but also to do so by splitting human capacities and attributes and giving them class or race or sex or gender assignations. The culturally desirable attributes go to the dominant group; the ones the culture least rewards to the subordinate. Thus, social processes such as gendering, racing, classing, and sexing are at the very heart of subjectivity and subjective trauma, not accidental add-ons (as they are conceived to be in most psychoanalytic theories). (pp.66–7)

These social processes determine attitudes to dependency which in turn explain 'how cultural demands to split off capacities such as vulnerability, assertion, connection, dependence are lived both intrapsychically and interpersonally' (ibid.). That is, social processes produce certain kinds of subjects in particular through their openness or otherwise to dependency, something tied up intimately with the class–gender–race nexus into which subjects are socialised.

For Layton, relationality is forged in a psychic space divided between tendencies to maintain the splits induced by cultural hierarchies, and hence shaped by 'relational trauma' that 'divide the subject against itself', and 'those parts of self that have known and are able to seek out relationships based in mutual recognition of self and other as separate but interdependent subjects' (p.67). This kind of theorising, as Rustin (1995) has persuasively argued, is based on a 'positive' view of psychoanalysis in which the emphasis is on finding alternatives to, or ways out from, the constraints on human capacities wrought by oppressive social processes alongside (for the Kleinians at least) psychic impulses that are themselves destructive in form. Conflict and destructiveness are recognised as real and are not wished away, but the psychological and political momentum is towards identifying means to overcome them and to produce a more settled society, characterised by more fulfilling ('based in mutual recognition') relationships. Along the way, this involves identification of requirements for healthy psychic development and the kinds of social arrangements that might promote this. So, for example, Winnicott's (1960) ideas about the conditions under which 'false', conformist selves arise have been influential amongst relational psychoanalysts in adumbrating the conditions of early parenting that result in secure subjects attuned to the possibility of trust and relational interdependence. In the hands of some sociologists, this account of the necessary conditions for secure development also provides one basis for opposition to alienating and oppressive political systems.

Many of these ideas have been taken up credibly in social theory, for instance in the work of Axel Honneth, to produce a reformist account of social change. Honneth (e.g. Fraser and Honneth, 2003) examines social and political conflict as derived from a 'fundamental struggle for recognition that itself is the key to understanding the long-term development of social interaction in capitalist societies' (McNay, 2008, p.271). Drawing directly on object-relational and intersubjectivist psychoanalysis, Honneth suggests that healthy development is dependent on an accurate and sustaining experience of recognition from the parent, and that this developmental necessity can be writ large as a simple fact of human experience. The argument here is that 'the desire for recognition is so fundamental to individual self-realization that it is the motivating force behind social development' (McNay, 2008, p.273). 'Affective recognition', grounded in childhood experiences in the family, is thus the source for the kind of emotional stability and security of selfhood that is necessary for sustaining social life. It gives rise to 'legal' and 'status' recognition in a triad that, as it develops, produces new forms of human opportunity, but if blocked evidences distortions and constraints on freedom. In particular, claims for legal and status recognition can become the fuel for social struggle and collective resistance; that is, an essentially affective condition (the demand for recognition rather than, for example, for resources) leads to political activity.

Honneth's model of social conflict has stirred up a great deal of interest and debate, with the positioning of affect at the heart of sociality being one of its attractive elements (because it counters the hyper-rationalism of much social theory), as well as a source of contention. What is of interest here is the use it makes of psychoanalytic theory as an account of recognition that is then extended into a description of the foundations of the human subject and thence as a prescription for social progress. Winnicott and Benjamin in particular are drawn on to provide a theory of the subject based on the idea of mutual recognition, with the resilience of the object in the face of the subject's demands being one key trope upon which personality and consequently social stability are based. As previously noted, this has much face-value plausibility, and in particular it evidences the possibility of linking the intimacies of the supposedly personal sphere (the parent–child encounter, for instance) with the rationalities and irrationalities of social action. This link might explain the passion with which people struggle for fairness and equality, for recognition of themselves and for all the other elements that go into an 'identity politics'. However, there is also a considerable amount of criticism of Honneth's reliance on this psychoanalytic model, which says something about the problems of importing psychoanalytic developmental thinking into political and sociological theory. Some of this relates to the familiar danger of reducing the political to the psychological. For instance, in her critique of Honneth's model of recognition, Fraser (in Fraser and Honneth, 2003) argues that its psychological focus 'displaces' and 'reifies' economic and social concerns to make all politics a matter of identity struggle. Not only is this unhelpfully reductionist in neglecting the specificity of the political domain, but it also tends towards conservatism (despite Honneth's attention to a wide range of modes of resistance) because of the adaptational tinge to it in which survival and acknowledgement in a particular social environment become central to healthy citizenship. McNay (2008) summarises the strengths and limitations of Honneth's reliance on a psychoanalytic formulation of social identity most comprehensively in the following passage:

> There is no doubt that Honneth's phenomenology of social suffering emphasizes a crucial realm of catalyzing emotional experience that remains hidden in the rational and instrumental orientation of other sociological perspectives. The difficulty is that the unidirectional causal dynamic of his ontology of recognition, where social relations are seen as extrapolations of social dynamics, reifies these emotions and the realm of experience in general. The prepolitical realm of social suffering is seen as some unmediated realm of experience characterized by spontaneous and authentic feelings with inherent moral status. It is not evident, however, that all suffering leads to any kind of political insight or can be accorded such moral significance in the politics of experience and this is partly because all experience is mediated through a web of potentially distorting symbolic relations. (p.218)

Amongst the issues raised by McNay here is the differentiation implicit in Honneth's writing between a realm of politics and a 'prepolitical' realm of feelings, which in essence involves relational immediacy and a mode of genuineness that lays down markers for later authenticity. In many respects, this derives from his specific choice of psychoanalytic model. Winnicottian developmental thinking, built upon by later relational and intersubjectivist work, assumes the possibility of a kind of ideal state in which the mirroring of the child's needs by the mother is accurate. Within this theory, the child's aggressive, even destructive, assaults on the maternal object are survived with an appropriate amount of loving resilience to enable the child both to feel recognised for what she or he is, and to recognise the other/mother as a separate being with whom a relationship can be forged, and on whom the child can reliably draw. As described in Chapter 5, in the work of Jessica Benjamin this model is extended into a subtle interrogation of the necessary conditions for recognition both in the psychotherapeutic and the political sphere, in both of which it also meets the issue of reconciliation as an approach to the resolution of conflict. For Honneth, the stakes are equally high: the conditions of recognition, based in fundamental psychological needs, are what govern social striving and antagonism. The power of this account is that it facilitates a focus on emotion in social life and so allows one to gain theoretical leverage on the intensity of people's investments in politics. The problem, as McNay points out, is that it makes the political and social sphere subsidiary to the psychological. As with the very different theory of Reich, this means that the needs of the subject come first; the social is restricted to either blocking or meeting these needs. Ontologically, this means that there is a psychic space which is non-political, or prior to politics, which then occupies an idealised position within the theory as a whole. Put more broadly, the relational model of psychoanalysis deployed in this way becomes one in which the subject loses its sociality through being postulated as an entity that is self-constituted prior to the operations of social forces. Relationality may be originary (as it is in Winnicott's thought), but it tends to be reduced to promoting or thwarting the growth of the subject rather than *structuring* the subject from the start. It is not that this necessarily leads to a neglect of economic and political factors in social life – in principle, there is no reason why it should do this – but it makes their function and significance that of servicing the needs of individuals, who themselves are described only in terms of necessary psychic and intersubjective processes, but not as formed in and of the social itself.

Lack and enjoyment in political thought

As noted in Chapter 5 in connection with Judith Butler's work, the psychoanalytic theorising of Jean Laplanche is currently being posited as an alternative basis for an understanding of identity politics that conceptualises the subject as split and socially riven from the start. The extrinsic formulation of the subject is expressed in the theory of enigmatic signifiers, those untranslatable messages from the adult which become the foundation for the infant's unconscious life and which are the residue of the process of unconscious seduction passed on through generations from parent to child. This adds a strand of 'alienness' at the core of subjecthood: central to each subject is an unconscious dimension, as we know, but this unconscious does not 'belong' to the 'person', but rather arises from an act of mis-communication, a mode of unwitting seduction, in which the parental desire excites the child, without being understood. 'So we have the reality of the message and the irreducibility of the fact of communication. What psychoanalysis adds is a fact of its experience, namely that this message is frequently compromised, that it both fails and succeeds at one and the same time. It is opaque to its recipient and its transmitter alike' (Laplanche, 1999, p.169). It is no longer a matter of intention; what comes from the other to the subject is something unknown to both, yet intense in its effect (and affect). The infant is invaded by an unconscious message, its private spaces inflicted with the sense of 'something else', something excessive and too strong, always hinting at its presence without ever letting itself be fully known. The adult, too, holds an alien message inside: there is something no one can ever properly know. If this model has force, it is very difficult to imagine what a personal, authentic pre-social space can be; however 'deep' we go, we find the other already there. In contrast to the object-relational stance, the split human subject 'hidden' behind the ego (which is really a Lacanian formulation, but has influenced a generation of French analysts) is brought into being by the other. It is not excisable from the other and hence is 'always-already' social. Identity struggle is consequently never going to be a matter of striving for recognition of what one authentically 'is'; it is rather a matter of *producing* a subject in line with certain aspired-for values, creating a subject with force in the world. Specifically, recognition of the subject as a being with rights, for instance as 'black' or 'gay', is not a matter of putting a name to a mode of authenticity that is pre-given, but rather of creating the conditions under which discursively constructed possibilities are given shape and allotted agentic power. Psychoanalysis of this kind would not by any means preclude identity struggle; but it also places under scrutiny the notion of 'identity' itself as something constructed rather than basic, something importantly flawed rather than assumed to be ideally whole.

This brings us back to the perspective offered by Lacanian psychoanalysis, the exponents of which have framed the issues somewhat differently. In the context of this discussion, a symptomatic element is the apparently arcane debate about 'lack' and 'fullness' in psychoanalytic thought. This refers specifically to whether the subject is driven by lack in seeking its desire, or whether there is a kind of overflowing of psychic activity out of which things happen as an expression of the essentially *sui generis* imaginative life of the human subject. In classic Lacanian theory, there is little doubt that it is lack, concretised in castration, which is the key element. The division between the registers of Imaginary, Symbolic and Real classifies a discrepancy between what is imagined to be true (the holistic fantasy of an ego that can function autonomously and with integrity, of a subject that can fully know the truth); what can be symbolised and consequently manipulated, investigated and analysed (so psychoanalysis itself operates in the domain of the Symbolic); and what can never be known, or can be known only at the edges or by its sudden appearance in moments of breakthrough, never fully symbolisable, always at work but never quite there. These elements of the Lacanian scheme frame a set of 'lacks' contributing in different ways to the subject as a social and political entity. One is the theorisation of the subject as riven with splits; a second portrays the subject as intrinsically lacking in the sense of being cut off from the source of power, which always lies outside it as an Other that gives form and force to the subject's being. Both these types of lack are central to the Lacanian account of how the human subject is constituted. Indeed, the second type, which is essentially a description of how the Symbolic works, is vital to Lacanian ideas on sexual difference and on the construction of the subject in language. It stresses that the subject is not *a centre to itself*, but rather, in line with Freudian theory, is displaced and inhabited by something outside it. The subject is always constructed according to the desire of the Other, always answerable to a 'big Other' that is over and beyond itself and can perhaps be thought of as 'society' (amongst other things).

What is of great importance here in distinguishing the Symbolic from the Imaginary relationship to the Other is the postulation of the Other itself as *lacking*, not as a fully formed answer to the subject's desire. That is, the subject is lacking because it is placed in a web of symbolic positioning which cuts it off from the source of its desire; but the Other is also lacking, because it makes demands on the subject, facing the subject with the question, 'What does the Other want?'

> A lack is encountered by the subject in the Other, in the very intimation that the Other makes to him by his discourse. In the intervals of the discourse of the Other, there emerges in the experience of the child something ... namely, *He is saying this to me, but what does he want?* The desire of the Other is apprehended by the subject ... in the lacks of the discourse of the Other, and all the child's *whys* reveal not so much an avidity for the reason of things, as a testing of the adult, a *Why are you telling me this?* ever-resuscitated from its base, which is the enigma of the adult's desire. (Lacan, 1973, p.214)

Hook (2008a) draws out the political implications of this position, commenting:

> Once we realize that the linked questions of desire *('What do I want?')* and social location *('What makes sense of the position I occupy in society?')* are really unanswerable – because they always rebound in the form of another question – then we start to understand the futility of such recourse to the Other, at least within the realm of the signifier, and the alienation of the subject that inevitably results. (p.279)

The interesting point here is that the Other is conceptualised not as a solid structure of power that acts over and against the subject, but as lacking, as having a desire of its own, which the subject is also immersed in. Out of this overlapping of lacks, if one can enunciate the Lacanian theory of desire in this way (desire as always being built on a lack), comes a nodal point for the investment of the subject in the social. If the Other is lacking (if 'it needs me'), then the subject is faced with the question of what it is in the subject that is desired, and hence of what kind of lack in the Other can be filled by the (also lacking) subject. This is linked to the Lacanian notion of the *objet a* as the object cause of desire – the thing in the other that provokes the desire of the subject, that moves it into action. In this complex array of interlinked abstractions surrounding lack, one can just about glimpse a political theory, one which has been taken up by an array of commentators (e.g. Bosteels, 2006): the mutual construction of lacking subjectivities produces a play of investments that circulate between subject and Other and operate in the social field.

There is a third type of lack here, however, produced by the impossibility of symbolisation of the Real. Stavrakakis (2007) frames it like this:

> In fact it is this constitutive and unbridgeable gap between the symbolic/imaginary nexus (the field of social construction and institution) and the always escaping real which also makes history possible: if it was feasible for a particular social construction to symbolise fully the real, then history would come to an end, together with the permanent play between human creativity (desire) and social dislocation (lack). (p.40)

The Real is constitutively unsymbolisable, and as such always features as a lack at the centre of the human subject: there is an impossibility always in play, and this has effects in generating a gap into which subjecthood must fall. Out of this come some possible political readings linked to the Lacanian endeavour. One is to conceptualise lack as promoting human creativity but also as always setting limits to it: there is never any closure in the political field, because there is always something left out. Whilst this is anti-utopian in its implications, it also creates a constant pressure for newness, for seeking something else. This has some implications resonant of Castoriadis' (e.g. 1995) divergence from Lacanian orthodoxy, in which he focuses on the constant creativity of the human subject *in the imaginary* as a kind of generator of a stream of signifiers that gets broken into and constrained by the institutions of society, but which nevertheless is the source for constant radical imagination. However, this approach suffers from dividing the originary, essential psychic 'monad' off from the social, returning them to an oppositional relationship akin to that fallen into by object relations theory. In contrast, the 'orthodox' Lacanian position maintains a stance that the Other (and hence the institutions of society) and the subject are never separable, that desire and creativity are produced by the Real. As Žižek (1994) states, in a different domain (in this case about the limitations of Habermas' theory):

> Here we confront the incommensurability between hermeneutics ('deep' as it may be) and psychoanalytic interpretation: Habermas can assert that distortions have meaning as such – what remains unthinkable for him is that *meaning as such results from a certain distortion* – that the emergence of meaning is based on a disavowal of some 'primordially repressed' traumatic kernel. (p.27)

That is, meaning – creativity and imagination included – is not something pulsing away which is shaped or distorted by social pressures; there is no pure, transparent communication between subjects, for example. Instead, the openness of the Lacanian field is given by the fact that there are always gaps in the functioning of the Symbolic. It can never quite hold together because of the presence of something unsymbolisable at its core – which does not mean that the effort is never to be made to symbolise it, but rather that it can never be mastered. Stavrakakis (2007) comments:

> From a Lacanian point of view, the fact that the imposition of the symbolic is never total can only mean that the real, being ultimately incommensurable with the symbolic, resists symbolisation and persists alongside our socio-symbolic identifications. ... First of all ... it persists through the continuous resurfacing of negativity, through the dislocation of subjective and social identities. By encircling these encounters with the real, Lacan seems to register the importance of a moment that, in social and political theory, could only be described as the moment of the political *par excellence*. (p.53)

The 'political' here is the response to the constitutive lack within the subject and the Other. It

> refers to the moment of failure of a given identity or social construction; a failure which not only dislocates the identity in question but also creates a lack, stimulating the desire for a rearticulation of the dislocated structure, stimulating, in other words, human creativity, becoming the condition of possibility for human freedom. (p.54)

That is, the fact of lack creates the desire for change – an idea which drives Stavrakakis' belief in and commitment to radical democracy.

The emphasis on lack in Lacanian political thought has been much criticised for its tendency to posit irrevocable exclusions to the social order and also for its abstractness (no doubt more than adequately represented in the description above), which to some has meant that it is more an account of ontology than of politics. It is also attacked for its negativism, even nihilism, which ironically can result in a conformism that reduces the prospects for change to that of coming to accept its impossibility. Robinson (2004), for instance, in a review of books by Žižek, Badiou, Laclau and Mouffe and Stavrakakis, complains:

> For Lacanians, the return of the Real is always a disruptive, almost revolutionary event which shatters the entire social totality constructed around its exclusion. Every social order, therefore, has a single touchy 'nodal point' which it must maintain, or else it will collapse. Since the exclusion of a Real element is supposed to be necessary, Lacanians urge that one reconcile oneself to the inevitability of lack. Lacanian politics is therefore about coming to terms with violence, exclusion and antagonism, not about resolving or removing these. The acceptance of lack takes the form of an Act or Event, in which the myth of subjective completeness is rejected and the incompleteness of the self is embraced. The primary ethical imperative in Lacanian politics is to 'accept' the primacy of antagonism, i.e. the central ontological claim of the Lacanian edifice itself. (p.260)

Whilst this is probably an extreme formulation, lumping together a variety of authors who have significant differences with one another, there is a genuine critical point arising here, which has to do with the extent to which social change can occur if one assumes that lack is constitutive and unavoidable. As is suggested by the query posed by Žižek to Adorno's work, quoted earlier, there is a difficulty about whether psychoanalysis is ever to be in a position to advocate change, or whether it will always retain a 'diagnostic' edge which means it can never commit to anything. In some of Žižek's writing, the result of this is a foregrounding of 'terror' and also a writing style that is often apparently wilfully contrary, working through a systematic process of unsettling expectations by reversals and provocations. 'Today's "mad dance"', he writes, '... awaits its resolution in a new form of Terror' (Butler, Laclau and Žižek, 2000, p.326); elsewhere he emphasises the difference between a false resistance and a radical act that basically smashes apart the symbolic order through the insurgence of the Real. Stavrakakis (2007) argues that this idea radically revises and is incompatible with the Lacanian emphasis on lack. It is a kind of impatience with it, which also relies on a belief in a 'divine miracle' that will dispense with negativity and create a new order. Faced with the Lacanian argument that the 'constitutive division' of the subject can never be displaced,

> Žižek's response is to reverse the argument and argue that the true source of evil is assuming finitude, mortality, and lack as such, ignoring the dimension

of 'divine miracles': '[acts] occur, on the contrary, as a totally unpredictable *tuche*, a miraculous event which shatters our lives. To put it in somewhat pathetic terms, this is how the "divine" dimension is present in our lives' (p.120)

Even Žižek's use of the Lacanian trope of *jouissance* buys into this, despite its efficacy in instigating a penetrating analysis of apparently 'irrational' investments in political turmoil. At its broadest, *jouissance* references the 'enjoyment' that comes with immersion in the Real – how the subject gets taken up in unsymbolisable, irrational activity that makes it feel alive, yet is also bizarre, overstated, excessive to the apparently realistic demands of the situation. The individual subject does this in relation to the symptom, which can be a nodal point holding the psyche together. Enjoyment also operates at the core of the political, as excessive phenomena (war, terror, nationalism) overwhelm the social order and subjects find themselves caught up in them. This is, as noted, an important idea that gives leverage on the extensive questions brought up by apparently irrational political and social acts – internecine conflicts, self-destructive political claims, obvious 'cost-benefit losers' that are clung onto until the bitter end. The idea that subjects might find these enlivening precisely because they draw on the unsymbolisable, excluded core of subjecthood is one that Lacanian theorists, and Žižek in particular, have contributed to political thought. But whether the Žižekian use of the concept is really 'Lacanian' and is not rather an appeal to a kind of vitalist life energy that fuels action, is a moot point. That is, if *jouissance* is the answer, then perhaps the Lacanian/Freudian emphasis on avoiding pretence that there is a cure – that the analyst actually knows the truth of the subject – has been forgotten.

That said, Žižek often shows an exemplary allegiance to the Lacanian lesson that psychoanalysis is not a programme or policy for action, but rather a critical discourse that is committed to returning subjects to what they can and cannot know. In *The Parallax View*, for example (2006b), he presents an extended examination of psychoanalysis' response to contemporary cultural shifts that are not only marginalising it institutionally, but also seem to reflect a move away from the Oedipal structures with which psychoanalysis is most familiar. Žižek identifies three conventional psychoanalytic responses to this:

1. In a disavowal similar to that of the few remaining 'orthodox' Marxists, it continues to act as if nothing has really changed: the fundamental structure of the Unconscious and its formations as formulated by Freud still reigns supreme, the changes are merely superficial, so one should resist the temptation of the fashionable calls for a 'new paradigm.'

2. While recognizing the shift, the move toward a 'post-Oedipal society,' it perceives this as a dangerous development, as a loss of our very fundamental ethico-symbolic coordinates; as a result it advocates some kind of return to the symbolic authority of the paternal Law as the only way to halt our slide toward the global chaos of autistic closure and violence.
3. It regularly tries to 'keep up with the times,' and thus acquire a new legitimacy: either by searching for proofs that the new neurosciences confirm its hypotheses, or by redefining its therapeutic role against the 'new anxieties' of our 'postmodern' epoch (for instance, focusing on 'pathological Narcissism'). (p.298)

Žižek asks which of these three ways is the right one, and gives a characteristic answer: 'The *fourth* one, of course: that of asserting that, on the contrary, it is only today that we encounter in our daily lives the basic libidinal deadlock around which psychoanalysis circulates' (ibid.). He then goes on to deliberately set up a straw-person argument that Lacanian psychoanalysis differentiates between two failed responses to the 'crisis of authority' (the crisis of the discourse of the Master, in more Lacanian terms): first, what Lacan calls the discourse of the University (total administration and bureaucratisation of knowledge) and, secondly, the discourse of the Hysteric ('the excess of doubt, of permanent questioning' [ibid.]). In contrast to these, the discourse of the Analyst stands for

> the emergence of revolutionary-emancipatory subjectivity that resolves the split into university and hysteria: in it, the revolutionary agent (*a*) addresses the subject from the position of knowledge which occupies the place of truth (that is, which intervenes at the 'symptomal torsion' of the subject's constellation), and the goal is to isolate, get rid of, the Master-Signifier which structured the subject's (ideologico-political) unconscious'. (ibid.)

This seems to make the analyst into the one who speaks the revolutionary truth, but as Žižek is quick to point out, this in itself is at odds with the Lacanian doctrine that no one knows the truth. Where, for example, many contemporary social theorists see the reflexivity of contemporary society as a move towards emancipation, Žižek argues that it is now precisely this reflexivity that operates to preserve things as they are, for example by making the interpretations that could be offered by a psychoanalyst into something already known to the subject, who thinks about her or himself in this way in the first place. That is, one comes to psychoanalysis to have confirmed the narrative of oneself as a psychological subject. The result is that the Symbolic is unable to provide effective interpretations, because interpretation is itself part of the 'symptom' of the contemporary world; hence, according to Žižek, the taste for violence which breaks through the Symbolic itself, which is, in important respects, a taste of the Real. 'What if', he asks (p..303), 'the gap between the Symbolic and the raw Real epitomized by the figure of the skinhead is a false one, since this Real of the outbursts of "irrational" violence is generated by the globalization of the Symbolic?'

Žižek's argument here is relatively subtle and is pursued into a consideration of superego violence and the changing role of the *objet a*, but for current purposes it is interesting mostly for its understanding of the efficacy of psychoanalysis as a model for activity in the current political culture. 'Reflexive modernity' of the kind that would be promoted for example by Giddens (1991), is seen by Žižek as an instance of the absorption of analytic discourse into the administered society. It is an example of what Ian Parker (1997) describes as 'psychoanalytic culture', the saturation of contemporary consciousness by psychoanalytic concepts. Rather than giving leverage for revolutionary activity, this tendency removes the sting from psychoanalysis; that is, it becomes another instance in a long history (as long as the history of psychoanalysis itself – see Jacoby, 1975; Frosh, 1999) of the blunting of the subversive edge of psychoanalysis, so that it becomes an agent, rather than a critic, of the status quo. If everyone is adept at using psychoanalytic ideas reflexively – if everyone already knows what their dreams mean in Freudian language – then psychoanalysis cannot surprise anyone, cannot any more speak from the margins in a way that will produce a radical shock. The question asked right at the beginning of this book, of how psychoanalysis can be rescued from its collapse into conformity, is therefore, *one shouldn't start from there*. In Žižek's account, psychoanalysis always has to stay one step ahead, doing the unexpected – just as he does, perhaps playing the fool:

> Traditionally, psychoanalysis was expected to allow the patient to overcome the obstacles which denied him or her access to 'normal' sexual enjoyment; today, however, when we are bombarded from all sides by different versions of the superego injunction 'Enjoy!', from direct enjoyment of sexual performance to enjoyment of professional achievement or spiritual awakening, we should move to a more radical level: today, psychoanalysis is the only discourse in which you are allowed *not* to enjoy (as opposed to 'not allowed to enjoy') ... The desire that no longer needs to be sustained by the superego injunction is what Lacan calls the 'desire of the analyst'. (2006b, p.304)

Much feeds into this idea of the desire of the analyst, including a set of images that more than border on antisemitism, in which Žižek claims that the correct model of the analyst is the 'Jewish moneylender, a shadowy figure to whom all the big figures of society come to borrow money, pleading with him and telling him all their dirty secrets and passions' (p.305). But at the end of it there is an important question about the outcome of Lacanian politics. Žižek writes:

> Lacan's claim is that the discourse of the Analyst prepares the way for a new Master ... The question, however, remains: how, *structurally*, does this new Master differ from the previous, overthrown one ...? If there is no structural difference, then we are back with the resigned conservative wisdom about (a political) revolution as a revolution in the astronomic sense of the circular movement which brings us back to the starting point (p.307)

Žižek's own aspiration seems to be to construct new 'Master-signifiers' based on the disappearance of the Freudian unconscious (collapsing under the weight of self-reflexivity) and its replacement with a revolutionary break. He acknowledges, however, that what this means is there could be a very narrow dividing line between the analyst and the totalitarian leader: 'both are objet petit a objects of transferential love; the difference between them is the difference between the perverse social link (in which the pervert knows what the other really wants) and the discourse of the analyst who, while occupying the place of supposed knowledge, keeps it empty' (p.380). Can one trust the analyst to do this? Can one trust any revolutionary leader to provoke a break without reverting to the authoritarian mastery that she or he supposedly seeks to replace? The Lacanian answer to this would seem to be that it is unlikely that one can. Perhaps once again we are back to the ambivalence found in the psychoanalytic concept of resistance: everything we intensely oppose, we also desire; every position we seek to overcome, we also wish to occupy. Žižek seems to try to avoid this by wriggling out of all expected positions, by remaining unsettled and continuously provocative, but it may be fair to say that in the course of doing this he becomes 'predictably unpredictable', his celebrity status generated not just by the extraordinary vivacity and depth of his discourse, but also by a search by his readers and audiences for a kind of entertainment that comes from being once more surprised. Without the surprise, without the fireworks, it would not be Žižek. Similarly, Lacan's apparently disruptive opacity became predictable, his anti-eloquence, which may initially have been produced by a genuine concern not to rush to simple conclusions, itself turning into Lacanian orthodoxy. The predictability and eventual mundanity of these recurring events possibly contributes to the appeal of the call to 'revolutionary terror' as a way of breaking through repetitions by sweeping them all away; until, that is, one thinks of the consequences. Psychoanalysis offers a great deal of leverage here, in outlining the patterns of desire in which subjects become stuck – whether due to lack or fullness, it does not really matter. But there is still little evidence that psychoanalysis can point a way through it to something 'more real than the Real', which will put a stop to the cycles of power that continually impose themselves and create subject positions of predictable kinds, whichever individuals end up occupying them.

Conclusion

This chapter has been concerned with how psychoanalysis is drawn on in political theory as a resource for radical critique. Moving from Freud's ideas on the psychology of the 'mass' to the parallel worlds of psychoanalytic and political resistance, it argued for the fertility of some basic psychoanalytic notions in generating ideas about the complex and ambivalent ways in which political investments occur. Classical 'Freudo-Marxist' theory such as that of the Frankfurt School trace the psychic operations of ideology, whilst contemporary relational theory provides insights into the intersubjective conditions that might be necessary for the production of a more equal society. Finally, the powerful and voguish application of Lacanian ideas in the political sphere was debated. Here, the emphasis on lack and on constant critique from a position of 'emptiness' offers a rallying point for those who regard radical politics as requiring suspicion of all fixed positions, including those advocated by radicals themselves. As such it is probably true to some basic Freudian premises, for instance that everything can and should be analysed, and that utopias are always imaginary consolations. One wonders, however, whether this position of continual criticism can ever form the basis for a political programme that might actually improve the conditions of people's lives.

The work described here is so disparate as to make it difficult to come to any straightforward conclusion about the contribution of psychoanalysis to this particular space outside the clinic. Nevertheless, there seems little doubt that this contribution is significant, supplying a vocabulary and a set of substantive ideas for exploring the investments of subjects in the political sphere. This is not just a matter of ideology, identity or affect. Psychoanalysis allows one to speak of the reasons people become deeply involved in politics, as well as of how the social order 'infects' them so that particular political arrangements come to feel necessary and absolute. But it also offers a broader set of concepts around resistance, desire, recognition and lack that might usefully feed into general political thought. At the very least, this would oppose the rationalism present in much conventional political theory, and offer leverage on the irruptions of violent and intense emotion that seem endemic to the lives of social groups, including whole nations. This might reflect back on psychoanalysis itself, not only as a motivation to examine the political stance taken by psychoanalysts (which has only been mentioned here but has been worked on quite extensively in the literature), but also as a set of questions about how social and political processes mediate the construction of individual subjects. As such, the questions raised are psychosocial in their import and orientation. That is, they question the convention of distinguishing between subject and society and suggest instead the need to look for what runs through both.

Chapter 7

Psychoanalysis and the 'Psychosocial'

Throughout this book, I have been claiming a general 'psychosocial' perspective that addresses ways in which what are conventionally taken to be the separate spheres of the 'personal' or 'individual' and the 'social' are actually bound up together. In each example of the application of psychoanalysis in social research, I have been interested in how psychoanalysis might help bridge this particular gap. This has partly been through appreciation of the structuring power of the social order (the 'big Other' of Lacanian thought), and of dynamic mechanisms such as identification that offer a model of how the subject might experience the 'external' world as 'internal'. In particular, the constitutive function of otherness, as theorised especially by Laplanche (1999), is an idea that has taken hold across a wide range of approaches, including relational and Lacanian psychoanalysis. Taking this seriously involves accepting that there is no subject without the other; that is, that the subject is permeated from the start by the 'interruption' represented by other subjects and by society.

Whilst the perspective adopted here is 'psychosocial' in this sense, the specific disciplinary locus of *psychosocial studies* is only just emerging in the social sciences. As this chapter will show, psychoanalysis plays a considerable part in this emergence, lending psychosocial studies some authority and providing it with one of its distinctive perspectives. Conversely, psychosocial studies is fast becoming an arena in which psychoanalysis can recover some of its ground within the academy. It is also a space for contestation between different forms and understandings of psychoanalysis, partly because as a new discipline it is as yet unclear about what it wants from it. Should psychosocial studies buy in completely to a world view in which its focus is on the affective and unconscious components of social being, with psychoanalysis offering the language and concepts that make this viable? In that case, psychoanalysis would be drawn on as an expert discipline that has the knowledge base available to it to make psychosocial studies possible. Alternatively, is psychoanalysis just one of a range of tools that can be used to make sense of psychological and social material? This too makes psychoanalysis an expert system, though a more circumscribed one, jostling with other approaches (for example, phenomenology) and being seen more as a technology than an ideology. Or is there something to be developed from the version of psychoanalysis that sees it as a universal methodology of 'undoing', provoking and questioning rather than supplying solutions to research questions? This would use it to prise open psychosocial studies, challenging it to produce understandings of the social human subject that are uncertain and equivocal, allowing breathing space for critical visions. This is, of course, the rather idealistic aspiration of much of what has been presented in this book to date; but it has its own difficulties. Not least, it might make one wonder whether this kind of critical instability is a sufficient basis on which an academic discipline can be founded.

This chapter debates some of these issues. It begins with a brief genealogy of psychosocial studies and a discussion about the kind of psychosocial studies with which a critical psychoanalysis could engage. It then looks at how two forms of psychoanalysis – loosely, Kleinian and Lacanian – have been advanced in British psychosocial studies, and examines some of the implications of this. It finishes with an account of some of the difficulties of 'applying' psychoanalysis in this field, an account which also draws together some of the broader challenges of the book as a whole.

Critical psychology and psychosocial studies

In the study of mind, behaviour and now brain, the discipline of academic psychology is a powerful force. Originating at roughly the same time as psychoanalysis, in the latter half of the nineteenth century, and partly in response to the same individualising tendencies in the surrounding culture, psychology has developed to become a field of astonishing virtuosity and extensive application, with vast cultural currency as well as research and vocational appeal. It is bought into by media and government; it is perhaps the predominant 'psy' discipline (Rose, 1998) in relation to the regulation or administration of the contemporary subject; and it has significant productive power in the organisation of health and education services, in management practices in organisations, and in judicial work. Its primary self-narrative is as a 'scientific' discipline, based on rigorous observation and experimentation and as far as possible following the traditions of the natural sciences in the grounding of its claims ('psychological science' and 'scientific psychology' being terms of approbation in the community of researchers). As such, it presents itself as an 'expert' discipline, a kind of advanced technology of knowledge, capable of offering independent information about people's psychology and not amenable – at least ideally – to subjective beliefs that distort the nature of its facts.

Psychology thus diverges from psychoanalysis particularly around the issue of subjectivity. Where psychoanalysis attends to the 'subjective' as its core project and also in its methodology (for instance in the transference but more broadly in its use of affective responses to guide interpretations), psychology has traditionally avoided anything that might interfere with the 'objectivity' of its observations. This also means that it has claimed independence as a scientific profession and presented itself as separate from political pressures and processes. However, as Nikolas Rose (1998) indicates, despite its apparently individualistic focus (the mind and behaviour of the individual subject, thought about as a mechanical and/or biological entity, is its proper topic of study), psychology operates in a *social* field. It is not just a body of knowledge, but a branch of activity that has its own ideological and hence political investments – rather a different point of view from the one adopted by those who claim for it some kind of scientific 'neutrality'. It is part of the state apparatus for selection, categorisation and treatment, as witnessed in its applications in education and health as well as in management, policing and the military (e.g. Burman, 2007). Psychologists have also not infrequently been co-opted by governments as participants in repressive policies. This has occurred in relation to psychiatric treatment of dissidents, for example in the Soviet Union (Bloch and Reddaway, 1984), but is not confined to countries where professional bodies lack strong ethical codes. A recent example is the involvement of US psychologists in military interrogations in Guantánamo Bay, a practice eventually repudiated by the American Psychological Association in August 2008, but only after an acrimonious debate within its ranks (Summers, 2007). Additionally, the emphasis on the individual as the object of knowledge makes specific ideological claims, which can be seen most clearly in assumptions about the separation between what is individual (seen as 'personal') and what is social. The sub-discipline of social psychology, for example, has rarely had much to say about the nature of the social itself, but has largely been restricted to investigations of cognitions in social settings (attitudes, prejudice, social judgements, etc.) and of people's behaviour in groups and other social situations. It thus studies the individual in social contexts but without deconstructing the notion of individuality itself. Instead, the separate status of the individual is assumed as a 'given' (and not as a historical construct), however much it might be acknowledged that the practices of individuals vary from one sociocultural setting to another. The individualising tendency of psychology can thus be seen as a particular kind of intervention in social science, paralleling the separation of 'private' from 'public' and 'personal' from 'political'. Within it, the links between what are separated out as 'social' and 'individual' are reduced or even removed absolutely, ostensibly either because they are indeed distinct elements, or because they consequently become easier to study; but perhaps actually as a further contribution to the smooth running of the administered society.

The development of psychology in this way can also be seen partly as a product of an intellectual division of labour with the contemporaneous development of an empirical discipline of sociology, which took on the study of the social (social structures, class and race, and so on), whilst psychology inhabited the domain of the individual. Whilst the demarcation could clearly never be absolute, it has been quite strong, and has limited the possibilities for exploration of the *intersection* of supposedly social and individual from within these two disciplines. In addition, the strict division between individual and social risks reducing one to the other (so that, for example, the social is seen as no more than the free interactions of individuals, or the individual is seen as fully constituted by her or his social class, or gender or 'race' position), or of essentialising each element so that the social is 'bracketed off' in discussions of the individual, or vice versa. The conceptualisation of the individual/social divide is itself the problem here. Whilst one might make tactical decisions in any research project to investigate at the level of the 'person' or the 'social', in fact these are not distinct entities, but simply ways of carving up the research field to make it manageable, with the effect of reproducing ideological assumptions about the nature of the social world. Both psychology and sociology have treated these distinctions as real, with repetitive and mostly fruitless debates about 'individual *versus* society' and 'nature *versus* nurture' being the consequence.

As happens within hegemonic disciplines, psychology has produced its own internal critics who have drawn on broader political and social theories to contextualise and analyse the discipline itself so that its conditions of emergence and modes of operation become more visible (e.g. Parker, 2007). Many of these critics have worked against oppressive psychological practices operating in the specific areas of 'race' and intelligence, mental health and evolutionary psychology (e.g. Gould, 1996; Banton et al., 1985; Rose and Rose, 2000). Others have sought a broader development in forming a 'critical psychology' that has two main tendencies: offering a political critique of psychology; and using psychology for 'emancipatory' ends, involving empowerment of oppressed groups and theoretical and practical critique of social forces. This latter tendency has been entwined with liberation movements of various kinds, including anti-psychiatry and patients' rights, and predominantly offers a 'social justice' perspective (e.g. Fox, Prilleltensky and Austin, 2009). Although psychoanalysis has occasionally been drawn on by exponents of this approach, on the whole the emancipatory agenda has been opposed to what is seen as psychoanalysis' own conformism, expressed in what are regarded as normative practices particularly in relation to sexism and ethnocentrism. This type of critical psychology is primarily activist in orientation and has had a powerful impact on community psychology in general.

The other perspective, which offers a critical account of psychology itself, is closer to the concerns of this chapter. It seeks to find a way to move beyond the complacent individualism of psychology not only to understand how the discipline itself collaborates in the apparatus of administration (e.g. Hook, 2007), but also to develop a set of theoretical tools that will make it possible to overcome the individual–social split and instead think through ways to bring together or 'suture' these supposedly opposed entities. Amongst other things, this type of critical psychology has fed into a set of approaches loosely grouped together as 'psychosocial studies'. These have their other origins in social work and sociology, but also in an applied psychoanalytic tradition associated with the Tavistock Institute from the 1950s onwards, committed to radical shifts in public and institutional practices (Frosh, 2003; Walkerdine, 2008). In addition to this basically psychoanalytically driven type of psychosocial thinking, social psychology has also spawned a set of new research perspectives that partake very actively of the 'turn to language' evident in all the social sciences since the 1970s. In this 'discursive' tradition, the human subject is understood as an entity produced in and by language – an understanding that has been implicit in much that has already been addressed in this book, albeit not necessarily arising from the same epistemological stable. As will be discussed, this discursive turn, whilst engaged in the same critical endeavour as much psychosocial studies research, has some significantly different views of the utility of psychoanalytic concepts for advancing this work.

Psychosocial studies is a fragile entity, perhaps reflecting the difficulty of maintaining the thinking-together of social and individual that are constantly pushed apart by the fundamental ideological impulses of liberalism and late capitalism. As noted elsewhere (Frosh, 2003), its characteristics include looking out from psychology and sociology towards interdisciplinary theories and methodologies that allow it critical leverage; and in doing this psychoanalysis has seemed to have much to offer. In many ways this seems obvious. Psychoanalysis, as evidenced throughout this book, has always ranged across conventional disciplines, never quite having a home in any of them, and at its best has managed to sustain a vision of the human subject as born in and of both bodily, internal drives and social relationships. More importantly, the central notion of psychoanalysis, that of the unconscious, has an evidently 'trans-individual' aspect to it (Hook, 2008b), in the sense that unconscious ideas are both 'in' and 'outside of' the subject, neither owned by the 'person' nor completely separate. This means that psychoanalysis has clear potential for offering theoretical models that traverse divides – neither inside nor out, neither one discipline nor another, going its own way, speaking from the margins (as it always has done), with a strong critical tradition behind it. It also offers the most developed vocabulary for theorising 'subjectivity' that is currently available, answering a significant need amongst researchers interested in exploring the construction of the subject in the social field. Additionally, as will be discussed further below, two of the dominant versions of psychoanalysis available in the 'academy' draw on and contribute to intellectual frameworks that are of considerable significance in the broader field of the social sciences: the Kleinian and relational psychoanalysts to 'intersubjectivity', and the Lacanians to the poststructuralist tradition of discursive constructionism. This all means that psychosocial researchers using psychoanalytic perspectives of this kind are also plugged into contemporary social theory and can draw on sophisticated developments in those areas, as well as (feeling that they are) contributing to a larger intellectual mission.

The gradual emergence of psychosocial studies has thus created a fresh opportunity for the reinsertion of psychoanalysis into academic social research. This has not been uncontroversial. For example, many psychosocial researchers share the traditional sociological suspicion of psychoanalysis because of its strongly individualising tendencies. Those who have been most influenced by poststructuralist and/or discursive perspectives resist the 'top-down', expert-knowledge epistemological claims of many psychoanalysts, with their apparent certainties about the 'true' nature of human subjectivity and their interpretive practice that seems to know best, or at least to know subjects better than they know themselves (e.g. Billig, 1997; Wetherell, 2003). The conservative or regressive tendencies in psychoanalysis are evident at times, here as in all fields. This includes the powerful sense that once one has developed a psychoanalytic perspective one has been transformed through a procedure that has often been compared with mystical conversion (Gellner, 1985), after which it becomes impossible to see things in any other way but through a psychoanalytic lens. This has understandably raised some hackles amongst psychosocial researchers struggling to develop more fluid and open ways of thinking. On the other hand, the concern of psychosocial studies with the interplay between what are conventionally thought of as 'external' social and 'internal' psychic formations has resulted in a turn to psychoanalysis as the discipline that might offer convincing explanations of how the 'out-there' gets 'in-here' and vice versa, especially through concepts such as projection, internalisation and identification. As with the other topics addressed in this book, the appeal of psychoanalysis as a critical approach 'from the margins' that can be deployed against common-sense readings of the surface of things, which are seen not only as superficial but also as ideologically constrained, is considerable. It reflects those elements of psychoanalysis that are open, disruptive and challenging to received ideas, without dogmatically asserting that there is some alternative 'truth' that only psychoanalysts know.

There is also a tussle visible about the kind of psychoanalysis that might be appropriate in psychosocial studies. In the British academic context in which much of this debate has been developed, this has produced a lively debate between thinkers influenced by Kleinian and Lacanian ideas, with the former being associated more strongly with an empirical outlook, and the latter with a more critical but also more abstract stance on the limits on what can and cannot be known. Amongst the issues that this throws up is a question about whether what some regard as the possible critical edge of psychoanalysis is being blunted by a humanistic rendering that appropriates psychosocial studies to what is effectively object relational thinking; or whether the influence of psychoanalysis can grant to this relatively new field a capacity to maintain an open, querying stance towards the objects of its study. As with the other areas discussed in this book, much depends on avoiding adoption of psychoanalytic certainty – of the type of reading of psychoanalysis that sees it as harbouring the deep truths of human nature – and developing a psychoanalytic stance that is both tentative and creatively disruptive.

Defining the psychosocial

It should be made clear first that the kind of psychosocial studies being discussed here is different from the common use of the term to describe normative work dealing with social adjustment or interpersonal relations. As Wendy Hollway (2006) comments: 'In the largely positivist tradition of health sciences, for example, it is often found hyphenated, along with biology ('bio-psycho-social'), to refer to the additive treatment of different levels of analysis in the same research framework' (p.467). Whilst such work addresses important issues, it is not distinctive or theoretically innovative – each of its components is left more or less untouched. In contrast, the tradition with which this chapter is concerned understands psychosocial studies as a critical approach interested in articulating a place of suture between elements whose contribution to the production of the human subject is normally theorised separately. Rustin (2008) describes the appeal of this trajectory as follows:

> The attractions of psychosocial studies, to students and researchers alike, arise from reaction to the continuing scientism, biologism, and individualism of much mainstream academic psychology, as well as to the limitations of academic sociology's understanding of individual subjects and subjectivity. Furthermore, the study of the emotions, central to psychosocial studies, has long been a marginal concern for both psychology and sociology. It has, therefore, been possible to create an educational and academic space in which the psychological and the sociological can be brought together, outside the control of either of the two main parent disciplines. (p.407)

The origins of this mode of psychosocial studies lie in psychoanalysis, sociology, applied social studies and social work, critical social psychology, poststructuralist theory, social constructionism, queer theory and feminist social research. Though deeply influenced by both Marx and Freud, its concerns have moved on considerably from those theoreticians whose primary interest was in how social repression operates to constrain the libidinal individual. Rather, contemporary psychosocial studies of this kind focuses on conceptualising and researching a type of subject which is both social and psychological, which is constituted in and through its social formations, yet is still granted agency and internality.

The main dilemma that this genealogy produces is one familiar from the previous chapters, that of finding ways of staying committed to an agenda that gives value to personal experience, interconnectedness, intersubjectivity, affect, embodiment, agency and most importantly the impulse to articulate a kind of ethical subject; whilst at the same time acknowledging and drawing on the complete disruption of this agenda through the force of the revelation that there is no such human subject. What we take to be the realm of the personal, including the famous 'inner world' of psychoanalysis, is either wavering and fragmentary, or a thoroughly fictional entity, produced and sustained by various manifestations of the 'big Other' (Hook, 2008a). Amongst the many problems this gives rise to is the repeated difficulty of uncovering a space for bringing together the psychological and the social without postulating these two spheres as distinct from one another. Their assumptions are so divergent, that often it seems that separating them completely for analytic purposes is all that can be done. In this respect, the apparently obsessional question about whether to have a hyphen between 'psycho' and 'social' has some meaning. Representing a mainly humanist, object relational and socialist tradition, Paul Hoggett (2008) argues that 'preserving the hyphen' is an important indicator of analytic clarity, in that it acknowledges that 'critique' demands the making of distinctions, the maintaining of a clear eye about the different components out of which an apparent whole is made. Blurring distinctions, he argues, including the distinction between 'inside' and 'out' and hence 'psycho' and 'social', is a way of losing touch with this important critical mode of thought, has ethical consequences in relation to ways of approaching otherness, and may even be an indication of a loss of mental health:

> Respect for difference necessitates a constant effort to resist the temptation to blur, assimilate, and merge. That is why I believe that the preservation of the difference between the psycho- and the social is crucial, a task I believe is best accomplished by preserving the hyphen, as in 'psycho-social', and by preserving the kinds of distinctions that we have between inner and outer, private and public, and so on. As a clinician, if I am working with a patient who constantly confuses inner and outer, I know I am in the presence of someone in serious difficulty. (pp.382–3)

Against this forceful idea, one might suggest that 'preserving the hyphen' results in taking as given precisely what needs to be analysed: how it is that social and psychological become separated from one another both as modes of 'reality' and also as structures of disciplinary knowledge. To a considerable degree, it might also be argued that holding on to the social–individual divide is a kind of political move, sometimes drawn on in order to oppose totalitarianism (the individual is precious; everyone has a right to exist), but more often used to obscure the mechanics of subjectification. It suggests that individual and society are irreducibly distinct, so whilst one might talk about their interaction, one never needs to examine how they are constructed, and hence how they necessitate analytic deconstruction and critique. The division is thus a way of doing politics, and the psychosocial becomes a contrary way of doing politics, a rebellion that asserts that one cannot be had without the other, that they are warp and weft and signifier and signified, and so on through the different ways of saying that they are two sides of the same thing.

In theorising what is meant by the 'unhyphenated' psychosocial, a potent image, with or without its Lacanian gloss (Lacan, 1973), is the Moebius strip: underside and topside, inside and outside flow together as one, and the choice of how to see them is purely tactical, just like the decision as to whether to look at the subject from a 'social' or 'psychological' perspective. Thinking through the implications of the psychosocial as a Moebius strip, however, rather than falling back into the relatively familiar opposition of psychological and social, is a difficult task, and as the quotation from Hoggett above indicates, this is complicated by the way in which psychoanalysis is drawn on in much of this work. Rather than following the agenda of offering a kind of critical deconstruction that develops from the history of psychoanalysis as a mode of radical critique, the more relational aspects of psychoanalysis often have ascendancy in psychosocial studies, fuelled by the politically reformist and emancipatory aims of certain modes of critical psychology and mental health practice. This means that the dominant impulse is a kind of humanistic, therapeutic one (particularly reflected in a concern with 'emotion' in the public sphere, as in the quote from Rustin, above, and in Perri 6 et al., 2006), a mode of personalising or humanising opposition to the industrial-military complex as it rolls over the vestiges of human feeling. This is a reason not only for the influence of relational psychoanalysis, valued for its rigorous attention to the quality of subjectivity as forged and understood in relational contexts, but also for the widespread use of qualitative research methods as the preferred empirical approach within psychosocial studies. As argued elsewhere,

> Qualitative psychology enters here as part of a turn in the so-called human sciences towards the rolling-up of experience into narrative form: without discounting the reality of events, the key research question becomes not what happens to a person, but how this is accounted for, how it is put into a frame that makes sense. This *humanizes* reality, placing the emphasis on the agentic, meaning-making activity of the research (and human) subject. (Frosh, 2007, pp.635–6)

Both the therapeutic agenda and the narrative one are responses to the acute awareness of the alienating structures of mainstream, normalising social practices (including those of research and of much that passes for mental health treatment), and so fall clearly within the traditions of community and emancipatory activism that have fuelled interest in the psychosocial in the first place. However, the main thrust of work that rescues agency and emotion in the name of the psychosocial is to reconstitute a holistic individual who still has to be theorised in relation to an often persecutory 'outside'.

The psychosocial as a 'sutured' unit consequently remains an ill-defined entity. This might actually be part of its productivity, allowing flexibility in the methods and foci of its research. Nevertheless, without a clear vision of its own object of study, or at least a detailed rendition of the ongoing difficulties with articulating such a vision, psychosocial studies is at risk of being reappropriated by its more conventional, 'foundational' disciplines. Philosophically and practically, this suggests that psychosocial studies is at a stage of development in which the priority is *reflexivity*, understood as an interactively critical practice that is constantly feeding back on itself and is always suspicious of the productions of its own knowledge. This stance also argues the necessity for the psychosocial and the critical to go together to develop a resistive practice based on what Marcuse (1965) and others have called 'negation'. Fundamentally, this is rooted in a constant probing of assertions and apparent knowledge in the light of the entities that constitute them; or in psychoanalytic terms, a refusal ever to abandon the 'analytic attitude' (Rieff, 1966). What are sought are ways of resisting the tendency to invest events and objects with too much familiarity, for instance dividing them into inner and outer or same and different; to oppose this, ways of 'making-strange' are needed, leading to encounters with the oddness and newness of these objects, their resistance to appropriation (Latour, 2007). In the same way, as psychosocial studies seeks to be a trans- (as opposed to inter-) disciplinary practice that negates the easy assumption of 'in here, out there', subject and object, psychic and social, it needs to constitute itself in such a way as to constantly unsettle its own activities and assumptions. This means testing itself through negation, querying its own premises, and always seeking to renew its engagement with a space that is neither 'psycho' nor 'social', and is definitely not both, but is something else again. The question here is whether and in what ways psychoanalysis can contribute to this agenda, given that many of the same issues apply to psychoanalysis itself. It too needs to rescue itself from its own claims to mastery, and in particular to a kind of universalised knowledge that pays insufficient attention to the conditions under which it arises. As discussed particularly in Chapter 1 and evident in the other applications of psychoanalysis that have been debated in this book, this especially concerns the question of what Hook (2008b, p.398) refers to as 'the epistemological and ethical disjunction that accompanies attempts to apply psychoanalysis' clinical forms beyond the confines of the clinic'.

Psychoanalysis and discourse

The engagement of psychosocial studies with psychoanalysis centres on questions about the nature of subjectivity and subjecthood, and also on ways in which psychoanalytic ideas can be employed in the collection and analysis of research data. For example, for those researchers seeking to use psychoanalysis as a methodological approach that can add something to empirical psychosocial studies, a likely contribution from psychoanalysis derives from the sophistication of its ideas about emotional investment and fantasy. These can offer a 'thickening' or enrichment of interpretive understanding brought to bear on personal narratives, especially those arising out of interview situations. Psychoanalytic interpretive strategies may be able to throw light on the psychological processes, or perhaps the conscious and unconscious 'reasons', behind a specific individual's investment in any rhetorical or discursive position. This may offer a more complete (because more individualised as well as emotion-inflected) interpretive re-description of interview material, with helpful links to clinical perceptions and practices.

There are many examples of this kind of work now available in the literature (e.g. Frosh et al., 2003), most of it from Britain and often formulated in the context of a debate with discursive psychology, which also uses qualitative research procedures to try to map identity and subjectivity, and to understand the construction of the social subject. The different approaches here generally follow from different theoretical principles. Psychoanalytically inclined researchers start from the position that unconscious processes infiltrate the narrative accounts given by research participants, so that interpretive strategies aimed at uncovering these unconscious processes will be needed. Discursive researchers, on the other hand, assume that these same accounts are produced through social activity and the linguistic transactions between subjects, and are not ghosted by any underlying unconscious presence. As an example of the former tendency, Wendy Hollway, delineating her use of the term 'psycho-social', assumes immediately the existence of a certain kind of psychoanalytic subject. Her usage, she writes,

> derives from a commitment to understand subjectivity and agency in a way that transcends individual–social dualism and draws on psychoanalysis for this purpose. In this perspective, we are *psycho*-social because we are products of a unique life history of anxiety- and desire-provoking life events and the manner in which they have been transformed in internal reality. We are psycho-*social* because such defensive activities affect and are affected by material conditions and discourses (systems of meaning which pre-exist any given individual), because unconscious defences are intersubjective processes (i.e. they affect and are affected by others with whom we are in communication), and because of the real events in the external, social world which are discursively, desirously and defensively appropriated. (Hollway, 2006, pp.467–8)

It is noticeable here that Hollway incorporates the psychoanalytic subject into both the 'psycho' and 'social' sections of her hyphenated term, but actually makes both of them psychological in the process. The former, as one might expect, is made up of the transformation of material conditions into 'internal reality'. This renders psychoanalysis as usefully explaining the way in which external events become incorporated 'into' the psyche or self, notably through concepts such as introjection and identification. But the social is also psychoanalytically invested. The social as intersubjective is inhabited by psychic defences; and the individual 'appropriates' aspects of the external world which thereby become saturated with psychological significance. This certainly seems like a legitimate attempt at using psychoanalysis psychosocially: in this model, it would be very difficult to separate out one sphere (the personal, say) from the other. However, there is also an imbalance produced by the psychoanalytic orientation. Although there is a space marked out for the 'social', it is given significance in the 'psycho-social' terrain primarily as the source of internalising strategies undertaken by the individual. That is, social practices act as a kind of fodder for the psychodynamic processes of the subject. In some ways this makes it hard to see the difference between the 'psycho' and 'social' elements of Hollway's formulation: both are described in terms of how events in the 'external' world have an impact on the subject's 'internal reality'. What seems to happen is that the external world is colonised by the internal, and in so doing the dichotomy between the two is obscured but not erased.

As Hollway herself notes, a variety of what she calls 'constructionist' approaches reject this view because of the assumption about 'innerness' that it involves. They also object to the presentation of psychoanalysis as an expert system that has access to this inner world and knows what it is like, and posits it as something that exists in and of itself, however linked it might be with a social order which is also permeated by unconscious processes. This is a key element in the dispute amongst often good psychosocial colleagues (e.g. Hollway and Jefferson, 2005; Wetherell, 2005) about 'top-down' and 'bottom-up' interpretive approaches; it is also part of the debate about the functioning of the 'discursive' and whether anything stands outside language (Frosh, 2002; see also Chapter 5). Many psychosocial researchers recognise differences between discursive social psychology and psychoanalysis, yet also argue that there is a degree of congruence between them deriving from a shared interest in subjective meaning and in the constructive role of language. In essence these relate to a concern with language or communication as the medium through which people compose themselves. However, the differences that exist between psychoanalysis and discursive psychology are significant. Michael Billig describes them like this:

> Discursive psychology ... argues that phenomena which traditional psychological theories have treated as 'inner processes' are, in fact, constituted through social, discursive activity. Accordingly, discursive psychologists argue that psychology should be based on the study of this outward activity rather than upon hypothetical, and essentially unobservable, inner states. In this respect, discursive psychology is inimical with psychoanalytic theory,

> which presumes that hidden unconscious motive-forces lie behind the surface of social life. Psychoanalytic theorists often treat outward social activity as a cipher for unobservable, inner motivational processes. (Billig, 1997, pp.139–40)

For most psychoanalysts, talk is primarily determined by relational dynamics and unconscious processes; while, for discursive psychology, talk is mediated by the availability of discourses in the social and political realm. While discursive psychology explores the cultural resources that people draw on when giving accounts of their experiences, the relational tradition is more interested in talk as suggestive of underlying psychic positions that organise individuals' internal worlds in particular ways. This psychic realm is seen as being informed by actual events and therefore social structures, but as being located 'in' and primarily constituted through unconscious processes. Individuals are 'unconsciously impelled' to express themselves in particular ways in discourse, resulting in discernible patterns that will differ from individual to individual. A relational psychoanalytic reading therefore goes 'behind' the text as the positions that individuals construct through their talk are taken to be indicative of anxieties, defences and particular ways of relating that develop in infancy and recur throughout their lives. By contrast, discursive psychology reads the text for the identity positions that are constructed for the person talking and the audience listening, and for the broader cultural discourses and subject positions it draws on in these constructions. This relates to Wetherell's (2003) criticisms of psychoanalysis as predicated on a problematic psychological–social dualism. She argues that the deep psychological properties or structures that psychoanalysis is interested in are separated from social relations and therefore presented as static, confined to early development, without any exploration of their possible transformation through subsequent and ongoing social relations and practices.

Whilst psychoanalytically oriented psychosocial researchers can justifiably claim that their acknowledgement of each person's 'unique life history of anxiety- and desire-provoking life events' (Hollway, 2006, p.467) introduces more developmental fluidity than Wetherell allows for, the deeply rooted infant-centredness of psychoanalysis, perhaps especially in its object-relational form, often produces rather predictable motivational accounts and interpretive strategies. Acceptance of a developmental account leads strongly to viewing adult relationships as structured by these developmental processes, with the task of analysis being largely to understand this structuring. By its very nature, it is difficult to escape a determinist viewpoint here, and this is what often makes discursive social psychologists, and hence some exponents of psychosocial studies, uneasy about psychoanalytic claims. This also links with a continuing prioritising of the 'inner' over the 'outer'. Despite the reference to material conditions in Hollway's description of the 'psychosocial', both elements are theorised as infiltrated by 'the' unconscious, which in turn is understood as residing in the 'inner world'. Hollway positions herself against what she calls the 'post-structuralist' anti-psychoanalytic position by arguing that it is 'insufficiently cognizant of the psychological processes whereby the recursive formation of selves within their life settings is not only mediated by complex material, discursive and relational influences but also by dynamic, intersubjective, unconscious processes' (2006, p.466). This seems to assume the thing it posits (the existence of 'dynamic, intersubjective, unconscious processes'), a problem aggravated by the further claim that what is lacking both from Foucauldian poststructuralism and from discursive psychology is 'that neither adopts a developmental account of subjectivity. In contrast, I want to ask, ... how subjectivity (or "self") is formed within primary relations, and for this I draw on the tradition of object relations psychoanalysis, even while critiquing certain individualized notions of the self' (2006, p.467). Object relations theory is thus made foundational for the psychosocial position, which is assumed to need a developmental account and also to require ways of specifying mechanisms which will link the 'out-there' with the 'in-here'. This is not to suggest that such an approach is illegitimate – quite the contrary, as questions of relationality and of ways in which notions of 'unconscious' and sociality can be brought together must be central to any discussion of critical uses of psychoanalysis. But it does not solve the problem of whether appealing to an inner mode of subjectivity, a 'depth' layer, is a way of achieving this – it simply restates that it is.

The terminology of 'internal reality' widely used by object-relational and Kleinian theorists can be interestingly contrasted with a more classic psychoanalytic notion of 'psychic reality'. Despite its reference to the 'psychic', this may actually be more psychosocial in the sense that it figures something that is never totally 'internal'. Psychic reality is what the subject *lives in*; this replaces an abstracted opposition of the 'outer' as against the 'inner' with a conceptualisation of the 'psychic' as that which stands in for both. Laplanche and Pontalis (1967, p.363) note: 'This notion is bound up with the Freudian hypothesis about unconscious processes: not only do these processes take no account of external reality, they also replace it with a psychical one.' This means that the subject is always immersed in a flux that is neither inside nor out, but something else – a folding of space that is perhaps closer to the Moebius ideal. Psychic reality is already hybrid, and deterministic renderings of psychoanalysis that differentiate between its elements by claiming that 'defensive activities affect and are affected by material conditions and discourses' and by postulating 'real events in the external, social world' may miss the psychoanalytic point. This links to an argument put forward by Hook (2008b) that what should be focused on in psychosocial studies of this kind is not the 'inner world' or unconscious of any individual subject, but rather 'analysis of the libidinal economy underlying specific discursive formations' (p.399). He goes on to say that this 'proposes a non-reductive analytical strategy, asserting that discourses themselves maintain the coherence, the repetitiveness – indeed, the cycles of jouissance – that mark certain well-established patterns of libidinal functioning, a strategy which does not attempt to fix such discursive patterns as merely the outcome of intra-psychic processes, of individual psychopathology' (ibid.). Examples that he draws on include nationalism, colonialism and apartheid. The key point is that instead of focusing on individuals and their separate anxieties and defensive structures, it is the swirling around of repetitive *discourses* or perhaps patterns of enjoyment ('cycles of jouissance') that can be observed on a social level, and which link the functioning of unconscious structures and libidinal economies with social formations. Hook (p.400) argues that certain beliefs or ideological elements garner 'a je ne sais quoi quality, something "in them more than themselves," and hence take on a disproportionate libidinal status by virtue of the degree of investment of a given community'. Examining the processes whereby this comes about, and the functions of these nodal objects in the social world, draws on psychoanalytic insights about the unconscious fixing of desire, without necessarily appealing to the separation of individual from social, or inner from outer. Instead, it is the flows and blockages of desire that become the focus of analysis, not an individual's anxieties. This kind of argument can be seen at work in the discussions on the application of psychoanalysis to political thought in the previous chapter; but it may be that it also has something to say to the more psychological orientation of psychosocial studies.

Types of psychoanalysis

This raises the broader issue of whether the deployment of psychoanalysis in much psychosocial studies works from the point of view of psychoanalysis itself – if it can be said to have a 'point of view' – or whether it is a way of sanitising psychoanalysis so that it loses its specificity, and becomes just a kind of verbal bridge that makes it seem like something new is known. This relates to the question of what kind of psychoanalysis one might draw on. In Britain, the two main approaches adopted in this kind of work have been Kleinian and Lacanian. Whilst there are many points of convergence and divergence between these (see Frosh, 1999), and whilst the broader contrast between relational (such as Kleinian) and structural (such as Lacanian) psychoanalytic models has been returned to several times in this book, the central point at issue in relation to psychosocial studies is about their different attitudes to the uncovering – or perhaps making – of 'meaning'. Loosely, Kleinian interpretive approaches, as they are used in psychosocial research, seek to make narrative sense of material, telling a story of a subject's unconscious life, for example, or her or his investments in certain problematic positions (Hollway and Jefferson, 2005). This connects with the way in which Kleinian theory retains a 'redemptive' element in it (Stonebridge, 1998), both explicitly in the notion of reparation and implicitly through its therapeutic trajectory. It recognises the split nature of the subject – hence is genuinely psychoanalytic – but pursues a sense-making agenda that makes everything come together in the end. For instance, the integrative capacity of the 'depressive position' is taken as the norm of mental health, even though there is usually an acknowledgment that people continue to oscillate throughout their whole lives between this and a more fragmentary 'paranoid-schizoid' mode of functioning, and that this is a necessary and creative process. The productive consequences of this 'positive' view of the psychoanalytic task have been very marked in British psychoanalysis and its applications (e.g. Rustin, 1995), as it presses a key question about social relations: how, given the prevalence of destructiveness in the social world, can it nevertheless be possible to produce a society in which violence can be kept at bay, envy ameliorated and community created? The application of this approach in studies of institutional dynamics has been a major area of real-world impact for psychoanalysis, and as noted in Chapter 6, its importance is considerable in political theory. It is particularly well attuned to investigations of destructiveness and envy as they manifest between people, both in therapy and in social and organisational life. Ironically, however, it is Kleinianism's unexpected *optimism* – its claim that paranoid-schizoid functioning can be topped by a depressive scenario in which reconciliation of ambivalent extremes can be managed and destruction made good – that defines what on the surface looks like a despondent and fateful theory. This can also lead an analyst (of texts as well as patients) to be propelled towards a 'curative' focus, one of reparation, of putting things together so that they will make narrative (or therapeutic) sense. The question is, what does this do to the subject understood as a fragmentary being made up of multiple, conflicting 'identities' and standing at the focal point of numerous forces? Or put more simply, what if the subject's experience does *not*, in fact, make sense?

Amongst the assumptions of Kleinian thinking, as taken up in psychosocial studies, that are at odds with a deconstructive approach, is the notion of the presence of a permanent, real unconscious – something inhabited by the truth of the subject, and sought for by the analyst whose task it is to comprehend apparently meaningless activity. This is part of its affiliation to 'depth', for it is below the 'surface' of observable phenomena that the truth of the subject lies. Rustin (2008) comments: 'The recognition or disclosure of such "depth" (of beliefs, desires, meanings, and intentions) is what psychoanalysis has always been about, both in its clinical and broader social applications' (pp.411–12). For Lacanians, however, as described particularly in Chapter 3, it is precisely the constant *deferral* of meaning that is at issue. The role of psychoanalysis is not to make narrative sense in which the depth unconscious is drawn on as an 'explanation', but rather to *disrupt* sense, to examine the building blocks out of which sense is being produced as a kind of epiphenomenon. The argument here is that narrative sense is always made post hoc. In relation to research it is always a process of the researcher rereading the subject's discourse in order to even it out, to find anchor points for it and consequently to make it safe and orderly, however complexly and aesthetically this may be done. It is in principle a *defensive* process. Just as a psychoanalytic patient might organise disturbing material into a satisfying narrative, so taking refuge in an attractive interpretation can be a way for a researcher to defend against the disturbance produced by the material that gave rise to the interpretation in the first place. Parker notes here: 'There is an important twist that Lacan adds to our understanding of the process of fixing meaning through repetition of certain signifiers or metaphorical substitutes in their function as quilting points or master signifiers, which is that the process of anchoring occurs *retroactively*' (Parker, 2005a, p.170). The *analytic* as opposed to interpretive process is geared to refusing this retroactive fixing of meaning, and instead to bringing out the 'non-meaning' (Lacan, 1973, p.250) of each component of the subject's discourse. The task is thus to avoid making something whole and integrative but instead to concentrate on the *productivity* of speech – on what it leads to and by what it is constrained.

This emphasis on what might be seen as the productivity of discourse is taken up in the Lacanian recasting of interpretation as *interruption*: something brought in to produce a new motion, a movement of signifiers freed by the analyst's response, but not thereby made meaningful. 'Rather than revealing a hidden unconscious that is already there,' writes Juan-David Nasio (1992, p.46) about the act that surprises and exceeds the intention of the analysand, 'this act produces the unconscious and causes it to exist.' The patient finds her- or himself speaking in an unexpected way, perhaps with more affect than intended, or possibly about a memory that she or he never realised was present, and – as in all psychoanalysis – this becomes the source of analytic attention. However, instead of seeing it as a product of an unconscious state that has always been there, secretly carried around by the patient wherever she or he goes, the Lacanian view is that it is a product of a very specific situation, the analytic encounter itself. 'When the "word" erupts in the analysand,' writes Nasio (p.24), 'we call it, among other things a symptom, a lapse, or a witticism, and when it erupts in the psychoanalyst, we call it an interpretation.' The unconscious comes into being only in the relationship between analysand and analyst. It is a specific product of that relationship, of, for example, the transference, which itself appears only in the special situation of the consulting room 'as the particular moment of the analytic relation when the analyst becomes a part of the patient's symptom' (p.17). Nasio describes the interpretive act of the analyst with great caution, in a way that links it with the desire to make sense of narrative. Both of them threaten to become a kind of over-enthusiastic therapeutic consciousness that tries to do too much: 'It is indeed the demand that engenders the blind passion to heal, a passion that is akin to another passion, that of wanting to understand' (p.74). Nasio encourages the analyst to withstand this temptation to understand and instead allow her or himself to be 'open to surprise' (p.75). Parker (2005a) relates this specifically to the psychosocial practices of discourse analysis, which he subjects to Lacanian interrogation:

> The reflexive position of the discourse analyst is an issue here, for when one approaches a text in hermeneutic mode as something we can 'understand' because it is like our own framework (or even because we recognize it as being the mirror opposite of what is familiar to us), this, for Lacanians, would betray the stance we are taking as lying on 'the line of the Imaginary' (imagining that we interpret from outside the text). The task of an analyst is to work on 'the line of the Symbolic' (working within the domain of the text), and to open up the text by disrupting and disorganizing it so that its functions become clearer, including its functions for us. (p.177)

There is no analytic knowledge that stands outside the symbolic, hence no true interpretation that can tie the fragments together to create an integrative meaning; only a constant probing and search, and where possible a set of unexpected moments in which both analyst and patient are thrown off balance.

There is something of a risk of apparent frivolity in some of these comments, when faced with the *clinical* reality of the distress brought to psychoanalysis by clients. 'Disruptive eruptions of meaninglessness against the comfortable backdrop of established reason', as Nobus and

Quinn (2005, p.4) name the psychoanalytic process, or 'disrupting and disorganizing', as Parker portrays the Lacanian imperative, do not seem quite adequate to the experience of suffering. There is a reasonable claim to be made that the stance of relational psychoanalysis, with its valorisation of the narrative worth of the subject's speech in the context of a listening, 'recognising' other, might have more to offer in a political context in which reducing people to meaninglessness is one of the *problems*. This is a point made in slightly different ways by Lynne Layton (2008) in her examination of psychoanalysis' response to neoliberalism (which pushes people into the position of being commodities) and by Rustin (2008) in his comment that 'The distinctiveness of this tradition is that it has upheld a commitment to analytic truth as the best way of enhancing the mental well-being of patients and refused to separate the pursuit of understanding and achievement of therapeutic benefit' (p.413). In terms of both therapeutic need and emancipatory practice it would be indefensible to criticise clinicians who engage with patients' feelings, who focus carefully on transference and countertransference in the consulting room, and who try to act ethically to give their patients an experience of being recognised and understood. Clearly, the theoretical apparatus of psychoanalysis facilitates this necessary work.

The situation of psychosocial studies, however, is different from that of clinical work, both as a mode of research (e.g. in the utility of its concepts in empirical investigations) and theoretically, as it lays out the nature of the 'psychosocial subject'. The 'non-sensical' stance of Lacanian psychoanalysis reflects a distinction to be made between the 'therapeutic' and 'analytic' elements of psychoanalysis, a distinction which has long been familiar from discussions of the 'analytic attitude' (e.g. Rieff, 1966), and has also resurfaced in critiques of narrative in psychoanalysis (Laplanche, 2003). The central idea promoted in this work is to oppose the normativeness present in assumptions around individualism and the priority of reparation and care. This produces a more analytic, so clearly a more 'austere' attitude, but also one that opens out possibilities for thought and action that might be closed down by too definite an interpretive stance. Parker's contention that we should not approach a text as something we can understand, but rather as something waiting to be opened up, derives in part from his reading of the end of a Lacanian analysis as 'bringing the subject to the point where they are a perfect Saussurean, such that they recognize that the language that bears them is made up only of differences without any positive terms' (Parker, 2005a, p.168). For him, this motif of 'absolute difference' sets up the task of the Lacanian as 'searching for patterns and connections between signifiers, but as connections that differentiate them from each other and hold them in tension rather than divining connections that reveal an underlying order' (ibid.). Not down and deep, that is, but out and wide – that is the motion whereby something started off in the subject, something unexpected and surprising, gives rise to something else, that might be a kind of tag or answer, or perhaps a new version of the unconscious. 'The unconscious', writes Nasio (1992), 'is a constantly active process that exteriorizes itself incessantly through acts, events or speech that meet the conditions that define a signifier, namely, to be an involuntary expression, opportune, devoid of meaning, and identifiable as an event in connection with other absent or virtual events' (p.3). If this is the reading we have of the unconscious, there is no pre-existing grid that can be drawn on to find the defended subject and trace her or his manoeuvres when faced with the anxiety that undoubtedly pervades everything. Such a grid would reflect an imaginary stance, in which the existence of an 'answer' to the subject's 'problem' (for instance, her or his confusion of narrative) is postulated. Rather, the unconscious emerges only in what happens when expectation is exceeded and some kind of response is drawn out of the other with whom the subject is in contact; this response might or might not be containing or interpretive, but most of all it will be a surprise.

Reflexivity, countertransference and psychosocial research

Both the productivity and restrictiveness of psychoanalysis applied in this area can be examined finally through reference to the issue of reflexivity. The familiar idea within psychosocial studies and more broadly in the critical social sciences is that the existence of an objective 'out there' that can be studied from a position of neutrality is not tenable, at least not in the social arena, because of the responsiveness of people to the ideas that surround them. People *use* ideas in order to create themselves; they are, in this specific sense, meaning-making machines. Reflexivity is thus part of a movement against objectivism in the social sciences (Bourdieu, 1999), and hence is an approach which challenges the claim that there can ever be a 'truth' that is separate from the practices that give rise to it. In this way, reflexivity points to a potentially subversive procedure in which the conditions of emergence of knowledge are analysed as well as the apparent objects of knowledge themselves. In research terms, this means that when faced with human subjects the researcher is not able to assume a naïve or external other to be investigated, but rather must think about the way in which the subject is a source of meaning-making agency, using the props of the research situation actively to reconstruct her or his consciousness in the flow of social experiences. An example here is the transformation of understanding of the research interview when one shifts from a classical view of language as representation to one of language as performative. The act of speaking about something changes the speaker; what the subject 'knows' shifts as a result of the interview, as it is co-constructed in and through the interchange with the researcher. So, for example, it would be reasonable for a respondent to answer an interview question with the phrase, 'I've never thought about it like that', and then go on to construct a response that is as new to her or him as it is to the interviewer. This poses considerable problems for traditional notions of reliability and validity in research, and makes awkward any assumption of knowledge about a subject, as all knowledge becomes temporally and interpersonally positioned. It does not, of course, make such knowledge *impossible*; rather, it makes it contingent, strategic and provisional, best construed as the closure of theory around an arbitrary fixed point or full stop, as Stuart Hall (1996) terms it, or perhaps linked with Lacan's (1956) idea of 'points de capiton' ('quilting points') knotting signifier and signified together. Nevertheless, reflexive theory emphasises how people construct themselves through positions taken on cultural axes, including that offered by psychoanalysis. That is, the 'truth' of psychoanalysis lies in its power as a social, sense-making discourse. Research is not a process of uncovering (even relative) 'truths' about people, but rather exposes the ways in which subjects are positioned by the theoretical structures used (by them as well as by researchers) to understand them.

Under these circumstances, researcher and research activity have to be theorised as contributing to the production of knowledge. For Bourdieu, reflexivity involves a type of objectification of the researcher, in which the researcher (and her or his discipline) is explored for the effect that she or he may be having on the subject, but also

> *to objectify the act of objectification*: to consider the position of the researcher within his or her own milieu alongside the field position of the object of research, and comparatively to reflect upon how positions within the field, both of the researcher and of the researched, might exert determinative influence upon the end product of social analysis. (Stepney, 2003, p.131)

Consistent with this is the vision of research as a mode of knowledge production that directly implicates the subjective presence of the researcher within the account of the object of study. In other words, social research operates in and through a particular relationship between researcher and subject, which, in Bourdieu's account, is not completely arbitrary but is determined by the social structure itself.

Doing social research requires knowledge of this structuring process and the way in which it positions the research that is generated. Such knowledge is achieved through reflection on how 'research' is constituted, how its power structures are realised, what is regarded as useful and meaningful, what expectations are generated, and so on. More prosaically, this kind of reflexivity requires the researcher to keep an honest gaze on what she or he brings to the research process: how it is set up, what is communicated to the subject, what differences of race, class, gender, etc., might prevail and what impact they might have, and how her or his actions might influence the subject's own active meaning-making activities. This is commonly addressed through transcription procedures that allow close scrutiny of the researcher's words (in interview research), diaries recording everything that strikes the researcher, feedback from and to the research subjects, and attempts to talk rigorously with supervisors and others about the nature and impact of the work.

These practices are important and indeed necessary in relation to the complexities of the research process (e.g. Potter and Hepburn, 2005). However, a major difficulty with them concerns what account can in fact be given of the investments of the researcher in the knowledge-making process. Hook (2008b) comments:

> inasmuch as reflexivity involves a type of ego-judgement on its own productions, it cannot but be part of the problem, a means of insulating the méconnaissance of ego-misrecognition within a closed circuit. Neither the perspective I have on my own perspective, nor my coresearcher's input on my own input entails an adequate degree of otherness; for reflexivity to work, a far more radical break, a more forceful discontinuity needs to be introduced. (p.410)

Here, psychoanalysis has considerably more sophisticated concepts available to it than can be found in much social science, but this very sophistication makes the issues more problematic. For example, some social researchers seem to imply that describing researchers' investments in their work might be a relatively simple, technical matter, perhaps an issue of confession or self-revelation. But what is to be revealed? The researcher's gender, class and 'race' positions may well be relevant and it may be important to declare them as a way to increase the transparency and richness of the data produced. This is, indeed, the strategy employed by some of the best practitioners of the new social science. For instance, Margaret Wetherell acknowledges that her work on racism in New Zealand is influenced by her own history as a white New Zealander (Wetherell and Potter, 1992). However, even where researchers have been scrupulous in laying out the ways in which they might have promoted certain 'responses' or narratives from their research participants, the most they are able to do is declare their conscious intentions and include material such as full transcripts to enable a reader to form an impression of the researcher's own contribution. Psychoanalysis would regard this kind of reflexivity as both too restricted and too general, in that it recognises social structures and can track interpersonal interactions, but has a deeply impoverished vocabulary for describing the intersubjectivity of the research process – the ways in which each person 'uses' the other, unacknowledged and unconsciously. Declarations of relatively explicit aspects of the researcher's persona will therefore never be complete enough to understand what her or his contribution to the research might be, let alone to comprehend the nuances of the interpretive strategy employed in data analysis. There are likely, for example, to be complex unconscious processes interacting with the research work, encouraging some ways of going about things, inhibiting others. Psychoanalysis draws attention to this and also shows how complicated it is. How does one attend to the moment-by-moment flows between, for instance, interviewer and interviewee, and what can be learnt from these that might pass muster under the heading of 'research'?

The reflexivity argument has a number of implications in relation to the employment of psychoanalysis in qualitative psychosocial research. For Parker (2005b) it focuses and limits the possibilities of psychoanalysis itself, understood as a compelling narrative that is culturally specific and even functional:

> What psychoanalytic research can do, then, is to turn psychoanalytic knowledge around against itself so we understand better the way that psychoanalytic ideas have themselves encouraged us to look for things deep inside us as the causes of social problems. Psychoanalytic subjectivity – our sense of ourselves as having hidden childhood desires and destructive wishes – is the perfect complement to economic exploitation in capitalist society, for both succeed in making the victims blame themselves. (p.105)

This takes to its logical conclusion the constructionist argument that subjects are produced discursively, though exactly how psychoanalysis will reveal the conditions of its own operation as an exploitative system is left open to speculation, and the claim in the quotation that psychoanalysis promotes self-blame misses an important distinction between blame and responsibility. More conventionally, Parker draws attention to the impact of psychoanalysis' emphasis on the ways knowledge (specifically of the analysand) is mediated through the person – the subjectivity – of the knower (the analyst). That is, knowing the other involves knowing the impact of the other on (or 'in') the self, and requires a capacity to reflect on this in a way that openly recognises both the pre-existing investment of the knower/researcher in the material, and what is added to this by the specific concerns of the other. Parker (2005b) comments on how this produces a reassessment of conventional research ideas on subjectivity as a problem:

> Subjectivity is viewed by psychoanalysis, as with much qualitative research, not as a problem but as a resource (and topic). To draw upon one's own subjectivity in the research process does not mean that one is not being 'objective', but that one actually comes closer to a truer account. In psychoanalytic terms, the 'investment' the researcher has in the material they are studying plays a major role in the interest that will eventually accrue from the research. (p.117)

This is a familiar point in relation to psychoanalytic infant observation, where it is held that knowledge of the child can *only* be obtained through registering the observer's emotional response to what she or he sees (Waddell, 1988). Coded more broadly as 'countertransference', it is also a feature of most contemporary psychoanalytic practice, especially that influenced by Kleinian and British School thinking. Hence Hollway and Jefferson's (2005) assertion that in their psychoanalytically-inflected qualitative work they can ground their interpretive claims through what they describe as an analysis of the 'countertransference'. Referring to their case study of 'Vince' from their research into anxiety and fear of crime, they claim that information is generated through comparing the different responses the two researchers had to the participant himself:

> We used these and the triangulation of them between the two of us. For example, while WH [Wendy Hollway] wanted to describe Vince as quiet-spoken and unassertive, TJ [Tony Jefferson] was more inclined to describe him as timid. We used this information to reflect on how we were differently positioned in relation to Vince through these different countertransference responses. Wendy, who conducted both interviews, found herself feeling suspiciously protective of him, while Tony, having met him briefly, listened to the audiotapes and read the transcripts, felt critical of his timidity. This observation is an example of how to use the psychoanalytic principle of unconscious intersubjectivity to theorize the effect of research relationship(s) on the production and analysis of data. (p.151)

The value of this procedure is that it provides a space for checking out the researchers' responses to the research participant and thinking through what these responses might signify. It also draws attention to the position of the researcher in qualitative work, where the end point of research might be various constructed versions of experience rather than full knowledge of an objective and fixed external reality. The task of the interviewer, therefore, shifts from one of eliciting the interviewee's 'real' views to creating the conditions under which a thoughtful conversation can take place. In doing work of this kind, the person of the researcher is deeply implicated. If it is the case that psychological knowledge is constructed in the context of an interchange between 'researcher' and 'researched', then understanding the determining characteristics of that interaction – including what the researcher brings to it – is crucial for evaluating the significance of any research 'findings'.

However, the practice Hollway and Jefferson describe is in some important respects significantly different from the kind of exploration of unconscious material characteristic of psychoanalytic reflection on the countertransference in the *clinical* situation. What the researchers do is notice how a participant made them feel (protective, critical) without the necessary limitations of the analytic session and contract which would allow one to understand the validity of this response. Vince does not come to them for help – does not announce that he feels something to be wrong, or that the researcher can offer him anything. Indeed, he does not set up that particular transference on which the whole analytic encounter is based. On the contrary, Hollway (who conducted this interview) goes to Vince, wants to interview him, wants to find out something about him, wants to 'make sense of him', so the interaction is primarily driven by *her* desire. In this context, her feelings and responses are better thought about as *her transference*, not her countertransference; they are rather like Freud's (1907) insertion of his own associations to the dreams in *Gradiva*, described in Chapter 2. Clearly, both Hollway and Jefferson have thoughts and feelings about their interviewees, but what might be termed the 'conditions of emergence' of these are so far removed from the analytic situation as to make their affiliation with psychoanalytic terminology strained and potentially misleading. Hook (2008b) summarises the more general version of this argument:

> We might admit that psychoanalytic interpretation remains always poised on the verge of wild analysis. This, it would seem, is the inherent epistemic risk posed by a discipline that hopes to trace the unconscious in its most unlikely and absurd manifestations. If this is indeed the case, then the factors of supervision, clinical technique, the provision of an appropriate ethical code, and the contextualization of a detailed and ongoing (week-by-week, year-by-year) life history – that is, precisely those factors that in part define the clinic

> – are all of absolute necessity. It is thus difficult to see how one can justifiably extend clinical psychoanalytic warrants (such as diagnosis and interpretation of individuals) beyond the parameters of the clinic. (p.399)

The grounding of psychoanalytic interpretive practices so that they do not wander away into complete speculative freedom requires numerous factors that have evolved over time to regulate the conduct of clinical encounters. As Hook suggests, these hedge the tendency of analysis to become 'wild' and make it into a more ordered process. This can of course always be challenged (it is part of the argument here that no interpretation can come near the 'truth'), but at least has the traditions of the clinic to bolster it and make it into a predictable framework in which the significance of events can be evaluated and judgements can be made about the reasonableness of what is claimed and said. Research has its own such traditions, but they are different, and this difference needs to be marked up rather than obscured by using the vocabulary of psychoanalysis as if the things referred to (for example, transference and countertransference) mean the same in whatever social context they appear.

A number of other psychoanalytically informed psychosocial researchers have tried out ways of incorporating this kind of sensitivity to subjectivity into their work. This has been done perhaps most notably through the use of group procedures to check and examine researchers' systematic responses to their material (e.g. Marks and Mönnich-Marks, 2003, who used this approach to identify possible unconscious motivational mechanisms at work in their sample of Nazi sympathisers) – a way of working congruent with the standard infant observation training methods mentioned above. Nevertheless, significant problems remain. Many of these are methodological and refer to the difficulty of knowing what to do with the richly subjective, suggestive texts that derive from free and evocative interviewing procedures and personal modes of interpretation (Frosh and Saville Young, 2008). More generally, however, there is the tendency already noted to adopt psychoanalytic ideas of countertransference as if they are the same as social-science notions of reflexivity. The difficulties with this are due to deployment in one context of psychoanalytic interpretive strategies and grounding procedures that have arisen most convincingly in another context with strikingly different characteristics – that of the clinical situation of the 'consulting room'. This returns us to some of the most intractable and general issues about psychoanalysis in psychosocial studies. Where psychoanalysis is mined for its *technology*, as for instance where notions of countertransference are applied to discussions of how researchers feel, there is a danger that it will be used as an ungrounded expert system of knowledge in precisely the way objected to by its critics. Even the more cautious approach of Marks and Mönnich-Marks (2003) relies on a pre-given idea that the emotional reactions of the researchers (all of whom will be socialised into a certain kind of consciousness and are likely to become more similar to one another through their repeated discussions and shared stories of their research) are meaningful as indicators of the actual *unconscious* state of mind of the participants. This is a direct result of the application of a Kleinian style of psychoanalysis in which the truth of the subject can be known through mediation by (or through the unconscious of) an interlocutor who has more knowledge and understanding than does the subject. In Lacanian terms, we are in the domain of the imaginary here, expecting there to be a real totality that can be understood from outside it, instead of appreciating the fictive nature of all totalities, and the way that necessarily means that all subjects – analysts as well as analysands, clever and reflective researchers as well as recalcitrant participants – relate *partially*. Psychoanalysis is normative (or in Lacanian terms, untruthful) when its reflexivity is seen as a way of knowing the subject 'better'. In that mode it has relatively little to contribute to psychosocial studies other than a set of rather mechanistic ideas that explain processes of internalisation but risk separating and reifying the 'inner' and 'outer' in a manner that goes against the psychosocial ambition to theorise them together. Psychoanalysis has more to offer when its disruptive and performative elements are placed in the foreground; that is, when the kind of reflexivity it advances is one that acknowledges the way the phenomena of the psychosocial are produced *through the actions of* analyst and analysand, researcher and researched as a way of 'throw[ing] us off the psychoanalytic subject' (Baraitser, 2008, p.426). This means that cherished psychoanalytic ideas have to be rethought for the different context of investigation and expression: transference and countertransference, for example, are simply not the same in and out of the consulting room. But it also holds onto an important psychoanalytic insight that helps significantly with the task of thinking 'psychosocially'. This is the claim that psychological and social, inner and outer, are only artificially separated, and are constituted by something else that runs through them, sometimes emerging in surprising ways that psychoanalysts code as the 'unconscious' in its signifying, 'non-sensical' materialisation.

Conclusion

Psychoanalysis has an important part to play in the establishment of psychosocial studies as a disciplinary practice in which the social and the psychological are 'thought together'. In contrast to the other areas discussed in this book, which have their own substantial traditions with which psychoanalysis has to contend if it is to intervene in their fields, psychosocial studies is relatively new, and is still seeking to fully define its methodological approach and its object of analytic interest. Indeed, in most respects psychoanalysis is the senior partner in the encounter between them. Rustin (2008) comments: 'Psychoanalysis is more securely rooted and institutionalized as a field of practice and (clinical) research than is psychosocial studies, not less' (p.409), and this is undoubtedly true, with the consequence that psychosocial studies often looks to psychoanalysis for intellectual bolstering of its own still nascent conceptual armoury. This seems to have resulted in a kind of three-way split amongst researchers in this area. On one side, there is a debate about whether psychoanalysis is the best place to look for an underpinning for psychosocial studies, with the major alternative being discursive psychology, but with others such as phenomenology and Deleuzian philosophy certainly being fully in the ring. Amongst those who do draw predominantly on psychoanalysis, there is a division between those adopting a relational, particularly Kleinian, perspective and those more enamoured of Lacanian ideas. Members of the former group have adopted a more empirical basis for their work, seeking ways of filling out narrative and discursive qualitative research with psychoanalytic methods and interpretive procedures. The latter group, as tends to be their wont, has more commonly taken the high ground of theoretical critique, although there are now a few examples of psychosocial research that employ Lacanian ideas when carrying out analysis of empirical data (e.g. Saville Young and Frosh, 2009).

In this chapter, some of these issues have been revolved from the point of view of considerations of what happens to psychoanalysis under these promising yet somewhat fraught conditions. There certainly seems to be a considerable space available for psychoanalysis to impact upon psychosocial studies, and considerable benefit in it doing so. This is not to say that it should automatically be hegemonic here. The debate with discursive psychology, for example, is potentially a very productive one and has already led to important clarifications about how to theorise people's investments in particular discursive positions, about the emotional and even 'therapeutic' significance of narrative, and about different meanings of the term 'interpretation', some of them deeply challenging to psychoanalysis. Divergence about the kind of psychoanalysis best deployed in psychosocial studies also has its productive side, though there is a risk that it will reduce to a contest over the 'purity' of the position taken by different protagonists. In this chapter, it has been argued that the critical practice of psychoanalysis requires considerable caution over the use of its concepts in research, without recognition of how far this means they must travel from the clinical situation which gives them meaning. This has been coupled with an attempt to hold onto a position in which psychoanalysis is used to query and disrupt attitudes towards psychosocial data, or indeed to psychosocial studies itself, that are too immediately 'knowing' and authoritative. This has meant that the primary advocacy has been of a Lacanian perspective that might stand back from offering interpretive expertise and instead concentrate on observing the kinds of traces of unconscious impulses that were met with much earlier in this book, in the chapter on psychoanalysis and literature. The reciprocally destabilising effect of texts on psychoanalysis and psychoanalysis on texts that was tracked there is still the requirement for maintaining an open psychoanalysis that can be reflexively located as *analytic* rather than as the source of institutional expertise. Nevertheless, the alternative psychoanalytic position taken up by more empirically minded psychosocial researchers offers some important correctives to this somewhat abstract and possibly idealised high-mindedness. For example, it raises very practical questions about the reading of interview texts, the role of the researcher in constructing psychosocial data and the place of emotions in interpretation. As noted here, the difficulty is that these questions cannot be answered by assuming straightforward translation of psychoanalytic concepts and principles from the clinic to the 'outside': the distance is too great.

Many of these issues relate to the general concerns of this book, as well as being salient in the particular domain of psychosocial studies. *Why* psychoanalysis and *which* psychoanalysis are questions that apply in all the areas in which psychoanalysis intrudes; and *how* this intrusion then feeds back into psychoanalysis itself is crucial for determining whether it can remain an open intellectual discipline. In psychosocial studies, the ground is still sufficiently unmarked for these various contestations to be visible and lively, perhaps creating some of the best opportunities for psychoanalytic 'implication' in another discipline that have been available for some time.

Conclusion: Reflexivity Outside the Clinic

Re-view

There is much that is unstated in this book, or at least hinted at but not completely articulated. My assumption is that this is true of all books, as it is of all texts, narratives and discourses. At least, that is what both psychoanalysis and contemporary cultural theory would suggest, and what the new 'discipline' of psychosocial studies has taken in from both these traditions. The question is really whether what is stated is enough to convey my argument, and also to unsettle it sufficiently to prevent it from drifting into becoming another 'master discourse' of the kind that I have been criticising. I have plenty of doubts about this and so want to use the small space of this conclusion to reflect back on the claims made here, to consider what perspective they reveal, and to ask what can be done to query this without losing whatever force it might have.

The broad argument itself can, I hope, be fairly baldly stated. Psychoanalysis grew up in, and derives its authority from, the clinic. It is essentially a practice rooted in a live encounter between analyst and patient, with theory abstracted from this. The 'clinic' can be defined as any space that promotes this kind of live encounter. Psychoanalysis *outside* the clinic consequently refers to the intervention of psychoanalytic ideas and practices of interpretation drawn from psychoanalysis into environments not characterised by such live encounters. This includes empirical settings in which there is contact between a researcher and a research participant (for example, interviews or ethnographic studies), but where these have neither duration nor intensity comparable to that which allows psychoanalysts to ground their claimed knowledge of their patients. This book has considered a range of such interventions, focusing on social theory and psychosocial studies, but acknowledging that many others could have been chosen. Of particular interest has been the extent to which psychoanalysis can hold on to an ambition which is in some ways modest, when faced with the temptation to pronounce as an 'expert system' in these interventions. This means holding back from explaining the 'truth' of social phenomena to the host disciplines concerned, and instead limiting itself to asking some provocative questions, ensuring that emotion and irrationality are included in the relevant discussions of subjectivity. That is, the task of psychoanalysis is to direct attention towards the unconscious, without asserting a privileged position in doing so.

Drawing on some historical encounters (Freud's writings on literature and religion; the reconsideration of psychoanalysis and literature that took place in the 1980s), I have preferred Shoshana Felman's (1982a) notion of *implication* to that of application as a framework for describing and evaluating this work. This signifies an approach dealing not only with what psychoanalysis offers *to* the fields in which it operates, but also with what is reflected back into psychoanalysis *from* these applications. I have been particularly anxious to present a critique of the 'normalising' tendencies in psychoanalysis that construct it as what one might loosely call a 'bourgeois science', in order to advance its claim that it might retain a critical edge that can contribute to some kind of progressive move in social research. What is suggested here obviously has some political connotations, but at its most general it simply means using psychoanalysis to gain increased leverage on how social forces act to construct the human subject, rather than assuming that any particular version of the subject is the *necessary* norm. Because psychoanalysis is concerned with subjectivity, this means drawing together perspectives usually thought of as separate. That is, where the subjects of sociological or psychological analysis currently reside, the psychosocial subject is sought.

Despite its limitations, this book has been quite wide-ranging. One aim has been to achieve something genuinely transdisciplinary that reflects the history of the use of psychoanalysis, but also retains a critical stance towards it. In this regard, some of the material covered looks carefully grounded and fits the bill relatively well. Some, however, retains a speculative dimension that is attractive in many ways (without flights of fancy, it is difficult to think new thoughts), but might lead us back into the seductions of mastery. This applies to both the psychoanalytic traditions focused on in this book: relational psychoanalysis (broadly described, to include Kleinian approaches) and Lacanian psychoanalysis. In the former case, the move from the clinic to social and psychosocial studies is sometimes made too easily, without proper consideration of what this radical shift of setting means for the psychoanalytic concepts being used. This problem was flagged up particularly in the final chapter, on psychosocial studies, where Kleinian ideas have been imposed rather uncritically in some empirical work. It can also be seen in some of the ways both classical and emerging clinical ideas such as 'resistance' and 'recognition' have been extended to the political field and to a general philosophy of ethics. The *suggestive* power of these translations from the clinic is great and means that they are worth taking very seriously; but the requirement is to retain awareness of how they function as metaphors rather than as identities. Lacanianism, on the other hand, has largely infiltrated the academy through its cultural, philosophical and political applications. As such, it is in some ways better attuned to the task of 'implication', because it functions more like the other theories in these domains. However, this very compatibility risks the loss of the specific contribution that psychoanalysis can make. If this form of Lacanianism has already moved out of the clinic, then what is it that it can offer that is distinct from, for example, poststructuralist theories of the subject? How can the unconscious be kept in mind if it is not grounded in the actuality of the clinical encounter? Perhaps here the issue is to ensure that the continuing clinical fertility of Lacanian psychoanalysis is held in contact with its theoretical work in the academy in ways that are more common amongst adherents of the relational and Kleinian schools.

The previous chapters have made claims for a number of contributions by psychoanalysis to the social sciences. Psychoanalysis has genuine insights to offer about the formations of subjectivity and the place of the social (for example, through the 'other') in the emergence of the human subject. It opposes rationalism and positivism as philosophical stances because it demonstrates the strength of the 'irrational' in human conduct and the need to think through the impact of the unconscious when considering social as well as personal events. It has a subtle understanding of trauma, language and memory, of fears and desires. It can be used productively to trace the way discourses operate in 'texts' of various kinds, understood to include social and cultural materials as well as speech and writing. At its best, at least within the framework adopted in this book, it can be seen as making excursions into the social sciences which disrupt their taken-for-granted positions and augment or even overturn them by insisting that knowledge of the human subject can never be as they believed. Instead, it is always partial, always potentially undercut by some other way of being. More broadly, I have been making claims for the development of a new mode of academic practice, *psychosocial studies*, which attempts exactly the 'transdisciplinarity' mentioned above. Psychoanalysis intervenes to disrupt this emerging field as well, even as it provides it with some of its vocabulary and methodological procedures. In being taken up both as a substantive contributor to psychosocial studies and as a point of tension within it, psychoanalysis may have found a new space for the kind of implication in social research that gives it value outside the clinic. But, as with all the areas discussed in this book, this requires a continuing folding back on itself, a practice of reflexivity which is not always easy to achieve.

Reflexive practice

The demands of reflexivity do not only apply to the doing of psychoanalysis or social science, but also to the writing of books. Without being on the couch, it is difficult to trace all the sources of the choices made here, but it is perhaps possible to track some of their implications. As noted in Chapter 1, I have been rather under-inclusive in my selection of psychoanalytic theories for consideration, notably in paying what many (especially those in psychosocial studies) might regard as insufficient attention to what is known as British School psychoanalysis. This refers primarily to the tradition of Klein and Bion, but also to much object relations theory. These have instead been incorporated in a broader category of relational psychoanalysis, but it has to be acknowledged that whilst relational psychoanalysis draws heavily on Winnicott, it is much less connected with Kleinian thought. Indeed, in some of its manifestations – including the 'intersubjectivist' work of Jessica Benjamin, which has been used extensively in this book – it is *opposed* to Kleinianism. As my previous work attests (Frosh, 1999, 2006), I am not dismissive of British School work and in fact see it as making a considerable contribution to psychoanalysis as a resource for social thought. However, my reasoning in reducing its role here has to do with the promise of relational theory and the way it encourages the kinds of encounters with social research that this book endorses. Particularly through the varied (and contrasting) uses of the notion of *recognition* by Benjamin and Butler, one can see the emergence of a productive engagement with philosophical work on otherness that can create an elaborated understanding of social subjectivity. Kleinianism has lent its own categories of intersubjectivity for use in this, projection, introjection and projective identification being chief amongst them. However, its unswerving postulation of a 'depth' model and its focus on a separable 'inner world' make it less congruent with the psychosocial model sought here, in which no distinction is made between 'inside' and 'out'. It is also, in many of its manifestations, an example of an expert system of psychoanalysis that 'knows' its subject too well, and is at odds with the approach advocated here. That said, there is a definite loss in omitting Klein from the central dynamic of this work. As noted in Chapter 2, the profound attention it gives to destructiveness has been an important source of the cultural currency that it has. Other approaches also deal with destructiveness, and it is here that the influence of Kleinianism can be seen in relational psychoanalysis, alongside that of Hegel. Lacanian thought is also attuned to it, as the material on the neighbour and the 'Thing' shows. But there can be little argument with the claim that Kleinian psychoanalysis has the most fully developed theory of, and the most unwavering focus on, the forces of destruction, and one might consider that the contribution made by psychoanalysis to some of the more pressing contemporary social concerns could be lessened without it.

Other psychoanalytic approaches are also relatively absent, as are other fields of potential application/implication. The reasons behind the selections and omissions of this book are given in Chapter 1. However, looking back over this, and over other elements in my writing, what it seems to reveal is the types of 'seduction' that certain encounters outside the clinic hold for those of us who are enamoured of psychoanalysis, however ambivalently. The *intellectual* reasons for seeking to inform contemporary social science through an encounter with psychoanalysis, and vice versa, have been given continually throughout this book, and one hopes that the demonstration of their mutual fertility is convincing. It is not really that difficult to argue that psychoanalysis has one of the most elaborate vocabularies and conceptual systems addressing subjectivity, so it has to be brought into any debate that deals with this area of academic activity. Its power to query the surface of things is invaluable both as a tool and also as a continuing counterweight to tendencies towards claiming the truth of knowledge. So much has been asserted repeatedly here. But one is still left with a legitimate question about what the appeal might be, particularly if – as in this book – some of the more esoteric aspects of psychoanalysis are constantly drawn on, pushing readers away from its core, relatively simple ideas.

For Baudrillard (1979), in one of the founding texts of postmodernism, 'seduction' is opposed to psychoanalytic 'interpretation' in the same way that surface is opposed to depth. As it happens, he mistrusts depth. 'Getting beyond appearances is an impossible task', he writes (p.149), because every approach that tries to do this becomes seduced by its own terms, forms and appearances, until it becomes over-enamoured with its own presence, which it uses to persuade, flatter and deceive others. 'The havoc interpretation wreaks in the domain of appearances is incalculable', Baudrillard states (ibid.). The search for meaning is instructive because it reveals the attraction of that search, not because it actually discovers something meaningful lurking in the depths. Lacan (1991) addresses some similar issues when he outlines a number of the 'lures' of psychoanalysis, amongst which, as Parker (2008) points out, is belief in the progressive possibilities of psychoanalysis ('I am not a man of the left', asserts Lacan, 1991, p.114). This suggests that psychoanalysis itself is a kind of lure, a seduction that may have less to do with its intellectual weightiness and more with what its *associations* are, its flashy surface, one might say, or at least its appearance. This is rather a disconcerting thought for someone trying to write in a scholarly way about psychoanalysis, but it does seem apposite if one is doing this whilst also distancing oneself from the everyday difficulty faced by psychoanalysts who are doing 'routine' clinical work. Without idealising the latter, for clinical work itself has plenty of seductions (how one thinks of oneself, how one presents oneself to others, the prospect of voyeurism, and so on), the grounding of clinical psychoanalysis in human suffering is real enough to act as a *memento mori*. Lacking it, perhaps we are only left with the *appearance* of something meaningful. This can drift into becoming a kind of intellectual game in which one can feel special because of the suggestion that speaking in a psychoanalytic voice puts one in touch with real human depths, when in fact it is just another way of talking about the same things, mostly in the same small rooms.

I hope, of course, that this is not the case, though my own predilection for Lacanian obscurity makes me wonder. There is clearly a need for care. Nevertheless, the presentation of examples or 'interventions' throughout this book has aimed to show that something real is added by and to psychoanalysis when it openly engages with the other disciplines of the academy. It is important to renounce claims of mastery, but it matters equally that we open something out here that will allow understanding of the social to develop further than it can with its current disciplinary constraints. The key argument, if one can put it like this, is that without psychoanalysis as an involved, critical body of theory and practice, social theory and research remain tied to rationalist models that find too little space for the irruptions of subjectivity. The domain of the psychosocial is called into being here as a possible arena in which this can be contested and in which the division between social and personal, which is a construct of disciplinary practices rather than something 'real', might be broken down. It is too early to tell whether this will work, but without psychoanalysis it has much less chance of doing so.

However, this has to be a certain kind of psychoanalysis. It needs to retain its awareness of its clinical grounding, whilst also being sensitive to how it loses its authority outside the clinic (and even within it when that authority is contested – though that is another discussion). It needs to adopt an attitude of curiosity to the results of its forays outside, and be willing to have even cherished theoretical premises challenged by what it finds there. It needs to engage with questions about its own seduction into mastery and try to find a way to maintain its analytic 'discourse' as something that throws itself, and everything else, off balance. It might need to withdraw at times, when it knows too little, and be critical of itself, when it seems to know too much. Most of all, if the implication of psychoanalysis outside the clinic is to produce rich encounters, it needs to step back from its own normativeness, its own conformist tendencies, and ask how it can be constantly renewed.

References

Abel, E. (1989) *Virginia Woolf and the Fictions of Psychoanalysis.* Chicago: University of Chicago Press.

Adorno, T. (1967) Sociology and Psychology, Part I and II. *New Left Review, 46*, 67–97.

Adorno, T., Frenkel-Brunswick, E., Levinson, D. and Sanford, R. (1950) *The Authoritarian Personality.* New York: Norton, 1982.

Agamben, G. (1995) *Homo Sacer: Sovereign Power and Bare Life.* Stanford, CA: Stanford University Press.

Agamben, G. (2002) *Remnants of Auschwitz.* New York: Zone Books.

Allen, J. and Fonagy, P. (eds) (2006) *Handbook of Mentalization-Based Treatment.* Chichester: John Wiley.

Althusser, L. (1971) Ideology and Ideological State Apparatuses. In L. Althusser, *Lenin and Philosophy and other Essays.* London: New Left Books.

Altman, N., Benjamin, J., Jacobs, T. & Wachtel, P. (2006) Is Politics the Last Taboo in Psychoanalysis? In L. Layton, N. Hollander and S. Gutwill (eds), *Psychoanalysis, Class and Politics.* London: Routledge.

Appignanesi, L. and Forrester, J. (1992) *Freud's Women.* London: Weidenfeld & Nicolson.

Badiou, A. (2004) *Theoretical Writings.* London: Continuum.

Banton, R., Clifford, P., Frosh, S., Lousada, J. & Rosenthall, J. (1985) *The Politics of Mental Health.* London: Macmillan.

Baraitser, L. (2006) Introduction to Seminar with Jessica Benjamin. Centre for Psychosocial Studies, Birkbeck College, London.

Baraitser, L. (2008) On Giving and Taking Offence. *Psychoanalysis, Culture & Society, 13*, 423–7.

Baraitser, L. (2009) *Maternal Encounters: The Ethics of Interruption.* London: Routledge.

Baudrillard, J. (1979) On Seduction. In J. Baudrillard, *Selected Writings.* Cambridge: Polity, 1988.

Beckett, S. (1984) *Worstward Ho.* London: Calder.

Benjamin, J. (1988) *The Bonds of Love.* London: Virago.

Benjamin, J. (1995) *Like Subjects, Love Objects: Essays on Recognition and Sexual Difference.* London: Yale University Press.

Benjamin, J. (1998) *Shadow of the Other: Intersubjectivity and Gender in Psychoanalysis.* New York: Routledge.

Benjamin, J. (2000) Response to Commentaries by Mitchell and by Butler. *Studies in Gender and Sexuality, 1*, 291–308.

Benjamin, J. (2004) Beyond Doer and Done To: An Intersubjective View of Thirdness. *Psychoanalytic Quarterly, 73*, 5–46.

Benjamin, J. (2009) A Relational Psychoanalysis Perspective on the Necessity of

Acknowledging Failure in Order to Restore the Facilitating and Containing Features of the Intersubjective Relationship (the Shared Third). *International Journal of Psychoanalysis, 90*, 441–50.

Berman, M. (1983) *All That is Solid Melts into Air.* London: Verso.

Bernheimer, C. and Kahane, C. (eds) (1985) *In Dora's Case.* London: Virago.

Billig, M. (1997) The Dialogic Unconscious: Psychoanalysis, Discursive Psychology and the Nature of Repression. *British Journal of Social Psychology, 36*, 139–59.

Billig, M. (2006) Lacan's Misuse of Psychology: Evidence, Rhetoric and the Mirror Stage. *Theory, Culture & Society, 23*, 1–26.

Bion, W. (1959) *Experiences in Groups.* London: Tavistock.

Bion, W. (1962) *Learning from Experience.* London: Heinemann.

Bion, W, (1963) *Elements of Psychoanalysis.* London: Heinemann.

Bion, W. (1967) *Second Thoughts.* London: Heinemann.

Bloch, S. and Reddaway, P. (1984) *Soviet Psychiatric Abuse: The Shadow over World Psychiatry.* London: Victor Gollancz.

Bonaparte, M. (1933) *The Life and Works of Edgar Allan Poe.* Humanities Press, New York, 1971.

Bosteels, B. (2006) Alain Badiou's Theory of the Subject. In S. Žižek (ed.), *Lacan: The Silent Partners.* London: Verso.

Bourdieu, P. (1999) *The Logic of Practice.* Stanford, CA: Stanford University Press.

Brah, A. (1996) *Cartographies of Diaspora.* London: Routledge.

Braidotti, R. (2006) *Transpositions.* Cambridge: Polity.

Brennan, T. (ed.) (1989) *Between Feminism and Psychoanalysis.* London: Routledge.

Brooks, P. (1982) Freud's Masterplot. In S. Felman (ed.), *Literature and Psychoanalysis: The Question of Reading: Otherwise.* Baltimore: Johns Hopkins University Press.

Buber, M. (1959) *I and Thou.* Edinburgh: T&T Clark.

Burman, E. (2007) *Deconstructing Developmental Psychology.* London: Routledge.

Butler, J. (1990) *Gender Trouble: Feminism and the Subversion of Identity.* London: Routledge.

Butler, J. (1997) *The Psychic Life of Power.* Stanford, CA: Stanford University Press.

Butler, J. (2000) Longing for Recognition. *Studies in Gender and Sexuality, 1*, 271–90.

Butler, J. (2005) *Giving an Account of Oneself.* New York: Fordham University Press.

Butler, J. (2008) *Frames of* War. London: Verso.

Butler, J., Laclau, E. and Žižek, S. (2000) *Contingency, Hegemony, Universality: Contemporary Dialogues on the Left.* London: Verso.

Casement, P. (2002) *Learning from our Mistakes: Beyond Dogma in Psychoanalysis and Psychotherapy.* Hove: Brunner-Routledge.

Castoriadis, C. (1995) Logic, Imagination, Reflection. In A. Elliott and S. Frosh (eds), *Psychoanalysis in Contexts.* London: Routledge.

Coward, R. and Ellis, J. (1977) *Language and Materialism*. London: Routledge & Kegan Paul.

Deleuze, G. and Guattari, F. (1977) *Anti-Oedipus*. New York: Viking.

Deleuze, G. and Guattari, F. (1988) *A Thousand Plateaus*. London: Athlone.

Derrida, J. (1975) The Purveyor of Truth. *Yale French Studies*, *52* (Graphesis: Perspectives in Literature and Philosophy), 31–113.

Ehrenzweig, A. (1967) *The Hidden Order of Art*. London: Weidenfeld & Nicolson.

Eickhoff, F. (2006) On Nachträglichkeit: The Modernity of an Old Concept. *International Journal of Psychoanalysis, 87*, 1453–69.

Eliot, T.S. (1922) The Waste Land. In *The Waste Land and Other Poems*. London: Faber, 1940.

Ellmann, M. (1990) Eliot's Abjection. In J. Fletcher and A. Benjamin (eds), *Abjection, Melancholia and Love: The Work of Julia Kristeva*. London; Routledge.

Ellmann, M. (1994) Introduction. In M. Ellmann (ed.), *Psychoanalytic Literary Criticism*. Harlow: Longman.

Empson, W. (1956) *Seven Types of Ambiguity*. London: Chatto & Windus.

Erikson, E. (1956) The Problem of Ego Identity. *Journal of the American Psychoanalytic Association, 4*, 56–121.

Ettinger, B. (2006) *The Matrixial Borderspace*. Minneapolis: University of Minnesota Press.

Evans, D. (1996) *An Introductory Dictionary of Lacanian Psychoanalysis*. London: Routledge.

Felman, S. (1982a) To Open the Question. In S. Felman (ed.), *Literature and Psychoanalysis: The Question of Reading: Otherwise*. Baltimore: Johns Hopkins University Press.

Felman, S. (1982b) Turning the Screw of Interpretation. In S. Felman (ed.), *Literature and Psychoanalysis: The Question of Reading: Otherwise*. Baltimore: Johns Hopkins University Press.

Flax, J. (1996) Taking Multiplicity Seriously: Some Implications for Psychoanalytic Theorizing and Practice. *Contemporary Psychoanalysis, 32*, 577–93.

Fletcher, J. (1999) Psychoanalysis and the Question of the Other. Introduction to J. Laplanche, *Essays on Otherness*. London: Routledge.

Fletcher, J. (2007) Seduction and the Vicissitudes of Translation: The Work of Jean Laplanche. *Psychoanalytic Quarterly, 76*, 1241–91.

Fonagy, P. and Target, M. (2007) The Rooting of the Mind in the Body: New Links between Attachment Theory and Psychoanalytic Thought. *Journal of the American Psychoanalytic Association, 55*, 411–56.

Foucault, M. (1976) *History of Sexuality: Vol. 1*. London: Allen Lane.

Fox, D., Prilleltensky, I. and Austin, S. (2009) *Critical Psychology: An Introduction*. London: Sage.

Fraser, N. and Honneth, A. (2003) *Redistribution or Recognition: A Political-Philosophical Exchange*. London: Verso.

Freud, S. (1905) Fragment of an Analysis of a Case of Hysteria. *The Standard Edition of the Complete Psychological Works of Sigmund Freud, Volume*

VII (1901–1905): A Case of Hysteria, Three Essays on Sexuality and Other Works, 1–122.

Freud, S. (1907) Delusions and Dreams in Jensen's *Gradiva*. *The Standard Edition of the Complete Psychological Works of Sigmund Freud, Volume IX (1906–1908): Jensen's 'Gradiva' and Other Works*, 1–96.

Freud, S. (1908a) Creative Writers and Day-Dreaming. *The Standard Edition of the Complete Psychological Works of Sigmund Freud, Volume IX (1906–1908): Jensen's 'Gradiva' and Other Works*, 141–54.

Freud, S. (1908b) 'Civilized' Sexual Morality and Modern Nervous Illness. *The Standard Edition of the Complete Psychological Works of Sigmund Freud, Volume IX (1906–1908): Jensen's 'Gradiva' and Other Works*, 177–204.

Freud, S. (1910a) Leonardo Da Vinci and a Memory of his Childhood. *The Standard Edition of the Complete Psychological Works of Sigmund Freud, Volume XI (1910): Five Lectures on Psycho-Analysis, Leonardo da Vinci and Other Works*, 57–138.

Freud, S. (1910b) 'Wild' Psycho-Analysis. *The Standard Edition of the Complete Psychological Works of Sigmund Freud, Volume XI (1910): Five Lectures on Psycho-Analysis, Leonardo da Vinci and Other Works*, 219–28.

Freud, S. (1913a) Totem and Taboo. *The Standard Edition of the Complete Psychological Works of Sigmund Freud, Volume XIII (1913–1914): Totem and Taboo and Other Works*, vii–162.

Freud, S. (1913b) The Theme of the Three Caskets. *The Standard Edition of the Complete Psychological Works of Sigmund Freud, Volume XII (1911–1913): The Case of Schreber, Papers on Technique and Other Works*, 289–302.

Freud, S. (1914) The Moses of Michelangelo. *The Standard Edition of the Complete Psychological Works of Sigmund Freud, Volume XIII (1913–1914): Totem and Taboo and Other Works*, 209–38.

Freud, S. (1915) The Unconscious. *The Standard Edition of the Complete Psychological Works of Sigmund Freud, Volume XIV (1914–1916): On the History of the Psycho-Analytic Movement, Papers on Metapsychology and Other Works*, 159–215.

Freud, S. (1917a) Introductory Lectures on Psycho-Analysis. *The Standard Edition of the Complete Psychological Works of Sigmund Freud, Volume XVI (1916–1917): Introductory Lectures on Psycho-Analysis (Part III)*, 241–463.

Freud, S. (1917b) Mourning and Melancholia. *The Standard Edition of the Complete Psychological Works of Sigmund Freud, Volume XIV (1914–1916): On the History of the Psycho-Analytic Movement, Papers on Metapsychology and Other Works*, 237–58.

Freud, S. (1919) The 'Uncanny'. *The Standard Edition of the Complete Psychological Works of Sigmund Freud, Volume XVII (1917–1919): An Infantile Neurosis and Other Works*, 217–56.

Freud, S. (1920a) The Psychogenesis of a Case of Homosexuality in a Woman. *The Standard Edition of the Complete Psychological Works of Sigmund Freud, Volume XVIII (1920–1922): Beyond the Pleasure Principle, Group Psychology and Other Works*, 145–72.

Freud, S. (1920b) Beyond the Pleasure Principle. *The Standard Edition of the Complete Psychological Works of Sigmund Freud, Volume XVIII (1920–1922): Beyond the Pleasure Principle, Group Psychology and Other Works*, 1–64.

Freud, S. (1921) Group Psychology and the Analysis of the Ego. *The Standard Edition of the Complete Psychological Works of Sigmund Freud, Volume XVIII (1920–1922): Beyond the Pleasure Principle, Group Psychology and Other Works*, 65–144.

Freud, S. (1923) The Ego and the Id. *The Standard Edition of the Complete Psychological Works of Sigmund Freud, Volume XIX (1923–1925): The Ego and the Id and Other Works*, 1–66.

Freud, S. (1925) The Resistances to Psycho-Analysis. *The Standard Edition of the Complete Psychological Works of Sigmund Freud, Volume XIX (1923–1925): The Ego and the Id and Other Works*, 211–24.

Freud, S. (1926) Psycho-Analysis. *The Standard Edition of the Complete Psychological Works of Sigmund Freud, Volume XX (1925–1926): An Autobiographical Study, Inhibitions, Symptoms and Anxiety, The Question of Lay Analysis and Other Works*, 259–70.

Freud, S. (1927) The Future of an Illusion. *The Standard Edition of the Complete Psychological Works of Sigmund Freud, Volume XXI (1927–1931): The Future of an Illusion, Civilization and its Discontents, and Other Works*, 1–56.

Freud, S. (1930) Civilization and its Discontents. *The Standard Edition of the Complete Psychological Works of Sigmund Freud, Volume XXI (1927–1931): The Future of an Illusion, Civilization and its Discontents, and Other Works*, 57–146.

Freud, S. (1933) New Introductory Lectures On Psycho-Analysis. *The Standard Edition of the Complete Psychological Works of Sigmund Freud, Volume XXII (1932–1936): New Introductory Lectures on Psycho-Analysis and Other Works*, 1–182.

Freud, S. (1937) Analysis Terminable and Interminable. *The Standard Edition of the Complete Psychological Works of Sigmund Freud, Volume XXIII (1937–1939): Moses and Monotheism, An Outline of Psycho-Analysis and Other Works*, 209–54.

Freud, S. (1939) Moses and Monotheism. *The Standard Edition of the Complete Psychological Works of Sigmund Freud, Volume XXIII (1937–1939): Moses and Monotheism, An Outline of Psycho-Analysis and Other Works*, 1–138.

Freud, S. (1961) *Letters of Sigmund Freud 1873–1939* (ed. E. Freud). London: Hogarth Press.

Freud, S. and Einstein, A. (1933) Why War? *The Standard Edition of the Complete Psychological Works of Sigmund Freud, Volume XXII (1932–1936): New Introductory Lectures on Psycho-Analysis and Other Works*, 195–216.

Frosh, S. (1989) *Psychoanalysis and Psychology*. London: Macmillan.

Frosh, S. (1991) *Identity Crisis: Modernity, Psychoanalysis and the Self*. London: Macmillan.

Frosh, S. (1994) *Sexual Difference: Masculinity and Psychoanalysis*. London: Routledge.

Frosh, S. (1999) *The Politics of Psychoanalysis: An Introduction to Freudian and Post-Freudian Theory*. 2nd edn. Basingstoke: Palgrave.

Frosh, S. (2002) *After Words: The Personal in Gender, Culture and Psychotherapy*. Basingstoke: Palgrave Macmillan.

Frosh, S. (2003) Psychosocial Studies and Psychology: Is a Critical Approach Emerging? *Human Relations, 56*, 1547–67.

Frosh, S. (2005) *Hate and the Jewish Science: Anti-Semitism, Nazism and Psychoanalysis*. Basingstoke: Palgrave Macmillan.

Frosh, S. (2006) *For and Against Psychoanalysis*. 2nd edn. London: Routledge.

Frosh, S. (2007) Disintegrating Qualitative Research. *Theory and Psychology, 17*, 635–53.

Frosh, S., Phoenix, A. and Pattman, R. (2002) *Young Masculinities: Understanding Boys in Contemporary Society*. Basingstoke: Palgrave Macmillan.

Frosh, S., Phoenix, A. and Pattman, R. (2003) Taking a Stand: Using Psychoanalysis to Explore the Positioning of Subjects in Discourse. *British Journal of Social Psychology, 42*, 39–53.

Frosh, S. and Saville Young, L. (2008) Psychoanalytic Approaches to Qualitative Psychology. In C. Willig and W. Stainton-Rogers, *The Sage Handbook of Qualitative Research in Psychology*. London: Sage.

Gabbard, G. (2001) Introduction. In G. Gabbard (ed.), *Psychoanalysis and Film*. London: Karnac.

Gay, P. (1988) *Freud: A Life for Our Time*. London: Dent.

Gellner, E. (1985) *The Psychoanalytic Movement*. London: Paladin.

Giddens, A. (1991) *Modernity and Self-Identity*. Cambridge: Polity.

Goffman, E. (1969) *The Presentation of Self in Everyday Life*. London: Allen Lane.

Goldner, V. (2003) Ironic Gender/Authentic Sex. *Studies in Gender and Sexuality, 4*, 113–39.

Gould, S. (1996) *The Mismeasure of Man*. New York: Norton.

Greenacre, P. (1958) Early Physical Determinants in the Development of the Sense of Identity. *Journal of the American Psychoanalytic Association, 6*, 612–27.

Grinberg, L. and Grinberg, R. (1974) The Problem of Identity and the Psychoanalytical Process. *International Review of Psychoanalysis, 1*, 499–507.

Grünbaum, A. (1984) *The Foundations of Psychoanalysis: A Philosophical Critique*. Berkeley: University of California Press.

Guntrip, H. (1968) *Schizoid Phenomena, Object Relations and the Self*. London: Hogarth Press.

Habermas, J. (1968) *Knowledge and Human Interests*. Cambridge: Polity, 1987.

Hall, S. (1990) Cultural Identity and Diaspora. In J. Rutherford (ed.), *Identity: Community, Culture, Difference*. London: Lawrence & Wishart.

Hall, S. (1996) Who Needs 'Identity'? In S. Hall and P. du Gay (eds), *Questions of Cultural Identity*. London: Sage.

Haraway, D. (1991) *Simians, Cyborgs and Women: The Reinvention of Nature.* New York: Routledge.

Haraway, D. (2006) Encounters with Companion Species: Entangling Dogs, Baboons, Philosophers, and Biologists. *Configurations, 14,* 97–114.

Haraway, D. (2007) *When Species Meet.* Minneapolis: University of Minnesota Press.

Herzog, J. (2009) Triadic reality, same sex parents and child analysis: A response to Ann Smolen's 'Boys only! No mothers allowed'. *International Journal of Psychoanalysis, 90,* 19–26.

Hinshelwood, R. (1991) *A Dictionary of Kleinian Thought.* London: Free Association Books.

Hirst, P. (1979) *On Law and Ideology.* Basingstoke: Macmillan.

Hoggett, P. (2008) What's in a Hyphen? Reconstructing Psychosocial Studies. *Psychoanalysis, Culture & Society, 13,* 379–84.

Hollway, W. (2006) Paradox in the Pursuit of a Critical Theorization of the Development of Self in Family Relationships. *Theory and Psychology, 16,* 465–82.

Hollway, W. and Jefferson, T. (2000) *Doing Qualitative Research Differently.* London: Sage.

Hollway, W. and Jefferson, T. (2005) Panic and Perjury: A Psychosocial Exploration of Agency. *British Journal of Social Psychology, 44,* 147–63.

Hook, D. (2007) *Foucault, Psychology and the Analytics of Power.* Basingstoke: Palgrave.

Hook, D. (2008a) Fantasmatic Transactions: On the Persistence of Apartheid Ideology. *Subjectivity, 24,* 275–97.

Hook, D. (2008b) Articulating Psychoanalysis and Psychosocial Studies: Limitations and Possibilities. *Psychoanalysis, Culture & Society, 13,* 397–405.

Irigaray, L. (1985) *This Sex Which is Not One.* Ithaca, NY: Cornell University Press.

Isay, R. (1985) On the Analytic Therapy of Homosexual Men. *The Psychoanalytic Study of the Child, 40,* 235–54.

Jacobson, E. (1964) *The Self and the Object World.* London: Hogarth Press.

Jacoby, R. (1975) *Social Amnesia.* Sussex: Harvester.

Jacoby, R. (1983) *The Repression of Psychoanalysis.* New York: Basic Books.

Jameson, F. (1982) Imaginary and Symbolic in Lacan: Marxism, Psychoanalytic Criticism, and the Problem of the Subject. In S. Felman (ed.), *Literature and Psychoanalysis: The Question of Reading: Otherwise.* Baltimore: Johns Hopkins University Press.

Johnson, B. (1996) The Frame of Reference: Poe, Lacan, Derrida. In S. Vice (ed.), *Psychoanalytic Criticism.* Cambridge: Polity.

Jones, E. (1910) The Oedipus-Complex as An Explanation of Hamlet's Mystery: A Study in Motive. *American Journal of Psychology, 21,* 72–113.

Kelsen, H. (1924) The Conception of the State and Social Psychology – With Special Reference to Freud's Group Theory. *International Journal of Psycho-Analysis, 5,* 1–38.

Kerr, J. (1993) *A Most Dangerous Method.* New York: Knopf.

Kingsbury, P. (2007) Psychoanalytic Approaches. In J. Duncan, N. Johnson and R. Schein (eds), *A Companion to Cultural Geography*. Oxford: Blackwell.

Klein, M. (1927) Symposium on Child Analysis. *International Journal of Psycho-Analysis, 8*, 339–70.

Klein, M. (1932) *The Psycho-Analysis of Children*. London: Hogarth Press.

Klein, M. (1935) A Contribution to the Psychogenesis of Manic-Depressive States. *International Journal of Psycho-Analysis, 16*, 145–74.

Klein, M. (1955) The Psychoanalytic Play Technique. In M. Klein, *Envy and Gratitude and Other Works*. New York: Delta, 1975.

Klein, M. (1957) Envy and Gratitude. In M. Klein, *Envy and Gratitude and Other Works*. New York: Delta, 1975.

Kovel, J. (1995) On Racism and Psychoanalysis. In A. Elliott and S. Frosh (eds), *Psychoanalysis in Contexts*. London: Routledge.

Kristeva, J. (1983) Freud and Love. In T. Moi (ed.), *The Kristeva Reader*. Oxford: Blackwell, 1986.

Lacan, J. (1949) The Mirror Stage as Formative of the Function on the I as Revealed in the Psychoanalytic Experience. In J. Lacan, *Écrits: A Selection*. London: Tavistock, 1977.

Lacan, J. (1953) The Function and Field of Speech and Language in Psychoanalysis. In J. Lacan, *Écrits*. New York: Norton, 2005.

Lacan, J. (1954–55) *The Seminars of Jacques Lacan, Book II: The Ego in Freud's Theory and in the Technique of Psychoanalysis*. Cambridge: Cambridge University Press.

Lacan, J. (1956) The Quilting Point. In J. Lacan, *The Psychoses: The Seminar of Jacques Lacan Book III, 1955–6*. London: Routledge.

Lacan, J. (1959–60) *The Ethics of Psychoanalysis: The Seminar of Jacques Lacan Book VII*. London: Routledge, 1992.

Lacan, J. (1973) *The Four Fundamental Concepts of Psychoanalysis*. Harmondsworth: Penguin, 1979.

Lacan, J. (1991) *The Other Side of Psychoanalysis: The Seminar of Jacques Lacan Book XVII*. New York: Norton, 2007.

Laplanche, J. (1999) The Unfinished Copernican Revolution. In J. Laplanche, *Essays on Otherness*. London: Routledge.

Laplanche, J. (2003) Narrativity and Hermeneutics: Some Propositions. *New Formations, 48*, 26–9.

Laplanche, J. and Pontalis, J.-B. (1967) *The Language of Psychoanalysis*. London: Hogarth Press, 1973.

Latour, B. (2007) *Reassembling the Social: An Introduction to Actor-Network-Theory*. Oxford: Oxford University Press.

Layton, L. (2008) What Divides the Subject? Psychoanalytic Reflections on Subjectivity, Subjection and Resistance. *Subjectivity, 22*, 60–72.

Lear, J. (2005) *Freud*. London: Routledge.

Levi, P. (1960) *If This is a Man*. London: Abacus, 1987.

Levinas, E. (1985) *Ethics and Infinity*. Pittsburgh, PA: Duquesne University Press.

Levinas, E. (1991) *Entre Nous: On Thinking of the Other*. London: Athlone Press, 1998.

Lingis, A. (1994) *The Community of Those Who Have Nothing in Common*. Indianapolis: Indiana University Press.

Marcus, S. (1975) Freud and Dora: Story, History, Case History. In C. Bernheimer and C. Kahane (eds), *In Dora's Case*. London: Virago, 1985.

Marcuse, H. (1955) *Eros and Civilization*. Boston: Beacon Press, 1966.

Marcuse, H. (1965) *Negations*. Harmondsworth: Penguin.

Marks, E. and de Courtivron, I. (eds) (1981) *New French Feminisms*. Sussex: Harvester.

Marks, S. and Mönnich-Marks, H. (2003) The Analysis of Counter-Transference Reactions Is a Means to Discern Latent Interview-Contents. *Forum: Qualitative Social Research, 4 (2)*, www.ph-freiburg.de/sozial/Marks/fqs.pdf (accessed 6 February 2008).

Mayes, L., Fonagy, P. and Target, M. (eds) (2007) *Developmental Science and Psychoanalysis: Integration and Innovation*. London: Karnac.

McNay, L. (2008) The Trouble with Recognition: Subjectivity, Suffering, and Agency. *Sociological Theory* 26, 271–96.

Metz, C. (1977) *Psychoanalysis and Cinema: The Imaginary Signifier*. London: Macmillan, 1982.

Mitchell, J. (1974) *Psychoanalysis and Feminism*. Harmondsworth: Penguin.

Mitchell, J. (2002) Reply to Lynne Segal's Commentary. *Studies in Gender and Sexuality*, 3, 217–28.

Moi, T. (1989) Patriarchal Thought and the Drive for Knowledge. In T. Brennan (ed.), *Between Feminism and Psychoanalysis*. London: Routledge.

Moore, B. and Fine, B. (1990) *Psychoanalytic Terms and Concepts*. New Haven, CT: Yale University Press.

Mulvey, L. (1975) Visual Pleasure and Narrative Cinema. In L. Mulvey, *Visual and Other Pleasures*. London: Macmillan, 1989.

Mulvey, L. (1989) *Visual and Other Pleasures*. London: Macmillan.

Nasio, J. (1992) *Five Lessons on the Psychoanalytic Theory of Jacques Lacan*. Albany: State University of New York Press, 1998.

Nobus, D. and Quinn, M. (2005) *Knowing Nothing, Staying Stupid*. London: Routledge.

Ogden, T. (1999) 'The Music of What Happens' in Poetry and Psychoanalysis. *International Journal of Psychoanalysis, 80*, 979–94.

Parker, I. (1997) *Psychoanalytic Culture: Psychoanalytic Discourse in Western Society*. London: Sage.

Parker, I. (2005a) Lacanian Discourse Analysis in Psychology: Seven Theoretical Elements. *Theory and Psychology, 15*, 163–82.

Parker, I. (2005b) *Qualitative Psychology: Introducing Radical Research*. Maidenhead: Open University Press.

Parker, I. (2007) *Revolution in Psychology: Alienation to Emancipation*. London: Pluto Press.

Parker, I. (2008) Temptations of Pedagogery: Seventeen Lures (review of Lacan's *Seminar XVII*). *Subjectivities, 24*, 376–9.

Perri 6, Radstone, S., Squire, C. and Treacher, A. (eds) (2006) *Public Emotions*. Basingstoke: Palgrave Macmillan.

Phillips, A. (1988) *Winnicott*. London: Fontana.

Phoenix, A. and Rattansi, A. (2005) Proliferating Theories: Self and Identity in Post-Eriksonian Context. *Identity, 5*, 205–25.

Pick, D. (1995) Freud's Group Psychology and the History of the Crowd. *History Workshop Journal, 40*, 39–61.

Potter, J. and Hepburn, A. (2005) Qualitative Interviews in Psychology: Problems and Possibilities. *Qualitative Research in Psychology, 2*, 281–307.

Quayson, A. (2007) Area Studies, Diaspora Studies, and Critical Pedagogies. *Comparative Studies of South Asia, Africa and the Middle East, 27*, 580–90.

Reinhard, K. (2005) Toward a Political Theology of the Neighbor. In S. ?i?ek, E. Santner and K. Reinhard, *The Neighbour: Three Inquiries in Political Theology.* Chicago: University of Chicago Press.

Rieff, P. (1966) *The Triumph of the Therapeutic.* Harmondsworth: Penguin.

Riley, D. (2005) *Impersonal Passion.* Durham, NC: Duke University Press.

Riviere, J. (1927) Symposium on Child Analysis. *International Journal of Psycho-Analysis, 8*, 370–7.

Riviere, J. (1936) On the Genesis of Psychical Conflict in Earliest Infancy. In J. Riviere, *Collected Papers 1920–1958*. London: Karnac, 1991.

Robinson, A. (2004) The Politics of Lack. *British Journal of Politics and International Relations, 6*, 259–69.

Rose, H. and Rose, S. (2000) *Alas, Poor Darwin: Arguments Against Evolutionary Psychology.* London: Vintage.

Rose, J. (1996) *States of Fantasy.* Oxford: Clarendon Press.

Rose, J. (2003) *On Not Being Able to Sleep*. London: Vintage.

Rose, J. (2005) *The Question of Zion.* Princeton: Princeton University Press.

Rose, J. (2007) *The Last Resistance.* London: Verso.

Rose, N. (1998) *Inventing our Selves: Psychology, Power and Personhood.* Cambridge: Cambridge University Press.

Roseneil, S. (2006) The Ambivalences of Angel's 'Arrangement': A Psychosocial Lens on the Contemporary Condition of Personal Life. *Sociological Review, 54*, 846–68.

Rustin, M. (1991) *The Good Society and the Inner World.* London: Verso.

Rustin, M. (1995) Lacan, Klein and Politics: The Positive and Negative in Psychoanalytic Thought. In A. Elliott and S. Frosh (eds), *Psychoanalysis in Contexts.* London: Routledge.

Rustin, M. (1999) Psychoanalysis: The Last Modernism? In D. Bell (ed.), *Psychoanalysis and Culture.* London: Duckworth.

Rustin, M. (2008) For Dialogue between Psychoanalysis and Constructionism. *Psychoanalysis, Culture & Society, 13*, 406–15.

Said, E. (2007) *On Late Style: Music and Literature against the Grain.* London: Bloomsbury.

Samuels, A. (1993) *The Political Psyche.* London: Routledge.

Sandler, J., Dare, C. and Holder, A. (1973) *The Patient and the Analyst.* London: Maresfield Reprints, 1979.

Saville Young, L. and Frosh, S. (2009) Discourse and Psychoanalysis: Translating Concepts into 'Fragmenting' Methodology. *Psychology in Society, 38*, 1–16.

Schwartz, J. (1999) *Cassandra's Daughter: A History of Psychoanalysis in Europe and America.* Harmondsworth: Allen Lane.

Segal, H. (1979) *Klein*. Glasgow: Fontana.
Segal, H. (1991) *Dream, Phantasy and Art*. London: Karnac.
Segal, H. (1995) From Hiroshima to the Gulf War and After: A Psychoanalytic Perspective. In A. Elliott and S. Frosh (eds), *Psychoanalysis in Contexts*. London: Routledge.
Segal, L. (2001) Psychoanalysis and Politics: Juliet Mitchell, Then and Now. *Studies in Gender and Sexuality*, 2, 327–43.
Smolen, A. (2009) Boys Only! No Mothers Allowed. *International Journal of Psychoanalysis, 90*, 1–11.
Spivak, G. Chakravorty (1988) Can the Subaltern Speak? In C. Nelson and L. Grossberg (eds), *Marxism and the Interpretation of Culture*. Urbana: University of Illinois Press.
Spurling, L. (2009) *An Introduction to Psychodynamic Counselling*. 2nd edn. Basingstoke: Palgrave.
Stavrakakis, Y. (2007) *The Lacanian Left*. Albany: State University of New York Press.
Stepney, E. (2003) Bourdieu on Bourdieu: Reflexive Sociology and the Sociologist in Society. *Crossing Boundaries, 1*, 126–43.
Stokes, A. (1955) *Michelangelo*. London: Tavistock.
Stokes, A. (1963) *Painting and the Inner World*. London: Tavistock.
Stolorow, R. (2006) Intersubjectivity Theory and Intersubjective Systems Theory. In R. Skelton (ed.), *The Edinburgh International Encyclopaedia of Psychoanalysis*. Edinburgh: Edinburgh University Press.
Stonebridge, L. (1998) *The Destructive Element: British Psychoanalysis and Modernism*. London: Macmillan.
Summers, F. (2007) Psychoanalysis, the American Psychological Association, and the Involvement of Psychologists at Guantanamo Bay. *Psychoanalysis, Culture & Society, 12*, 83–92.
Tausk, V. (1933) On the Origin of the 'Influencing Machine' in Schizophrenia. *Psychoanalytic Quarterly* 2, 519–56.
Trilling, L. (1951) *The Liberal Imagination*. Harmondsworth: Penguin, 1970.
Ungar, V. (2009) A Contemporary Child Case Discussion. *International Journal of Psychoanalysis, 90*, 27–34.
Venn, C. (2006) *The Postcolonial Challenge: Towards Alternative Worlds*. London: Sage.
Venn, C. (2009) Identity, Diasporas and Subjective Change: The Role of Affect, the Relation to the Other, and the Aesthetic. *Subjectivity, 26*, 3–28.
von Dohnyani, K. (1986) Opening Ceremony, 34th IPA Congress. *International Journal of Psychoanalysis, 67*, 2–4.
Waddell, M. (1988) Infantile Development: Kleinian and Post-Kleinian Theory, Infant Observational Practice. *British Journal of Psychotherapy, 4*, 313–28.
Waddell, M. (1998) *Inside Lives: Psychoanalysis and the Development of the Personality*. London: Duckworth.
Walkerdine, V. (2008) Contextualizing Debates about Psychosocial Studies. *Psychoanalysis, Culture & Society, 13*, 341–5.
Wallerstein, R. (1998) Erikson's Concept of Ego Identity Reconsidered. *Journal of the American Psychoanalytic Association, 46*, 229–47.

Wetherell, M. (2003) Paranoia, Ambivalence and Discursive Practices: Concepts of Position and Positioning in Psychoanalysis and Discursive Psychology. In R. Harré and F. Moghaddam (eds), *The Self and Others: Positioning Individuals and Groups in Personal, Political and Cultural Contexts*. New York: Praeger/Greenwood.

Wetherell, M. (2005) Unconscious Conflict or Everyday Accountability? *British Journal of Social Psychology*, 44, 169–73.

Wetherell, M. (2008) Subjectivity or Psycho-Discursive Practices? Investigating Complex Intersectional Identities. *Subjectivity*, 22, 73–81.

Wetherell, M. (2010) Introduction: The Field of Identity Studies. In M. Wetherell and C. Mohanty (eds), *The Sage Handbook of Identities*. London: Sage.

Wetherell, M. and Potter, J. (1992) *Mapping the Language of Racism*. London: Harvester Wheatsheaf.

Whitebook, J. (1995) *Perversion and Utopia*. Cambridge, MA: MIT Press.

Wilson, E. (1934) The Ambiguity of Henry James. In F. Dupee (ed.), *The Question of Henry James: A Collection of Critical Essays*. New York: Holt & Co., 1945.

Winnicott, D. (1960) Ego Distortion in Terms of True and False Self. In D.W. Winnicott, *The Maturational Process and the Facilitating Environment*. London: Hogarth Press, 1965.

Winnicott, D. (1967) The Mirror-role of Mother and Family in Child Development. In D. Winnicott, *Playing and Reality*. (1969).

Winnicott, D. (1969) The Use of an Object. *International Journal of Psychoanalysis*, 50, 711–16.

Wolfenstein, V. (1981) *The Victims of Democracy*. London: Free Association Books.

Zaretsky, E. (2004) *Secrets of the Soul*. New York: Knopf.

Žižek, S. (1991) *Looking Awry*. Cambridge, MA: MIT Press.

Žižek, S. (1994) *The Metastasis of Enjoyment*. London: Verso.

Žižek, S. (2005) *Neighbours and Other Monsters: A Plea for Ethical Violence*. In S. Zicek, E. Santner and K. Reinhard (eds), *The Neighbor: Three Inquiries in Political Theology*. Chicago: University of Chicago Press.

Žižek, S. (2006a) *How to Read Lacan*. London: Granta.

Žižek, S. (2006b) *The Parallax View*. Cambridge, MA: MIT Press.

Zweig, S. (1943) *The World of Yesterday*. London: Cassell.

Index

SUNY BROCKPORT
3 2815 00917 9873

DRAKE MEMORIAL LIBRARY
WITHDRAWN
THE COLLEGE AT BROCKPORT